VOGUE

DICTIONARY OF

KNITTING STITCHES

VOGUE

DICTIONARY OF

KNITTING STITCHES

Anne Matthews

Quill New York

Library of Congress Catalog Card Number: 84-61900

ISBN: 0-688-04687-8
ISBN: 0-688-04688-6 (pbk)

Printed in The Netherlands

First Quill Edition

1 2 3 4 5 6 7 8 9 10

Contents

Introduction

There are many knitting books, magazines and leaflets but few that show stitch patterns in a format that leaves the knitter free to create her own designs. This book sets out to fill this need.

It is over 400 years since knitting was first practised in Britain. From Spain to France, France to Britain, knitting spread through Europe through the 15th and 16th centuries. By the end of the 15th century, the knitting of caps was an established industry in Britain, closely followed by the knitting of stockings. A pair of knitted silk stockings was presented to Queen Elizabeth 1 by a Mrs. Montague, knitted in a stitch now known as Mrs. Montague's pattern and shown on page 85.

The creative skills of these early knitters developed stitches that reflected the life of a community, the shapes and forms found in nature, as is shown in the names by which stitches are known – Little Leaf Lace, Travelling Vine, Tree of Life, Trinity Stitch. Over 450 of these stitches are illustrated together with instructions for a classic, round necked sweater to pattern as you wish.

Early patterns were not written down. They passed from master to apprentice, father to son, mother to daughter. Printed instructions began to appear last century and over the years they have been simplified into the easy to follow instructions now in use. Many magazines now regularly show knitting patterns and there are attractive designs in a number of foreign magazines. Not all print translations for the instructions and so a glossary of knitting terms in French, German, Italian and Spanish has been compiled for this book by Pingouin, one of Europe's major hand knitting yarn spinners.

This book would not have been possible without the generous help of many. My thanks go to Pingouin, Wendy, Twilleys, Rowan Wools, Patons and Jaeger for their yarns, their help and encouragement; to Winifred Muir at Pingouin in particular for undertaking to provide the glossary of Continental knitting terms. My thanks must go too to Alex Kroll for his guidance throughout, to Rupert Kirby for the layout and design of the pages and to the many colleagues, friends and neighbours who knitted the patterns.

The full page colour illustrations are taken from Knitting in Vogue by Christina Probert. The picture on page 73 is from volume 1, photographed by Anthony Crickmay. All the other pictures are from volume 2, photographed by Perry Ogden.

Basic Stitches

Fundamental to all knitting, basic plain and purl stitches used in rib, garter, moss and stocking stitch

Stocking Stitch

Row 1: (right side) Knit.
Row 2: Purl.

Twisted Stocking Stitch

Row 1: Knit each st through back of loop.
Row 2: Purl.

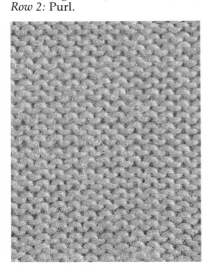

Reverse Stocking Stitch

Row 1: (wrong side) Knit.
Row 2: Purl.

2 × 2 Rib

multiple of 4
Row 1: ∗K2, p2; repeat from ∗ to end of row.
Row 2: as row 1.

Moss Stitch

multiple of 2
Row 1: *K1, p1; repeat from * to end of row.
Row 2: *P1, k1; repeat from * to end of row.

1 × 1 Rib

multiple of 2
Row 1: *K1, p1; repeat from * to end of row.
Row 2: as row 1.

Garter Stitch

Every row: Knit.

1 × 1 Twisted Rib

Multiple of 2
Row 1: *K1 tbl, pl; repeat from * to end of row.
Row 2: as row 1.

Simple Knit and Purl

Simple designs using plain and purl stitches in combination to provide interesting and effective patterns

Andalusian Stitch

multiple of 2
Row 1: Knit.
Rows 2 and 4: Purl.
Row 3: *K1, p1; repeat from * to end of row.

Reverse Ridge Stitch

Rows 1 and 3: Knit.
Row 2: Purl.
Rows 4 and 6: Knit.
Row 5: Purl.

Roman Stitch

Even number of stitches
Rows 1 and 3: Knit.
Rows 2 and 4: Purl.
Row 5: *K1, p1; repeat from * to end of row.
Row 6: *P1, k1; repeat from * to end of row.

Spindle Pattern

multiple of 6 plus 2
Row 1: *P2, k4; repeat from * to last 2 sts, p2.
Row 2 and foll alt rows: Knit the k sts and purl the p sts.
Row 3: *P2, k4; repeat from * to last 2 sts, p2.
Rows 5 and 7: P3, *k2, p4; repeat from * to last 5 sts, k2, p3.
Row 9: Purl.
Row 10: Knit.

Plain, round necked sweater patterned on sleeves and saddle shoulders with garter stitch ridges and knitted in George Picaud Laine et Coton

Ridged Slip Stitch

multiple of 4
Row 1: *K3, sl.1 purlwise; repeat
from * to end of row.
Row 2: *Sl.1 purlwise, p3; repeat
from * to end of row.
Row 3: *K3, sl.1 purlwise; repeat
from * to end of row.
Row 4: Knit.
Row 5: *K1, sl.1, k2; repeat from *
to end of row.
Row 6: *P2, sl.1, p1; repeat from *
to end of row.
Row 7: *K1, sl.1, k2; repeat from *
to end of row.
Row 8: Knit.

Moire Stitch

multiple of 2
Rows 1 and 3: *Sl.1 purlwise, k1,
yon to m1, psso the k1 and the
m1; repeat from * to end of row.
Rows 2, 4 and 6: Purl.
Row 5: Knit.

Gathered Stitch

Use 2 sizes of knitting needles for
this stitch.
Rows 1 to 6: Using finer needles,
knit.
Row 7: Change to larger needles
and knit twice into each stitch.
Rows 8, 10 and 12: Purl.
Rows 9 and 11: Knit.
Row 13: Change to finer needles
and k2 tog across the row.
Rows 14 to 18: Knit.

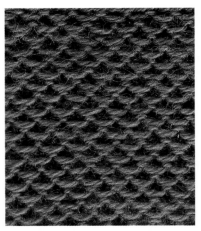

Stamen Stitch

multiple of 2
Row 1 and foll alt rows: Knit.
Row 2: *K1, sl.1 purlwise; repeat
from * to last 2 sts, k2.
Row 4: K2,* sl.1 purlwise, k1;
repeat from * to end of row.

Bamboo Stitch

multiple of 2
Row 1: ✴ Yon to m1, k2, pass m1 over k2; repeat from ✴ to end of row.
Row 2: Purl.

Woven Basket Stitch

multiple of 2
Row 1: ✴With right hand needle behind 1st st, k 2nd st tbl, k 1st st; repeat from ✴ to end of row.
Row 2: P1, ✴p 2nd st, p 1st st; repeat from ✴ to last st, p1.

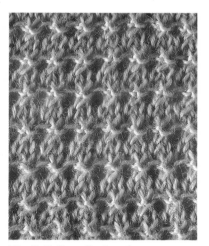

Pebble Stitch

multiple of 2
Row 1: Knit.
Row 2: Purl.
Row 3: K2 tog across row.
Row 4: ✴K1, pick up loop before next st and knit it; repeat from ✴ to end of row.

Ant Stitch

multiple of 4
Row 1: ✴K2, sl 2 purlwise; repeat from ✴ to end of row.
Row 2: ✴P2, k2; repeat from ✴ to end of row.
Row 3: ✴Sl 2 purlwise, k2; repeat from ✴ to end of row.
Row 4: ✴K2, p2; repeat from ✴ to end of row.

Linen Stitch

multiple of 2 plus 1
Row 1: *K1, yfwd, sl.1 purlwise, ybk; repeat from * to last stitch, k1.
Row 2: *P1, ybk, sl.1 purlwise, yfwd; repeat from * to last stitch, p1.

Irish Moss Stitch

multiple of 2
Row 1: *K1, p1; repeat from * to end of row.
Rows 2 and 4: Knit the k sts and purl the p sts.
Row 3: *P1, k1; repeat from * to end of row.

Striped Moss Stitch

multiple of 11 plus 5
Row 1: K5, *(k1, p1) 3 times, k5; repeat from * to end of row.
Row 2: *P5, (p1, k1) 3 times; repeat from * to last 5 sts, p5.

Star Stitch

multiple of 3 plus 1
Row 1: (wrong side) Purl.
Row 2: K1, *yon to m1, k3, pass the 1st of these 3 sts over the foll 2 sts; repeat from * to end of row.
Row 3: Purl.
Row 4: *M1, k3, pass the 1st of these 3 sts over the foll 2 sts; repeat from * to last st, k1.
Row 5: Purl.
Row 6: K2, *m1, k3, pass the 1st of these 3 sts over the foll 2 sts; repeat from * to last 2 sts, m1, k2 tog.
NOTE this stitch should not be used for large areas of knitting because of its tendency to slant.

Diagonal
Caterpillar Stitch

multiple of 8
Row 1: *K6, p2; repeat from * to end of row.
Row 2: *P1, k2, p5; repeat from * to end of row.
Row 3: *K4, p2, k2; repeat from * to end of row.
Row 4: *P3, k2, p3; repeat from * to end of row.
Row 5: *K2, p2, k4; repeat from * to end of row.
Row 6: Purl.

Garter Ridge Stitch

Rows 1 and 3: Knit.
Row 2: Purl.
Row 4: Knit.

Tweed Stitch

multiple of 2
Row 1: *K1, yfwd, sl.1 purlwise, ybk; repeat from * to end of row.
Row 2: Purl.
Row 3: *Yfwd, sl.1 purlwise, ybk, k1; repeat from * to end of row.
Row 4: Purl.

Alternating Link Stitch

multiple of 7 plus 4
Row 1: *P5, k1, p1; repeat from * to last 4 sts, p4.
Row 2 and foll alt rows: Knit the k sts and purl the p sts.
Row 3: *P5, k1, p1; repeat from * to last 4 sts, p4.
Rows 5 and 7: *P4, k1, p1, k1; repeat from * to last 4 sts, p4.

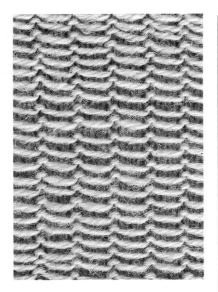

Horizontal Bat Stitch

multiple of 3 plus 1
Row 1: Knit.
Row 2: *K1, sl 2 purlwise; repeat from * to last st, k1.

Hindu Pillar Stitch

multiple of 4 plus 1
Row 1: (wrong side) K1, *k3 tog keeping sts on left hand needle, p the sts tog and then k them tog, k1; repeat from * to end of row.
Row 2: Purl.

Grain of Powder Stitch

multiple of 2
Row 1: *P1, ybk, sl.1 purlwise, yfwd; repeat from * to end of row.
Rows 2 and 4: Purl.
Row 3: *Ybk, sl.1 purlwise, yfwd, p1; repeat from * to end of row.

Sand Stitch

multiple of 2
Rows 1 and 3: Knit.
Row 2: *K1, p1; repeat from * to end of row.
Row 4: *P1, k1; repeat from * to end of row.

Medallion Stitch

multiple of 4
Row 1: *Ybk, sl 2 purlwise, k into back of 4th st then k the 3rd st; repeat from * to end of row.
Row 2: *Yfwd, sl 2 purlwise, p the 4th st then p the 3rd st; repeat from * to end of row.
Row 3: Knit.
Row 4: Purl.

Coral Knot Stitch

multiple of 2 plus 2
Row 1: K1, *k2 tog; repeat from * to last st, k1.
Row 2: K1, *k1, pick up loop between this and next st and knit it; repeat from * to last st, k1.
Row 3: Knit.
Row 4: Purl.

Hurdle Stitch

multiple of 2
Rows 1 and 2: Knit.
Rows 3 and 4: *K1, p1; repeat from * to end of row.

Horizontal Ridge Stitch

multiple of 2
Row 1: Purl.
Row 2: *K1, (k1, p1, k1) into next st; repeat from * to end of row.
Row 3: *K3, p1; repeat from * to end of row.
Row 4: *K1, p3 tog; repeat from * to end of row.
Row 5: Purl.
Row 6: *(K1, p1, k1) into next st, k1; repeat from * to end of row.
Row 7: *P1, k3; repeat from * to end of row.
Row 8: *P3 tog, k1; repeat from * to end of row.

Vertical Granite Stitch

multiple of 4
Rows 1, 3 and 5: *Yfwd, sl 2
purlwise, pass yarn over sl 2,
k2; repeat from * to end of row.
Rows 2, 4 and 6: *P2, k2 tog tbl
(next st and yo of previous row),
k1; repeat from * to end of row.
Rows 7, 9 and 11: *K2, yfwd, sl.1
purlwise, yon, sl.1 purlwise, ybk;
repeat from * to end of row.
Rows 8, 10 and 12: *K1, k2 tog tbl,
p2; repeat from * to end of row.

Braid Stitch

multiple of 10
Row 1: *P3, k5, p2; repeat from *
to end of row.
Row 2: *K2, p5, k3; repeat from *
to end of row.
Row 3: *P3, inc 1 by knitting into
back of loop below last st, k1, p3
tog, k1, inc 1 by knitting into loop
below next st, p2; repeat from * to
end of row.
Row 4: *K2, p5, k3; repeat from *
to end of row.

Swag Stitch

multiple of 5 plus 2
Rows 1, 3 and 5: Purl.
Row 2: Knit.
Rows 4 and 6: P2, *yfwd, sl 3, p2;
repeat from * to end of row.

Harris Tweed Stitch

multiple of 4
Rows 1 and 2: *K2, p2; repeat
from * to end of row.
Row 3: Knit.
Row 4: Purl.
Rows 5 and 6: *K2, p2; repeat
from * to end of row.
Row 7: Purl.
Row 8: Knit.

Horizontal Caterpillar Stitch

multiple of 10
Row 1: *K4, p6; repeat from * to end of row.
Rows 2, 4, 6 and 8: Purl.
Row 3: Knit.
Row 5: *P5, k4, p1; repeat from * to end of row.
Row 7: Knit.

Double Moss Stitch

multiple of 4
Row 1: *K2, p2; repeat from * to end of row.
Row 2: as row 1.
Row 3: *P2, k2; repeat from * to end of row.
Row 4: as row 3.

Diagonal Seed Stitch

multiple of 5
Row 1: *K4, p1; repeat from * to end of row.
Row 2: *P1, k1, p3; repeat from * to end of row.
Row 3: *K2, p1, k2; repeat from * to end of row.
Row 4: *P3, k1, p1; repeat from * to end of row.
Continue in this way working a purl st one further to the right on each row.

Granite Ridge Stitch

multiple of 2
Rows 1, 3 and 5: Knit.
Rows 2 and 4: Purl.
Row 6: K2 tog across row.
Row 7: *(K1, p1) into each st.
Row 8: Purl.

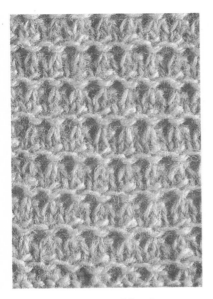

Granite Relief Stitch

multiple of 2
Row 1: Knit.
Row 2: K2 tog across row.
Row 3: K into the front and back of each st.
Row 4: Purl.

Plaited Cord Stitch

multiple of 5
Row 1: *K3, sl.1 purlwise, k1, yon to m1, psso the k1 and the m1; repeat from * to end of row.
Row 2: Purl.

Brick Stitch

multiple of 8
Rows 1 and 3: *P6, k2; repeat from * to end of row.
Rows 2 and 4: *P2, k6; repeat from * to end of row.
Rows 5 and 7: K2, *p2, k6; repeat from * to last 6 sts, p2, k4.
Rows 6 and 8: P4, *k2, p6; repeat from * to last 4 sts, k2, p2.

Double Andalusian Stitch

multiple of 12
Rows 1 and 3: Knit.
Row 2: *K2, p4; repeat from * to end of row.
Row 4: P3, *k2, p4; repeat from * to last 3 sts, k2, p1.

Purl Twist Diagonal Stitch

even number of stitches
Row 1: Knit.
Row 2: * P2 tog keeping sts on needle, p 1st st again and sl both sts off needle tog; repeat from * to end of row.
Row 3: Knit.
Row 4: P1, *p2 tog keeping sts on needle, p 1st st again and sl both sts from needle; repeat from * to last st, p1.

Slipped Granite Stitch

multiple of 4 plus 2
Row 1: (wrong side) *K1, p1; repeat from * to end of row.
Row 2: *P1, ybk, sl.1 knitwise, k2, m1, psso the k2 and m1; repeat from * to last 2 sts, p1, k1.
Row 3: as row 1.
Row 4: P1, k1, *p1, ybk, sl.1 knitwise, k2, m1, psso the k2 and m1; repeat from * to end of row.

Double Seed Stitch

multiple of 5
Row 1: *P3, k2; repeat from * to end of row.
Rows 2 and 4: Purl.
Row 3: *P1, k2, p2; repeat from * to end of row.

Hunters Stitch

multiple of 11 plus 4
Row 1: *P4, (k1 tbl, p1) 3 times, k1 tbl; repeat from * to last 4 sts, p4.
Row 2: K4, p1 tbl, *(k1, p1 tbl) 3 times, k4; repeat from * to end of row.

Double Pique Stitch

multiple of 2
Row 1: *K1, p1; repeat from * to end of row.
Rows 2 and 4: Purl.
Row 3: *P1, k1; repeat from * to end of row.

Heel Stitch

an uneven number of stitches
Row 1: Purl.
Row 2: K1, *ybk, sl.1, k1; repeat from * to end of row.

Alternating Garter Stitch Rectangles

multiple of 6 plus 4
Row 1: *K4, p2; repeat from * to last 4 sts, k4.
Row 2 and foll alt rows: Purl.
Rows 3, 5, 7 and 9: *K4, p2; repeat from * to last 4 sts, k4.
Rows 11, 13, 15, 17 and 19: K1, *p2, k4; repeat from * to last 3 sts, p2, k1.

Knotted Stitch

multiple of 3 plus 1
Row 1: *K1, sl.1 purlwise, k1, psso and put on left hand needle and knit it; repeat from * to last st, k1.
Row 2: Purl.

Vertical Caterpillar Stitch

multiple of 6
Rows 1, 3 and 5: *K3, p1 tbl, k2; repeat from * to end of row.
Rows 2, 4 and 6: *P2, k1 tbl, p3; repeat from * to end of row.
Rows 7, 9 and 11: *P1 tbl, k5; repeat from * to end of row.
Rows 8, 10 and 12: *P5, k1 tbl; repeat from * to end of row.

Embossed Cord Stitch

multiple of 6 plus 4
Row 1: P4, *k2, p4; repeat from * to end of row.
Row 2: *K4, cross 2 (p 2nd st and then k 1st st); repeat from * to last 4 sts, k4.

Double Ric Rac Pattern

multiple of 9 plus 5
Row 1: *P5, Tw2R, Tw2L; repeat from * to last 5 sts, p5.
Row 2: Knit the k sts and purl the p sts.
Row 3: *P5, Tw2L, Tw2R; repeat from * to last 5 sts, p5.
Row 4: Knit the k sts and purl the p sts.

Simple Seed Stitch

multiple of 4
Row 1: *K3, p1; repeat from * to end of row.
Rows 2 and 4: Purl.
Row 3: Knit.
Row 5: K1, *p1, k3; repeat from * to last 3 sts, p1, k2.
Rows 6 and 8: Purl.
Row 7: Knit.

Rib Patterns

*Used to give a good fit
at cuff and hem, ribs can also make
attractive designs*

2 × 2 Eyelet Rib

multiple of 6 plus 1
Row 1: P1, *k1, yon to m1, p3 tog, m1, k1, p1; repeat from * to end of row.
Row 2: *K1, p1, k3, p1; repeat from * to last st, k1.
Row 3: P1, *k1, p3, k1, p1; repeat from * to end of row.
Row 4: *K1, p1, k3, p1; repeat from * to last st, k1.

Fancy Slip Stitch Rib

multiple of 5
Row 1: *P2, k1, sl.1, k1; repeat from * to end of row.
Row 2: *P3, k2; repeat from * to end of row.

Fishermans Rib

Even number of stitches
Row 1: Purl.
Row 2: *P1, knit next st in the row below; repeat from * ending with p2.
Repeat row 2 only.

Slip Stitch Rib 1

multiple of 4
Row 1: *K3, sl.1 purlwise; repeat from * to end of row.
Row 2: Purl.
Row 3: *K3, sl.1 purlwise; repeat from * to end of row.
Row 4: Purl.

Easy fitting, chunky wool sweater in a twisted rib pattern, with saddle set shoulders and deeply ribbed neckband, knitted in Jaeger Naturgarn

Alternating 2 × 2 Rib

multiple of 4 plus 2
Rows 1 and 3: *K2, p2; repeat from * to last 2 sts, k2.
Rows 2 and 4: *P2, k2; repeat from * to last 2 sts, p2.
Row 5: *Tw2L, p2; repeat from * to last 2 sts, Tw2L.
Rows 6 and 8: *K2, p2; repeat from * to last 2 sts, k2.
Rows 7 and 9: *P2, k2; repeat from * to last 2 sts, p2.
Row 10: *K2, p2; repeat from * to last 2 sts, k2.
Row 11: *P2, Tw2L; repeat from * to last 2 sts, p2.
Row 12: *P2, k2; repeat from * to last 2 sts, p2.

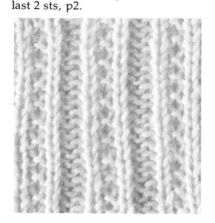

Beaded Rib

multiple of 5 plus 2
Row 1: *P2, k1, p1, k1; repeat from * to last 2 sts, p2.
Row 2: K2, *p3, k2 ; repeat from * to end of row.

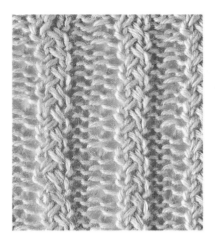

Braided Rib

multiple of 5 plus 2
Row 1: P2, * With right hand needle between 1st and 2nd sts, k the 2nd st, k the 1st st and slip both sts off left hand needle, k1, p2; repeat from * to end of row.
Row 2: *K2, p the 2nd st, p the 1st st and slip off left hand needle, p1; repeat from * to last 2 sts, k2.

Herringbone Rib

multiple of 9 plus 3
Row 1: *P3, (k2 tog keeping sts on needle and k into the first st again) three times; repeat from * to last 3 sts, p3.
Row 2: K3, *p6, k3; repeat from * to end of row.
Row 3: *P3, k1, (k2 tog keeping sts on needle and k into the first st again) twice, k1; repeat from * to last 3 sts, p3.
Row 4: K3, *p6, k3; repeat from * to end of row.

Crossed Rib 1

multiple of 4 plus 1
Rows 1 and 3: ∗(P1, k1) twice;
repeat from ∗ to last st, p1.
Rows 2 and 4: ∗(K1, p1) twice;
repeat from ∗ to last st, k1.
Row 5: ∗P1, C3R (k the 3rd st, p
the 2nd st, k the 1st st and let all
three drop from left hand needle);
repeat from ∗ to last st, p1.
Row 6: ∗(K1, p1) twice; repeat
from ∗ to last st, k1.

Barred Rib Stitch

multiple of 2 plus 1
Row 1: ∗P1, k1; repeat from ∗ to
last st, p1.
Row 2: K1, ∗p1, k1; repeat from ∗
to end of row.
Row 3: ∗P1, knit into front and
back of knit stitch; repeat from ∗
to last stitch, p1.
Row 4: ∗K1, p2 tog; repeat from ∗
to last stitch, k1.

Granite Stitch Rib

multiple of 7
Row 1: ∗K1, p1, k1, (yon to m1, k2
tog tbl) twice; repeat from ∗ to end
of row.
Row 2: ∗(M1, p2 tog) twice, k1, p1,
k1; repeat from ∗ to end of row.

Open Twisted Rib

multiple of 5 plus 3
Row 1: ∗P1, k1 tbl, p1, k2; repeat
from ∗ to last 3 sts, p1, k1 tbl, p1.
Row 2: K1, p1 tbl, k1, ∗p2, k1, p1
tbl, k1; repeat from ∗ to end of
row.
Row 3: ∗P1, k1 tbl, p1, k1, yrn to
m1, k1; repeat from ∗ to last 3 sts,
p1, k1 tbl, p1.
Row 4: K1, p1 tbl, k1, ∗p3, k1, p1
tbl, k1; repeat from ∗ to end of
row.
Row 5: ∗P1, k1 tbl, p1, k3 passing
3rd st over first 2 sts; repeat
from ∗ to last 3 sts, p1, k1 tbl, p1.
Repeat from row 2.

Lace Rib Pattern

multiple of 5 plus 2
Row 1: (wrong side) K2, *p3, k2;
repeat from * to end of row.
Row 2: P2, *k1, yon, sl.1, k1, psso,
p2; repeat from * to end of row.
Row 3: K2, *p3, k2; repeat from *
to end of row.
Row 4: P2, *k2 tog, yon, k1, p2;
repeat from * to end of row.

Double Corded Rib

multiple of 7 plus 3
Row 1: *K3, (sl.1 purlwise, k1, yon
to m1, psso the k1 and m1) twice;
repeat from * to last 3 sts, k3.
Row 2: K3, *p4, k3; repeat from *
to end of row.

Triple Twist Rib

multiple of 14 plus 1
Rows 1, 3 and 5: *P1, k6, p1, ** (sl
2 sts on to cable needle and hold at
back of work, k1, then k the 1st
and 2nd sts from cable needle, sl 1
st to cable needle and hold at front
of work, k2, then k st from cable
needle) **; repeat from * to last
st, p1.
Row 2 and following alt rows: K the k
sts and p the p sts.
Rows 7, 9, 11: *P1, work from **
to ** of row 1, p1, k6; repeat
from * to last st, p1.

Garter Stitch Rib

multiple of 6
Row 1: *K3, p3 ; repeat from * to
end of row.
Row 2: Knit.

Zigzag Twisted Rib

multiple of 18
Row 1: *P5, k2, p5, ybk, Tw2R, Tw2L, Tw2R, yfwd; repeat from * to end of row.
Row 2: *Tw2R purlwise three times, k5, Tw2R purlwise, k5; repeat from * to end of row.

Corded Rib

multiple of 5 plus 2
Row 1: *P2, Tw2R, k1; repeat from * to last 2 sts, p2.
Row 2: K2, *p1, sl 2 purlwise, k2; repeat from * to end of row.

Row 3: *P2, Tw2L, k1; repeat from * to last 2 sts, p2.
Row 4: K2, *p3, k2; repeat from * to end of row.

Acorn Rib

multiple of 3 plus 2
Rows 1, 3 and 5: *P2, k1; repeat from * to last 2 sts, p2.
Rows 2, 4 and 6: k2, *p1, k2; repeat from * to end of row.
Row 7: *P2, k three times in next st (k1 tbl, k1, k1 tbl); repeat from * to last 2 sts, p2.
Rows 8, 9 and 10: K the k and p the p sts.
Row 11: *P2, sl.1, k2 tog, psso; repeat from * to last 2 sts, p2.
Repeat from row 2.

Fancy Eyelet Rib

multiple of 4
Rows 1 and 3: *K1, p3; repeat from
* to end of row.
Rows 2 and 4: *K3, p1 ; repeat from
* to end of row.
Row 5: *K1, p2 tog, yon to m1,
p1; repeat from * to end of row.
Row 6: *K3, p1; repeat from * to
end of row.

Figure of Eight Twisted Rib

multiple of 10 plus 7
Row 1: (wrong side) K2, *p3, k2;
repeat from * to end of row.
Row 2: P2, *C3R, p2; repeat
from * to end of row.
Row 3 and foll alt rows: as row 1.
Row 4: P2, *k3, p2, C3R, p2;
repeat from * to last 5 sts, k3, p2.
Row 6: as row 2.
Row 8: as row 4.
Row 10: as row 2.
Row 12: P2, *C3R, p2, k3, p2;
repeat from * to last 5 sts, C3R,
p2.
Row 14: as row 2.
Row 16: as row 12.

Blackberry Rib

multiple of 9
Row 1: (wrong side) *P5, k4;
repeat from * to end of row.
Rows 2 and 4: *P4, k into back of
loop before next st, k2 tog, k1, k2
tog tbl, k into back of loop before
next st; repeat from * to end of
row.
Row 3: *P5, p3 tog, (k1, p1, k1)
into next st; repeat from * to end
of row.
Row 5: *P5, (k1, p1, k1) into next
st, p3 tog; repeat from * to end.
Repeat from row 2.

Little Hourglass Rib

multiple of 4 plus 2
Row 1: (wrong side) K2, *p2, k2;
repeat from * to end of row.
Row 2: P2, *k2 tog tbl and knit
again through front loops, p2;
repeat from * to end of row.
Row 3: K2, *p1, yon, p1, k2; repeat
from * to end of row.
Row 4: P2, *SSK, k1, p2; repeat
from * to end of row.

Double Eyelet Rib

multiple of 7 plus 2
Row 1: (wrong side) K2, *p5, k2;
repeat from * to end of row.
Row 2: P2, *k5, p2; repeat from *
to end of row.
Row 3: K2, *p5, k2; repeat from *
to end of row.
Row 4: P2, *k2 tog, yon, k1, yon,
SSK, p2; repeat from * to end of
row.

Little Shell Rib

multiple of 5 plus 2
Row 1: P2, *k3, p2; repeat from *
to end of row.
Row 2: K2, *p3, k2; repeat from *
to end of row.
Row 3: P2, *sl.1, k2 tog, psso, p2;
repeat from * to end of row.
Row 3: K2, *(p1, k1, p1) in front of
next st, k2; repeat from * to end of
row.

Raised Moss Stitch Rib

multiple of 7 plus 3
Row 1: P3, *k1, p1, k2, p3; repeat
from * to end of row.
Row 2: K3, *p2, k1, p1, k3; repeat
from * to end of row.
Row 3: P3, *k2, p1, k1, p3; repeat
from * to end of row.
Row 4: K3, *p1, k1, p2, k3; repeat
from * to end of row.

Italian Chain Rib

multiple of 6 plus 2
Row 1: (wrong side) K2, *p4, k2;
repeat from * to end of row.
Row 2: P2, *k2 tog, y2on, SSK, p2;
repeat from * to end of row.
Row 3: K2, *p1, p into front of 1st
yo, p into back of 2nd yo, p1, k2;
repeat from * to end of row.
Row 4: P2, *yon, SSK, k2 tog, yon,
p2; repeat from * to end of row.

Travelling Rib

multiple of 6
Row 1: *P2, Tw2L, k2; repeat from
* to end of row.
Rows 2, 4 and 6: *P4, k2; repeat
from * to end of row.
Row 3: *P2, k1, Tw2L, k1; repeat
from * to end of row.
Row 5: P2, k2, Tw2L; repeat from *
to end of row.

Granite Rib

multiple of 8 plus 2
Row 1: *K2, Tw2R three times;
repeat from * to last 2 sts, k2.
Rows 2 and 4: Purl.
Row 3: *K2, C3R (k the 3rd st,
then the 2nd st and then the 1st st)
twice; repeat from * to last 2 sts,
k2.

Puff Rib * repeat twice (3 in all)

multiple of 3 plus 2
Row 1: P2, *yon, k1, yon, p2;
repeat from * to end of row.
Row 2: K2, *p3, k2; repeat from *
to end of row.
Row 3: P2, *k3, p2; repeat from *
to end of row.
Row 4: K2, *p3 tog, k2; repeat
from * to end of row.

Pique Rib

multiple of 10
Row 1: *P3, k1, p3, k3; repeat from
* to end of row.
Row 2: *P3, k3, p1, k3 ; repeat
from * to end of row.
Row 3: *P3, k1, p3, k3 ; repeat
from * to end of row.
Row 4: Knit.

Double Twisted Rib

multiple of 6
Row 1: *P2, ybk, sl.1, k1, keeping the st on needle psso and then k into the back of k st again, k into back of 2nd st then k 1st st; repeat from * to end of row.
Row 2: *P4, k2; repeat from * to end of row.

Wheat Ear Rib

multiple of 5 plus 2
Row 1: *P3, Tw2L; repeat from * to last 2 sts, p2.
Row 2: *K3, Tw2R purlwise; repeat from * to last 2 sts, k2.

Slip Stitch Rib 2

multiple of 8
Row 1: (wrong side) *K3, yfwd, sl.1 purlwise, k3, p1; repeat from * to end of row.
Row 2: *K1, p3, ybk, sl.1 purlwise tbl, yfwd, p3; repeat from * to end of row.
Row 3: *K3, yfwd, sl.1 purlwise, k3, p1; repeat from * to end of row.
Row 4: *K1, p3, k1, p3; repeat from * to end of row.

Woven Rib

multiple of 2 plus 1
Row 1: *K1, yfwd, sl.1 purlwise, ybk; repeat from * to last st, k1.
Row 2: Purl.

Curled Rib

multiple of 6 plus 6
Row 1: *P4, k2; repeat from * to end of row.
Row 2 and foll alt rows: K all k sts and p all p sts.
Row 3: *P3, k3; repeat from * to end of row.
Row 5: *P2, k4; repeat from * to end of row.
Row 7: P1, *k4, p2; repeat from * to last 5 sts, k4, p1.
Row 9: P1, *k3, p3; repeat from * to last 5 sts, k3, p2.
Row 11: P1, *k2, p4; repeat from * to last 5 sts, k2, p3.

Farrow Rib

multiple of 3
Row 1 and every row: *K2, p1; repeat from * to end of row.

Crossed Rib 2

multiple of 10
Row 1: *K3, p1, k2, p1, k3; repeat from * to end of row.
Rows 2 and 4: K the k sts and p the p sts.
Row 3: *K3, p1, Tw2L, p1, k3; repeat from * to end of row.

Mock Cable Rib

multiple of 8
Row 1: *P5, k3; repeat from * to end of row.
Rows 2 and 4: *P3, k5; repeat from * to end of row.
Row 3: *P5, sl.1, k2, yon to m1, psso the k2 and the m1 ; repeat from * to end of row.

Kate - white

Wide Rib

multiple of 10
Row 1: *K7, p3; repeat from * to
end of row.
Row 2: *K3, p7; repeat from * to
end of row.

Moss Stitch Rib

multiple of 4
Row 1: *K3, p1; repeat from * to
end of row.
Row 2: *K2, p1, k1; repeat from *
to end of row.

Supple Rib

multiple of 3
Row 1: *K1, k the next st keeping
it on left hand needle, yfwd, p this
st and the next st tog, ybk; repeat
from * to end of row.
Row 2: Purl.

Broken Rib

multiple of 7
Row 1: *Tw2L, k3, p2 ; repeat from
* to end of row.
Row 2 and foll alt rows: *K2, p5 ;
repeat from * to end of row.
Row 3: *K1, Tw2L, k2, p2; repeat
from * to end of row.
Row 5: *K2, Tw2L, k1, p2; repeat
from * to end of row.
Row 7: *K3, Tw2L, p2; repeat from
* to end of row.

Crossover Rib

multiple of 4
Row 1: *P2, k2; repeat from * to
end of row.
Row 2: K the k sts and p the p sts.
Row 3: *P2, work 5 sts (k1, p1, k1,
p1, k1) into the next 2 sts tog;
repeat from * to end of row.
Row 4: K the k sts and p the p sts
and purl the extra sts.
Row 5: *P2, k3, k2 tog; repeat from
* to end of row.
Rows 6, 8 and 10: K the k sts and p
the p sts.
Row 7: *P2, k2, k2 tog; repeat from
* to end of row.
Row 9: *P2, k1, k2 tog; repeat from
* to end of row.

Tweed Stitch Rib

multiple of 6
Row 1: *P3, sl.1 purlwise, ybk, k1,
yfwd, sl.1 purlwise; repeat from *
to end of row.
Rows 2 and 4: *P3, k3; repeat
from * to end of row.
Row 3: *P3, k1, yfwd, sl.1
purlwise, ybk, k1; repeat from * to
end of row.

Mistake Stitch Rib

multiple of 4 plus 3
Row 1 and every row: *K2, p2;
repeat from * to last 3 sts, k2, p1.

Yes! Yes! Yes!

I want to order a subscription to *YANKEE* and receive a *FREE* copy of *Yankee's Main Dish Church Supper Cookbook.*

☐ Please send me twelve issues for just **$17.97**
   . . . that's a **$5.43** savings from the single-copy price!

☐ Please send me twenty-four issues for just **$31.97**
   . . . that's a **$14.83** savings from the single-copy price!

☑ Please send me a *free* copy of *Yankee's Main Dish Church Supper Cookbook.*

Name _____

Address _____

City _____ State _____ Zip _____

☐ Payment Enclosed   ☐ Bill Me

Give a gift subscription to a friend . . . receive a
free cookbook . . . and we'll send you
a card that can be used to announce your gift.

Gift for _____

Address _____

City _____ State _____ Zip _____

For Canadian/foreign subscriptions add $4 per year. U.S. funds only.   E85YK1D

Slip Stitch Rib 3

multiple of 6 plus 3
Rows 1, 3 and 5: *P3, k3; repeat
from * to last 3 sts, p3.
Rows 2, 4, and 6: K3, *p1, ybk,
sl.1, yfwd, p1, k3; repeat from * to
end of row.
Row 7: Purl.
Row 8: P3, *p1, sl.1, p4; repeat
from * to end of row.

Loop Stitch Rib

multiple of 8 plus 4
Row 1: *P4, k4 winding yarn
round needle 3 times for each st;
repeat from * to last 4 sts, p4.
Rows 2 and 4: K4, *yfwd, sl the 4
long sts, ybk, k4; repeat from * to
end of row.
Row 3: *P4, ybk, sl 4, yfwd; repeat
from * to last 4 sts, p4.

Alternating Rib

multiple of 6 plus 2
Row 1: K1, *sl.1, k2 tog, psso, p3;
repeat from * to last st, k1.
Row 2: P1, *sl.1, k2 tog, psso, k3
times into next st; repeat from * to
last st, p1.
Row 3: K1, *p3, k3 times into next
st; repeat from * to last st, k1.
Rows 4 to 12: K the k sts and p the
p sts.
Row 13: K1, *p3, sl.1, k2 tog,
psso; repeat from * to last st, k1.
Row 14: P1, *k3 times into next st,
sl.1 purlwise, p2 tog, psso; repeat
from * to last st, p1.
Row 15: K1, *k3 times into next st,
p3; repeat from * to last st, k1.
Rows 16 to 24: K the k sts and p the
p sts.

Mock Rib

multiple of 2
Row 1: *P1, ybk, sl.1 purlwise,
yfwd; repeat from * to end of row.
Row 2: Purl.

Textured Patterns

A family of stitch designs in widely different patterns with strong surface and textural interest

Reverse Stocking Stitch Check

multiple of 12 plus 12
Rows 1 and 3: Knit.
Rows 2 and 4: Purl.
Rows 5 and 7: K3, *p6, k6; repeat to last 9 sts, p6, k3.
Rows 6 and 8: K the k sts and p the p sts.

Ridged Stitch

multiple of 8 plus 4
Row 1: *K4, Tw2R, Tw2L; repeat from * to last 4 sts, k4.
Row 2: Purl.

Cell Stitch

multiple of 2 plus 1
Row 1: K1, *put right hand needle between 1st and 2nd sts and draw through a loop leaving loop on right hand needle, k2; repeat from * to end of row.
Row 2: *P1, p2 tog; repeat from * to last st, p1.
Row 3: K2, *put right hand needle between 1st and 2nd sts and draw through a loop leaving loop on right hand needle, k2; repeat from * to last st, k1.
Row 4: P2, *p1, p2 tog; repeat from * to last st, p1.

Long-line, loose fitting tunic sweater with dropped shoulders and neat shirt collar, all in moss stitch, knitted in ANI Homespun Shetland wool

Embossed Leaf Stitch Pattern 1

multiple of 10.
Row 1: Purl.
Row 2: Knit.
Rows 3 and 4: Purl.
Row 5: *P5, k5; repeat from * to end of row.
Row 6: *K1, p5, k4; repeat from * to end of row.
Row 7: *P3, k5, p2; repeat from * to end of row.
Row 8: *K3, p5, k2; repeat from * to end of row.
Row 9: *P1, k5, p4; repeat from * to end of row.
Row 10: Knit.
Row 11: *K1, p5, k4; repeat from * to end of row.
Row 12: *P3, k5, p2; repeat from * to end of row.
Row 13: as row 8.
Row 14: as row 9.
Row 15: *K5, p5; repeat from * to end of row.
Row 16: Purl.

Looped Honeycomb Stitch

multiple of 6
Row 1: *Sl.1 purlwise, k2, psso, k3; repeat from * to end of row.
Row 2: *P4, yon to m1, p1; repeat from * to end of row.
Row 3: *K3, sl.1 purlwise, k2, psso; repeat from * to end of row.
Row 4: *P1, m1, p4; repeat from * to end of row.

Pennant Pattern

multiple of 10
Row 1: *P2, k8; repeat from * to end of row.
Row 2: *P7, k3; repeat from * to end of row.
Row 3: *P4, k6; repeat from * to end of row.
Row 4: *P5, k5; repeat from * to end of row.
Row 5: *P6, k4; repeat from * to end of row.
Row 6: *P3, k7; repeat from * to end of row.
Row 7: *P8, k2; repeat from * to end of row.
Row 8: as row 6.
Row 9: as row 5.
Row 10: as row 4.
Row 11: as row 3.
Row 12: as row 2.

Pique Squares

multiple of 12
Row 1: ∗K6, ∗∗p2, replace on left hand needle, take yarn across front to back, replace on right hand needle∗∗ three times; repeat from ∗ to end of row.
Row 2 and foll alt rows: Purl.
Rows 3 and 5: as row 1.
Rows 7, 9 and 11: ∗From ∗∗ to ∗∗ in row 1 three times, k6; repeat from ∗ to end of row.

Cabled Squares Pattern

multiple of 8
Row 1: Knit.
Row 2: ∗P3, k2, p3; repeat from ∗ to end of row.
Rows 3, 5 and 7: as row 1.
Rows 4, 6 and 8: as row 2.
Row 9: ∗P2, ybk, sl.1, k2, sl.1, yfwd, p2; repeat from ∗ to end of row.
Row 10: ∗K2, yfwd, sl.1, ybk, k2, yfwd, sl.1, ybk, k2; repeat from ∗ to end of row.
Row 11: ∗K2, sl 3 sts on to cable needle and hold at back of work, k next st, sl. 1st st on cable needle to left hand needle in front of other 2 sts, k these 2 sts, k the next 3 sts; repeat from ∗ to end of row.
Repeat from row 2.

Twisted Leaf Pattern

multiple of 14
Row 1: ∗K2, Tw2R, Tw2L, k8; repeat from ∗ to end of row.
Row 2 and foll alt rows: Purl.
Row 3: ∗K1, Tw2R, k2, Tw2L, k7; repeat from ∗ to end of row.
Row 5: as row 1.
Row 7: ∗K3, sl.1, k1, psso and k the sl. st, k9; repeat from ∗ to end of row.
Row 9: Knit.
Row 11: ∗K8, Tw2R, Tw2L, k2; repeat from ∗ to end of row.
Row 13: ∗K7, Tw2R, k2, Tw2L, k1; repeat from ∗ to end of row.
Row 15: as row 11.
Row 17: ∗K9, sl.1, k1, psso and k the sl. st, k3; repeat from ∗ to end of row.
Row 19: Knit.

Moss Stitch Diamond Pattern 1

multiple of 12 plus 2
Row 1: ∗K6, p2, k4; repeat from ∗ to last 2 sts, k2.
Rows 2 and 6: P2, ∗(p2, k2) twice, p4; repeat from ∗ to end of row.
Rows 3 and 5: ∗K2, p2, k6, p2; repeat from ∗ to last 2 sts, k2.
Row 4: K2, ∗p10, k2; repeat from ∗ to end of row.

Chevron Pattern 1

multiple of 12
Row 1: ✳K3, p5, k3, p1; repeat
from ✳ to end of row.
Row 2 and foll alt rows: K the k sts
and p the p sts.
Row 3: P1, ✳k3, p3; repeat from ✳
to last 5 sts, k3, p2.
Row 5: P2, ✳k3, p1, k3, p5; repeat
from ✳ to last 10 sts, k3, p1, k3,
p3.
Row 7: ✳P3, k5, p3, k1; repeat from
✳ to end of row.
Row 9: K1, ✳p3, k3; repeat from ✳
to last 5 sts, p3, k2.
Row 11: K2, ✳p3, k1, p3, k5; repeat
from ✳ to last 3 sts, k3.

Ladder Stitch

multiple of 8 plus 1
Row 1: ✳K5, yfwd, sl 3 purlwise,
ybk; repeat from ✳ to last st, k1.
Row 2: P1, ✳ybk, sl 3 purlwise,
yfwd, p5; repeat from ✳ to end of
row.
Row 3: as row 1.
Row 4: Purl.
Rows 5 and 7: K1, ✳yfwd, sl 3
purlwise, ybk, k5; repeat from ✳ to
end of row.
Row 6: ✳P5, ybk, sl 3 purlwise
yfwd; repeat from ✳ to last st, p1.
Row 8: Purl.

Scattered Oats Pattern

multiple of 4 plus 1
Row 1: ✳K2, sl.1 purlwise, k1;
repeat from ✳ to last st, k1.
Row 2: P1, ✳p1, sl.1 purlwise, p2;
repeat from ✳ to end of row.
Row 3: ✳Sl 2 sts on to a double
pointed needle and leave at back
of work, k the sl st, k the 2 sts
from the double pointed needle,
k1; repeat from ✳ to last st, k1.
Row 4: Purl.
Row 5: as row 1.
Row 6: as row 2.
Row 7: K1, ✳k1, place sl st of
previous row on a double pointed
needle and leave at front of work,
k2, k the st from the double
pointed needle; repeat from ✳ to
end of row.
Row 8: Purl.

Fancy Basket Pattern

multiple of 8
Rows 1, 2, 3 and 4: ✳P4, k4; repeat
from ✳ to end of row.
Rows 5 and 6: ✳K4, p4; repeat from
✳ to end of row.
Rows 7 and 8: ✳P4, k4; repeat from
✳ to end of row.
Rows 9 and 10: as rows 5 and 6.

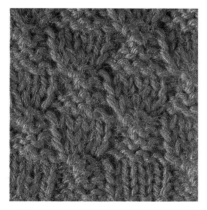

Chalice Stitch

multiple of 8
Rows 1, 2, 3 and 4: *K4, p4; repeat from * to end of row.
Row 5: *P4, sl 2 sts on to cable needle and leave at front of work, k2, k 2 sts from cable needle; repeat from * to end of row.
Rows 6, 7 and 8: *P4, k4; repeat from * to end of row.
Row 9: *Sl 2 sts to cable needle and leave at front of work, k2, k2 sts from cable needle, p4; repeat from * to end of row.
Repeat from row 2.

Ridged Almond Pattern

multiple of 4 plus 2
Row 1: P2, *(k1, p1, k1) into next st, p3; repeat from * to end of row.
Row 2 and foll alt rows: Purl.
Rows 3 and 5: P2, *k3, p3; repeat from * to end of row.
Row 7: P2, *k3 tog tbl, p3; repeat from * to end of row.
Rows 9 and 11: Knit.

Cornflower Pattern

multiple of 10
Rows 1 and 3: *P5, ybk, sl.1 purlwise, yfwd, p4; repeat from * to end of row.
Rows 2 and 4: *K4, yfwd, sl.1 purlwise, ybk, k5; repeat from * to end of row.
Row 5: *P3, k5, p2; repeat from * to end of row.
Row 6: *K2, p5, k3; repeat from * to end of row.
Row 7: *P3, ** with crochet hook, pick up the sl st of row 4 (wrh, draw loop through) twice, wrh, draw through both loops and put st on right hand needle **, k5, repeat from ** to **, p2; repeat from * to end of row.
Row 8: *K2, p2 tog, p3, p2 tog, k3; repeat from * to end of row.
Row 9: *P5, k1, p4; repeat from * to end of row.
Row 10: Knit.
Rows 11 and 13: *Ybk, sl.1 purlwise, p9; repeat from * to end of row.
Rows 12 and 14: *K9, yfwd, sl.1 purlwise, ybk; repeat from * to end of row.
Row 15: K3, *p5, k5; repeat from * to last 2 sts, k2.
Row 16: P2, *k5, p5; repeat from * to last 3 sts, p3.
Row 17: K3, work from ** to ** of row 7, *p5, work from ** to **, k5, work from ** to **; repeat from * to last 2 sts, k2.
Row 18: P2, p2 tog, *k5, p2 tog, p3, p2 tog; repeat from * to last 7 sts, k5, p2.
Row 19: *K1, p9; repeat from * to end of row.
Row 20: Knit.

Relief Diagonal Stitch

multiple of 6
Row 1: *P1, Tw2R, Tw2L, p1:
repeat from * to end of row.
Row 2 and foll alt rows: K the k sts
and p the p sts.
Row 3: *Tw2R, Tw2L, p2; repeat
from * to end of row.
Continue to move one st to the
right on alt rows.

Stepped Pattern

multiple of 18
Row 1: *K15, p3; repeat from * to
end of row.
Row 2 and foll alt rows: K the k sts
and p the p sts.
Row 3: *K15, p3; repeat from * to
end of row.
Rows 5 and 7: *K3, p15; repeat
from * to end of row.
Rows 9 and 11: *K3, p3, k12; repeat
from * to end of row.
Rows 13 and 15: *P6, k3, p9; repeat
from * to end of row.
Rows 17 and 19: *K9, p3, k6; repeat
from * to end of row.
Rows 21 and 23: *P12, k3, p3;
repeat from * to end of row.

Diamond Quilting Pattern

multiple of 6 plus 4
Row 1: Purl.
Row 2: K4, *(k1 y2on) twice, k4;
repeat from * to end of row.
Row 3: P4, *yfwd, sl next 2 sts
purlwise dropping the extra loops,
p4; repeat from * to end of row.
Row 4: K4, *yb, sl next 2 sts
purlwise, k4; repeat from * to end
of row.
Row 5: P4, *yfwd, sl next 2 sts
purlwise, p4; repeat from * to end
of row.
Row 6: K2, *k 3rd st on left hand
needle through front of loop, k the
1st and 2nd sts, sl next st on to a
double pointed needle and leave at
front, k2, k the st from the double
pointed needle; repeat from * to
last 2 sts, k2.
Row 7: Purl.
Row 8: K2, k1 y2on, k4, *(k1 y2on)
twice, k4; repeat from * to last 3
sts, k1, y2on, k2.
Row 9: P2, yfwd, sl 1 st dropping
the extra loop, p4, *yfwd, sl 2 sts
dropping the extra loops, p4;
repeat from * to last 3 sts, yfwd, sl
1 st dropping the extra loop, p2.
Row 10: K2, yb, sl next st
purlwise, *k4, yb, sl 2 sts
purlwise; repeat from * to last 7
sts, k4, yb, sl next st purlwise, k2.
Row 11: P2, yfwd, sl next st
purlwise, *p4, yfwd, sl next 2 sts;
repeat from * to last 7 sts, p4,
yfwd, sl next st, p2.
Row 12: K2, *sl next st on to a
double pointed needle and leave at
front, k2, k the st from the double
pointed needle, k the 3rd st on left
hand needle through front of loop,
k 1st and 2nd sts; repeat from * to
last 2 sts, k2.

Irish Moss Diamond Stitch

multiple of 14
Row 1: ✳(P1, k1) 4 times, k6; repeat from ✳ to end of row.
Row 2 and foll alt rows: K the k sts and p the p sts.
Row 3: ✳(K1, p1) 3 times, k4, p1, k3; repeat from ✳ to end of row.
Row 5: ✳K2, p1, k1, p1, k4, p1, k1, p1, k2; repeat from ✳ to end of row.
Row 7: ✳K3, p1, k4, (p1, k1) 3

times; repeat from ✳ to end of row.
Row 9: ✳K6, (k1, p1) 4 times; repeat from ✳ to end of row.
Row 11: as row 7.
Row 13: as row 5.
Row 15: as Row 3.

Turkish Stitch (with bias to left)

multiple of 2 plus 2
Row 1: Knit.
Row 2: P1, ✳yon, p2 tog tbl; repeat from ✳ to last st, p1.
Row 3: K1, ✳sl.1, k1, psso, yon; repeat from ✳ to last st, k1.
Repeat from row 2.

Turkish Stitch (with bias to right)

multiple of 2 plus 2
Row 1: Knit.
Row 2: P1, ✳yon to make 1, p2 tog; repeat from ✳ to last st, p1.
Row 3: K2, ✳yon to make 1, k2 tog; repeat from ✳ to end of row.
Row 4: P2, ✳yon to make 1, p2 tog; repeat from ✳ to end of row.
Row 5: K1, ✳yon to make 1, k2 tog; repeat from ✳ to last st, k1.
Repeat from row 2.

Chevron Seed Pattern

multiple of 22 plus 1
Row 1: K1, *p3, (k1, p1) twice, k1, p5, k1, (p1, k1) twice, p3, k1; repeat from * to end of row.
Row 2: P1, *p1, k3, (p1, k1) twice, p1, k3, p1, (k1, p1) twice, k3, p2; repeat from * to end of row.
Row 3: K1, *k2, p3, (k1, p1) five times, k1, p3, k3; repeat from * to end of row.
Row 4: K1, *p3, k3, (p1, k1) four times, p1, k3, p3, k1; repeat from * to end of row.
Row 5: P1, *p1, k3, p3, (k1, p1) three times, k1, p3, k3, p2; repeat from * to end of row.
Row 6: K1, *k2, p3, k3, (p1, k1) twice, p1, k3, p3, k3; repeat from * to end of row.
Row 7: K1, *p3, k3, p3, k1, p1, k1, p3, k3, p3, k1; repeat from * to end of row.
Row 8: K1, *p1, k3, (p3, k3) twice, p1, k1; repeat from * to end of row.
Row 9: K1, *p1, k1, p3, k3, p5, k3, p3, k1, p1, k1; repeat from * to end of row.
Row 10: K1, *p1, k1, p1, (k3, p3) twice, k3, (p1, k1) twice; repeat from * to end of row.
Row 11: K1, *(p1, k1) twice, p3, k3, p1, k3, p3, (k1, p1) twice, k1; repeat from * to end of row.
Row 12: K1, *(p1, k1) twice, p1, k3, p5, k3, (p1, k1) three times.
Row 13: P1, *(p1, k1) three times, p3, k3, p3, (k1, p1) twice, k1, p2; repeat from * to end of tow.
Row 14: K1, *k2, (p1, k1) twice, (p1, k3) twice, (p1, k1) three times, k2; repeat from * to end of row.

Chain Stitch

multiple of 8 plus 4
Row 1: *P4, Tw2L, Tw2R; repeat from * to last 4 sts, p4.
Row 2: *K4, p4; repeat from * to last 4 sts, k4.
Rows 3 and 5: *P4, k1, p2, k1; repeat from * to last 4 sts, p4.
Rows 4 and 6: *K4, p1, k2, p1; repeat from * to last 4 sts, k4.

Pique Diamond Pattern

multiple of 10 plus 10
Row 1: *K9, p1; repeat from * to end of row.
Row 2: K2, *p7, k3; repeat from * to last 8 sts, p7, k1.
Row 3: P2, *k5, p5; repeat from * to last 8 sts, k5, p3.
Rows 4 and 6: K4, *p3, k7; repeat from * to last 6 sts, p3, k3.
Row 5: P4, *k1, p9: repeat from * to last 6 sts, k1, p5.
Row 7: P2, *k5, p5; repeat from * to last 8 sts, k5, p3.
Row 8: K2, *p7, k3; repeat from * to last 8 sts, p7, k1.

Embossed Leaf Pattern 1

multiple of 7 plus 6
Row 1: P6, *yon to m1, k1, m1, p6; repeat from * to end of row.
Row 2: *K6, p3; repeat from * to last 6 sts, k6.
Row 3: P6, *k1, yon to m1, k1, m1, k1, p6; repeat from * to end of row.
Row 4: *K6, p5; repeat from * to last 6 sts, k6.
Row 5: P6, *k2, yon to m1, k1, m1, k2, p6; repeat from * to end of row.
Row 6: *K6, p7; repeat from * to last 6 sts, k6.
Row 7: P6, *k3, yon to m1, k1, m1, k3, p6; repeat from * to end of row.
Row 8: *K6, p9; repeat from * to last 6 sts, k6.
Row 9: P6, *sl.1, k1, psso, k5, k2 tog, p6; repeat from * to end of row.
Row 10: *K6, p7; repeat from * to last 6 sts, k6.
Row 11: P6, *sl.1, k1, psso, k3, k2 tog, p6; repeat from * to end of row.
Row 12: *K6, p5; repeat from * to last 6 sts, k6.
Row 13: P6, *sl.1, k1, psso, k1, k2 tog, p6; repeat from * to end of row.
Row 14: *K6, p3; repeat from * to last 6 sts, k6.
Row 15: P6, *sl.1, k2 tog, psso, p6; repeat from * to end of row.
Rows 16, 18 and 20: Knit.
Rows 17 and 19: Purl.

Large & Small Diamond Pattern

multiple of 15
Row 1: *K1, p13, k1; repeat from * to end of row.
Row 2: *P2, k11, p2; repeat from * to end of row.
Row 3: *K3, p9, k3; repeat from * to end of row.
Row 4: *P4, k7, p4; repeat from * to end of row.
Row 5: *K5, p5, k5; repeat from * to end of row.
Row 6: *K1, p5, k3, p5, k1; repeat from * to end of row.
Rows 7 and 9: *P2, k5, p1, k5, p2; repeat from * to end of row.
Row 8: *K3, p9, k3; repeat from * to end of row.
Row 10: as row 6.
Row 11: as row 5.
Row 12: as row 4.
Row 13: as row 3.
Row 14: as row 2.

Spine Stitch

multiple of 4
Row 1: Tw2R, Tw2L; repeat from *
to end of row.
Row 2: Purl.

Brocade Pattern

multiple of 8 plus 2.
Rows 1, 2, 3 and 4: Knit.
Row 5: *K2, p6; repeat from * to
last 2 sts, k2.
Row 6: Knit.
Row 7: *K2, p1, (p1 y2on) four
times p1; repeat from * to last 2
sts, k2.
Row 8: K2, *k1, sl next 4 sts on to
right hand needle dropping the
extra loops and replace on left
hand needle working k4 tog, p4
tog, k4 tog, p4 tog into the 4 sts
tog, k3; repeat from * to end of
row.
Row 9: *K2, p6; repeat from * to
last 2 sts, k2.
Row 10: Knit.

Rosebud Pattern

multiple of 8
Rows 1 and 3: *K4, k1 tbl, k3;
repeat from * to end of row.
Rows 2 and 4: *P3, p1 tbl, p4;
repeat from * to end of row.
Row 5: *K2, with crochet hook,
place hook under the loop before
the 4th (tbl) st, ** draw through a
long loop, wrh, draw through loop
**, leaving st on hook, repeat
from ** to ** twice, wrh, draw
through 3 sts, put this st on right
hand needle, k2, k1 tbl, k2, put
hook under loop after the tbl st
and work from ** to **, k1;
repeat from * to end of row.
Row 6: *P2 tog, p2, p1 tbl, p2, p2
tog, p1; rep from * to end of row.
Row 7: *K1 tbl, k3, (k1, p1, k1, p1)
into next st, turn, p4 tog, k3;
repeat from * to end of row.
Rows 8 and 10: *P7, p1 tbl; repeat
from * to end of row.
Row 9: *K1 tbl, k7; repeat from *
to end of row.
Row 11: K1 tbl, k2, put hook under
loop after tbl st and work ** to
** as in row 5, k1, *k2, work **
to **, k2, k1 tbl, k2, ** to **, k1;
repeat from * to last 4 sts, k4.
Row 12: P4, *p2 tog, p2, p1 tbl, p2,
p2 tog, p1; repeat from * to last 5
sts, p2 tog, p2, p1 tbl.
Row 13: *K1 tbl, k3, (k1, p1, k1,
p1) into next st, turn, p4 tog, k3;
repeat from * to end of row.
Repeat from row 2.

Basket Weave Pattern

multiple of 8 plus 8
Rows 1 and 3: ∗K2, p6; repeat from ∗ to end of row.
Rows 2 and 4: ∗K6, p2; repeat from ∗ to end of row.
Row 5: ∗K2, p2; repeat from ∗ to end of row.
Rows 6 and 8: K2, p2, ∗k6, p2; repeat from ∗ to last 4 sts, k4.
Rows 7 and 9: P4, ∗k2, p6; repeat from ∗ to last 4 sts, k2, p2.
Row 10: as row 5.

Stepped Diagonal Rib Pattern

multiple of 8
Rows 1, 2, 3 and 4: ∗P4, k4; repeat from ∗ to end of row.
Row 5: ∗P2, k4, p2; repeat from ∗ to end of row.
Row 6: ∗K2, p4, k2; repeat from ∗ to end of row.
Row 7: as row 5.
Row 8: as row 6.
Rows 9, 10, 11 and 12: ∗K4, p4; repeat from ∗ to end of row.
Row 13: as row 6.
Row 14: as row 5.
Row 15: as row 6.
Row 16: as row 5.

Ridged Square Pattern 1

multiple of 5
Row 1 and foll alt rows: Knit.
Rows 2, 4 and 6: ∗P4, k1: repeat from ∗ to end of row.
Row 8: Knit.

Block Stitch

multiple of 9 plus 6
Row 1: ∗P6, k3; repeat from ∗ to last 6 sts, p6.
Row 2 and foll alt rows: K the k sts and p the p sts.
Rows 3 and 5: as row 1.
Rows 7 and 9: ∗K6, p3; repeat from ∗ to last 6 sts, k6.

Linked Check Pattern

multiple of 10
Row 1: ∗K4, p2, Tw2R, p2; repeat
from ∗ to end of row.
Row 2: ∗K2, Tw2L purlwise, k2,
p4; repeat from ∗ to end of row.
Rows 3 and 5: as row 1.
Rows 4 and 6: as row 2.
Row 7: ∗P1, Tw2R, p2, k4, p1;
repeat from ∗ to end of row.
Row 8: ∗K1, p4, k2, Tw2L, k1;
repeat from ∗ to end of row.
Rows 9 and 11: as row 7.
Rows 10 and 12: as row 8.

Herringbone Pattern

multiple of 14
Row 1: (wrong side) K3, p1 y2on,
p6, p1 y2on, k3; repeat from ∗ to
end of row.
Row 2: ∗P3, sl next st to cable
needle dropping the extra loop
and leave at front of work, k3,
place loop st on left hand needle
and k it; put next 3 sts on cable
needle at back of work, k1
dropping the extra loop, k3 from
cable needle, p3; repeat from ∗ to
end of row.

Chevron Pattern 2

multiple of 12
Row 1: ∗P2, k2, p2, k1, p2, k2, p1;
repeat from ∗ to end of row.
Row 2 and foll alt rows: K the k sts
and p the p sts.
Row 3: ∗P1, k2, p2, k3, p2, k2;
repeat from ∗ to end of row.
Row 5: ∗K2, p2, k2, p1, k2, p2, k1;
repeat from ∗ to end of row.
Row 7: ∗K1, p2, k2, p3, k2, p2;
repeat from ∗ to end of row.

Banded Zigzag Stitch

multiple of 14

Row 1: *P5, Tw2R, k4, Tw2R, p1; repeat from * to end of row.
Row 2 and foll alt rows: K the k sts and p the p sts.
Row 3: *P4, Tw2R, k4, Tw2R, p2; repeat from * to end of row.
Row 5: *P3, Tw2R, k4, Tw2R, p3; repeat from * to end of row.
Row 7: *P2, Tw2R, k4, Tw2R, p4; repeat from * to end of row.
Row 9: *P1, Tw2R, k4, Tw2R, p5; repeat from * to end of row.
Row 11: *P1, Tw2L, k4, Tw2L, p5; repeat from * to end of row.
Row 13: *P2, Tw2L, k4, Tw2L, p4; repeat from * to end of row.
Row 15: *P3, Tw2L, k4, Tw2L, p3; repeat from * to end of row.
Row 17: *P4, Tw2L, k4, Tw2L, p2; repeat from * to end of row.
Row 19: *P5, Tw2L, k4, Tw2L, p1; repeat from * to end of row.

Embossed Leaf Pattern 2

multiple of 9

Rows 1 and 3: Purl.
Rows 2 and 4: Knit.
Row 5: *P4, k into front, back, front, back and front of next st, p4; repeat from * to end of row.
Row 6: *K4, p5, k4; repeat from * to end of row.
Row 7: *P4, k5, p4; repeat from * to end of row.
Row 8: as row 6.
Row 9: *P4, k2 tog tbl, k1, k2 tog, p4; repeat from * to end of a row.
Row 10: *K4, p3, k4; repeat from * to end of row.
Row 11: *P4, sl.1, k2 tog, psso, p4; repeat from * to end of row.
Row 12: *K4, p1, k4; repeat from * to end of row.
Rows 13 and 15: Purl.
Rows 14 and 16: Knit.

Twisted Column Pattern 1

multiple of 6 plus 2
Row 1: P2, *k4, p2; repeat from *
to end of row.
Row 2: *K2, (p2 tog) twice; repeat
from * to last 2 sts, k2.
Row 3: P2, * **k st of previous
row that slants to the right then k
st on left hand needle** twice,
p2; repeat from * to end of row.
Row 4: *K1, (p2 tog) twice, k1;
repeat from * to last 2 sts, k2.
Row 5: P2, *p1, repeat from ** to
** twice, p1; repeat from * to end
of row.
Repeat from row 2.

Lozenge Pattern 1

multiple of 5
Row 1: *P1, k4; repeat from * to
end of row.
Row 2: *P3, k2; repeat from * to
end of row.
Row 3: as row 2.
Row 4: *P1, k4; repeat from * to
end of row.
Row 5: as row 4.
Row 6: *K2, p3; repeat from * to
end of row.
Row 7: as row 6.
Row 8: *K4, p1; repeat from * to
end of row.

Barleysugar Rib

multiple of 6
Rows 1, 2 and 3: *K3, p3; repeat
from * to end of row.
Rows 4 and 6: *P1, k3, p2; repeat
from * to end of row.
Rows 5 and 8: K the k sts and p the
p sts.
Rows 7 and 9: *K1, p3, k2; repeat
from * to end of row.
Rows 10, 11 and 12: *P3, k3; repeat
from * to end of row.
Row 13: *P2, k3, p1; repeat from *
to end of row.
Row 14: as row 5.
Row 15: as row 13.
Row 16: *K2, p3, k1; repeat from *
to end of row.
Row 17: as row 5.
Row 18: as row 16.

Woven Diagonal Pattern

multiple of 6
Row 1 and foll alt rows: (wrong side)
Purl.
Row 2: *Yfwd, sl 3, ybk, k3; repeat
from * to end of row.
Row 4: K1, *yfwd, sl 3, ybk, k3;
repeat from * to last 5 sts, yfwd, sl
3, ybk, k2.
Row 6: K2, *yfwd, sl 3, ybk, k3;
repeat from * to last 4 sts, yfwd, sl
3, ybk, k1.
Row 8: *K3, yfwd, sl 3, ybk; repeat
from * to end of row.
Row 10: Sl.1, *k3, yfwd, sl 3, ybk;
repeat from * to last 5 sts, k3,
yfwd, sl 2, ybk.
Row 12: Sl.2; *k3, yfwd, sl 3, ybk;
repeat from * to last 4 sts, k3,
yfwd, sl.1, ybk.

Lattice Pattern

multiple of 8 plus 7.
Row 1: K1, p1, *p3, k5; repeat
from * to last 5 sts, p4, k1.
Row 2: P1, k4, *p5, y2on, k3;
repeat from * to last 2 sts, k1, p1.
Row 3: K1, p1, *p3, **drop yo,
with right hand needle, pull out
next st to make a long loop leaving
it at front of work, k4, pick up loop
purlwise and place on right hand
needle without knitting it **;
repeat from * to last 5 sts, p4, k1.
Rows 4 and 6: as row 2.
Rows 5 and 7: as row 3.
Row 8: P1, k4, *p5, k3; repeat from
* to last 2 sts, k1, p1.
Row 9: K1, *k5, p3; repeat from *
to last 6 sts, k6.
Row 10: P6, *y2on, k3, p5; repeat
from * to last st, y2on, p1.
Row 11: K1, *work from ** to **
of row 3 but ending p3; repeat
from * to last st, k1.
Rows 12 and 14: as row 10.
Rows 13 and 15: as row 11.
Row 16: P6, *k3, p5; repeat from *
to last st, p1.

Daisy Pattern

multiple of 18 plus 2
Row 1: K5, *(k1, yon, k1, yon, k1)
in next st, k17; repeat from * to
last 14 sts, k14.
Row 2: P14, *(p1 y2on) five
times, p17; repeat from * to last 5
sts, p5.
Row 3: K1, *ybk, sl 4, drop next
long st to front, sl 4 sts back to left
needle, pick up long loop knitwise
and sl it on to left hand needle, k2
tog tbl, k3, ybk, sl 3 dropping yon,
drop next long st to front, ybk, sl
4, pick up long st on left needle, sl
4 sts back on to left hand needle,
k3, k2 tog, k9; repeat from * to last
st, k1.
Row 4: P14, *yfwd, sl 3, p17;
repeat from * to last 5 sts, p5.
Row 5: K2, *ybk, sl 3, drop next
long st at front, sl 3 sts back to left
hand needle, pick up long st on
left needle, k2 tog tbl, k2, yb, sl.1,
drop next long st to front, sl.3, pick up st on left
needle, sl.3 sts back to left hand
needle, k2, k2 tog, k11; repeat
from * to end of row.
Row 6: Purl.
Row 7: K14, *(k1, yon, k1, yon, k1)
in next st, k17; repeat from * to
last 5 sts, k5.
Row 8: P5, *(p1 y2on) five
times, p17; repeat from * to
last 14 sts, p14.
Row 9: K10, * repeat from * in 3rd
row to last st, k1.
Row 10: P5, *yfwd, sl 3, p17;
repeat from * to last 14 sts, p14.
Row 11: K11, * repeat from * in
5th row to last 2 sts, k2.
Row 12: Purl.

Threaded Cross Stitch

multiple of 2
Use 2 sizes of knitting needles, one size about 4 sizes larger than the other. Cast on with the larger needle size.
Row 1: Knit using the smaller needle size.
Row 2: Purl using the larger needle size.
Row 3: With the smaller needle, *insert point of right hand needle through 1st st purlwise, k the 2nd st leaving it on the left hand needle then k the 1st st through the back loop. Slide both sts tog from the left hand needle. Repeat from * to end of row.
Row 4: Purl using the larger needle.
Row 5: With the smaller needle, k1, *insert the needle through the 2nd st purlwise, k the 1st st leaving it on left hand needle, k the previous st through the back loop as before. Repeat from * to last st, k1.
Repeat from row 2.

Embossed Diagonal Rib

multiple of 4
Row 1: *K3, yfwd, sl.1 purlwise, ybk; repeat from * to end of row.
Row 2 and foll alt rows: Purl.
Row 3: *K2, yfwd, sl.1 purlwise,

ybk, k1; repeat from * to end of row.
Row 5: *K1, yfwd, sl.1 purlwise, ybk, k2; repeat from * to end of row.
Row 7: *Yfwd, sl.1 purlwise, ybk, k3; repeat from * to end of row.

Stepped Diagonal Stitch

multiple of 6 plus 3
Row 1: *K3, p1, k1, p1; repeat from * to last 3 sts, k3.
Row 2 and foll alt rows: K the k sts and p the p sts.
Row 3: K1, *p1, k2, p1, k2; repeat from * to last 2 sts, p1, k1.
Row 5: *K3, p1, k1, p1; repeat from * to last 3 sts, k3.
Row 7: *P1, k1, p1, k3; repeat from * to last 3 sts, p1, k1, p1.

Basket Pattern 1

multiple of 20
Row 1: *P2, k2, p2, k2, p2, k10;
repeat from * to end of row.
Row 2 and foll alt rows: K the k sts
and p the p sts.
Row 3: *P2, k2, p2, k2, p12: repeat
from * to end of row.
Row 5: as row 1.

Row 7: as row 3.
Row 9: as row 1.
Row 11: *K10, p2, k2, p2, k2, p2;
repeat from * to end of row.
Row 13: *P12, k2, p2, k2, p2;
repeat from * to end of row.
Row 15: as row 11.
Row 17: as row 13.
Row 19: as row 11.

Ridged Square Pattern 2

multiple of 3
Row 1: *K2, p1; repeat from * to
end of row.
Row 2: *K1, p2; repeat from * to
end of row.
Row 3: as row 1.
Row 4: Knit.

Dice Pattern

multiple of 10 plus 5
Row 1: K5, *p5, k5; repeat from *
to end of row.
Row 2: P5, *k5, p5; repeat from *
to end of row.
Rows 3, 5, 6 and 8: as row 1.
Rows 4, 7 and 9: as row 2.
Row 10: K5, *p5, k5; repeat from *
to end of row.

Window Stitch

multiple of 12
Row 1: *K2, p6, k4; repeat from *
to end of row.
Row 2 and foll alt rows: K the k sts
and p the p sts.
Rows 3, 5, 7 and 9: *P2, k6, p2, k2;
repeat from * to end of row.
Row 11: *K2, p6, k4; repeat from *
to end of row.
Row 13: Knit.
Row 14: Purl.

Chevron Pattern 3

multiple of 10 plus 1
Row 1: *K1, inc 1 by knitting into
loop in the previous row behind
the next st to be knitted, k2, k2 tog
tbl and place this st back on left
hand needle passing the next st
over it, replace st on right hand
needle, k2, inc 1 as before; repeat
from * to last st, k1.
Row 2 and foll alt rows: Purl.

Eiffel Tower Pattern

multiple of 8
Row 1: *Yon to m1, p2 tog, p6;
repeat from * to end of row.
Rows 2, 4 and 6: *K7, p1; repeat
from * to end of row.
Rows 3, 5 and 7: *K1, p7; repeat
from * to end of row.
Row 8: Purl.
Row 9: P4, yon to m1, p2 tog, p2;
repeat from * to end of row.
Rows 10, 12 and 14: *K3, p1, k4;
repeat from * to end of row.
Rows 11, 13 and 15: *P4, k1, p3;
repeat from * to end of row.
Row 16: Purl.

Broken Diagonal Pattern

multiple of 4 plus 2
Row 1: K1, *p2, k1, sl.1 purlwise;
repeat from * to last st, k1.
Row 2: P1, *sl.1 purlwise, p3;
repeat from * to last st, p1.
Row 3: as row 1.
Row 4: as row 2.
Row 5: K1, *with right hand
needle in front of next 3 sts, insert
needle knitwise into sl. st and then
into 1st st and k, k next 2 sts and sl
st; repeat from * last st, k1.
Row 6: Purl.

Diamond & Lozenge Pattern

multiple of 12
Rows 1 and 2: *K6, p6; repeat
from * to end of row.
Rows 3 and 4: *P1, k5, p5, k1;
repeat from * to end of row.
Rows 5 and 6: *K1, p1, k4, p4, k1,
p1; repeat from * to end of row.
Rows 7 and 8: *P1, k1, p1, k3, p3,
k1, p1, k1; repeat from * to end of
row.
Rows 9 and 10: *(K1, p1) twice, k2,
p2, (k1, p1) twice; repeat from * to
end of row.
Rows 11 and 12: *P1, k1; repeat
from * to end of row.
Rows 13 and 14: *K1, p1; repeat
from * to end of row.
Rows 15 and 16: *(P1, k1) twice,
p2, k2, (p1, k1) twice; repeat from
* to end of row.
Rows 17 and 18: *K1, p1, k1, p3,
k3, p1, k1, p1; repeat from * to
end of row.

Rows 19 and 20: *P1, k1, p4, k4,
p1, k1; repeat from * to end of
row.
Rows 21 and 22: *K1, p5, k5, p1;
repeat from * to end of row.
Rows 23 and 24: *P6, k6; repeat
from * to end of row.
Rows 25 and 26: *P5, k1, p1, k5;
repeat from * to end of row.
Rows 27 and 28: *P4, (k1, p1)
twice, k4; repeat from * to end of
row.
Rows 29 and 30: *P3, (k1, p1) 3
times, k3; repeat from * to end of
row.
Rows 31 and 32: *P2, (k1, p1) 4
times, k2; repeat from * to end of
row.
Rows 33 and 34: *P1, k1; repeat
from * to end of row.
Rows 35 and 36: *K1, p1; repeat
from * to end of row.
Rows 37 and 38: *K2, (p1, k1) 4
times, p2; repeat from * to end of
row.
Rows 39 and 40: *K3, (p1, k1) 3
times, p3; repeat from * to end of
row.
Rows 41 and 42: *K4, (p1, k1)
twice, p4; repeat from * to end of
row.
Rows 43 and 44: *K5, p1, k1, p5;
repeat from * to end of row.

Pinnacle Crepe Pattern

multiple of 18
Row 1: *K1, (p2, k2) twice, p1, (k2, p2) twice; repeat from * to end of row.
Row 2: *(K2, p2) twice, k1, (p2, k2) twice, p1; repeat from * to end of row.
Row 3: as row 1.
Row 4: as row 2.
Row 5: *(P2, k2) twice, p3, k2, p2, k2, p1; repeat from * to end of row.
Row 6: *K1, p2, k2, p2, k3, (p2, k2) twice; repeat from * to end of row.
Row 7: as row 5.
Row 8: as row 6.
Row 9: *P1, (k2, p2) twice, k1, (p2, k2) twice; repeat from * to end of row.
Row 10: *(P2, k2) twice, p1, (k2, p2) twice, k1; repeat from * to end of row.
Row 11: as row 9.
Row 12: as row 10.
Row 13: *(K2, p2) twice, k3, p2, k2, p2, k1; repeat from * to end of row.
Row 14: *P1, k2, p2, k2, p3, (k2, p2) twice; repeat from * to end of row.
Row 15: as row 13.
Row 16: as row 14.

Lazy Daisy Stitch

multiple of 10 plus 5
Row 1: (wrong side) Purl.
Rows 2 and 4: Knit.
Rows 3 and 5: Purl.
Row 6: K5, *insert needle into a st 5 rows below the 3rd st on the left hand needle and pull up a loop, k5, insert the needle in same st and make a second loop, k5; repeat from * to end of row.
Row 7: P4, *p2 tog tbl, p5, p2 tog, p3; repeat from * to last 4 sts, p4.
Row 8: K7, pull up a loop from the same st as before and place on left hand needle, k loop and next st tog tbl, k9; repeat from * to last 7 sts, k7.
Rows 9, 11 and 13: Purl.
Rows 10 and 12: Knit.
Row 14: K10, insert needle into a st 5 rows below the 3rd st on the left hand needle and pull up a loop, k5, make a second loop, k5; repeat from * to last 10 sts, k10.
Row 15: P9, *p2 tog tbl, p5, p2 tog tbl, p3; repeat from * to last 9 sts, p9.
Row 16: K12, pull up a loop from the same st as before and place on left hand needle, k loop and next st tog tbl, k9; repeat from * to last 12 sts, k12.
Row 17: Purl.
Repeat from row 2.

Alternating V's Pattern

multiple of 28
Row 1: *K6, Tw2R, Tw2L, k6,
Tw2L, k8, Tw2R; repeat from * to
end of row.
Row 2 and foll alt rows: Purl.
Row 3: *K5, Tw2R, k2, Tw2L, k6,
Tw2L, k6, Tw2R, k1; repeat from *
to end of row.

Row 5: *K4, Tw2R, k4, Tw2L, k6,
Tw2L, k4, Tw2R, k2; repeat from *
to end of row.
Row 7: *K3, Tw2R, k6, Tw2L, k6,
Tw2L, k2, Tw2R, k3; repeat from *
to end of row.
Row 9: *K2, Tw2R, k8, Tw2L, k6,
Tw2L, Tw2R, k4; repeat from * to
end of row.

Irregular Lattice Pattern

multiple of 8
Row 1 and foll alt rows: Purl.
Row 2: *LT, k2, LT, RT; repeat
from * to end of row.
Row 4: K1, *LT, k2, RT, k2; repeat
from * to last st, k1.
Row 6: *RT, LT, RT, k2; repeat
from * to end of row.
Row 8: K3, *LT, k2, RT, k2; repeat
from * to last 5 sts, LT, k3.

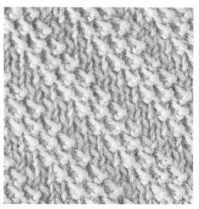

Diagonal Pique Pattern

multiple of 5
Row 1: (wrong side) *P2, **(inc 1
by knitting into front and back of
next st) 3 times**; repeat from
* to end of row.
Row 2: * **K2 tog tbl 3 times**,
k2; repeat from * to end of row.
Row 3: *P1, from ** to ** as in
row 1, p1; repeat from * to end of
row.
Row 4: *K1, from ** to ** as in
row 2, k1; repeat from * to end of
row.
Continue pattern by moving 1 st to
the right every alt. row.

Rectangular Check Pattern

multiple of 6
Row 1 and foll alt rows: Knit.
Rows 2, 4, 6, 8, 10 and 12: ✳K3, p3;
repeat from ✳ to end of row.
Rows 14, 16, 18, 20, 22 and 24: ✳P3,
k3; repeat from ✳ to end of row.

Diagonal Crossed Stitch

multiple of 8
Row 1: ✳(Sl.1 purlwise, k1, yon,
psso the k1 and made st.) twice,
k4; repeat from ✳ to end of row.
Row 2 and foll alt rows: Purl.
Row 3: ✳K2, (sl.1 purlwise, k1,
yon, psso the k1 and made st.)
twice, k2; repeat from ✳ to end of
row.
Continue to move 2 sts to the left
on alt rows.

Diagonal Rib

multiple of 4
Row 1: ✳K2, p2; repeat from ✳ to
end of row.
Row 2 and foll alt rows: K the k sts
and p the p sts.
Row 3: ✳K1, p2, k1; repeat from ✳
to end of row.
Row 5: ✳P2, k2; repeat from ✳ to
end of row.
Row 7: ✳P1, k2, p1; repeat from ✳
to end of row.

Ridged Chevron Pattern 1

multiple of 13
Row 1: ✳Inc 1 (k into front and
back of st), k4, sl.1, k2 tog, psso,
k4, inc 1 as before; repeat from ✳
to end of row.
Row 2: Purl.
Row 3: as row 1.
Row 4: Knit.

Square Pattern

multiple of 6 plus 2
Row 1: K2, *p4, k2; repeat from *
to end of row.
Row 2: P2, *k4, p2; repeat from *
to end of row.
Rows 3, 5 and 7: as row 2.
Rows 4, 6 and 8: as row 1.

Pique Zigzag Pattern

multiple of 10.
Row 1: *K5, (p1, k1) twice, p1;
repeat from * to end of row.
Row 2: *(P1, k1) 3 times, p4: repeat
from * to end of row.
Row 3: *K3, (p1, k1) twice, p1, k2;
repeat from * to end of row.
Row 4: *P3, (k1, p1) twice, k1, p2;
repeat from * to end of row.
Row 5: *(K1, p1) 3 times, k4;
repeat from * to end of row.
Row 6: P5, (k1, p1) twice, k1;
repeat from * to end of row.
Row 7: as row 5.
Row 8: as row 4.
Row 9: as row 3.
Row 10: as row 2.

Raised Leaf Pattern

multiple of 7
Rows 1 and 3: Knit.
Row 2: Purl.
Row 4: *P3, k1, p3; repeat from *
to end of row.
Row 5: *K3, p into front, back and
front of next st, k3; repeat from *
to end of row.
Row 6: *P3, k3, p3; repeat from *
to end of row.
Row 7: *K3, p into front and back
of next st, p1, p into front and
back of next st, k3; repeat from *
to end of row.
Row 8: *P3, k5, p3; repeat from *
to end of row.
Row 9: *K3, p into front and back
of next st, p3, p into front and
back of next st, k3; repeat from *
to end of row.
Row 10: P3, k7, p3; repeat from *
to end of row.
Row 11: K3, p into front and back
of next st, p5, p into front and
back of next st, k3; repeat from *
to end of row.
Row 12: *P3, k9, p3; repeat from *
to end of row.
Row 13: *K3, p2 tog, p5, p2 tog tbl,
k3; repeat from * to end of row.
Row 14: as row 10.
Row 15: *K3, p2 tog, p3, p2 tog tbl,
k3; repeat from * to end of row.
Row 16: as row 8.
Row 17: *K3, p2 tog, p1, p2 tog tbl,
k3; repeat from * to end of row.
Row 18: as row 6.
Row 19: *K3, p3 tog, k3; repeat
from * to end of row.
Row 20: as row 4.

Seed Block Pattern

multiple of 10 plus 2
Row 1: K1, *p1, k1, p1, k1, p6;
repeat from * to last st, k1.
Row 2: K1, *k5, p1, k1, p1, k1, p1;
repeat from * to last st, k1.
Rows 3, 5 and 7: as row 1.
Rows 4, 6 and 8: as row 2.
Row 9: K1, *p6, k1, p1, k1, p1;
repeat from * to last st, k1.
Row 10: K1, *p1, k1, p1, k1, p1,
k5; repeat from * to last st, k1.
Rows 11, 13 and 15: as row 9.
Rows 12, 14 and 16: as row 10.

Looped Stitch Pattern

multiple of 4 plus 1.
Row 1: Knit.
Row 2: Purl.
Row 3: *K1, put right hand needle
between 3rd and 4 sts on left hand
needle and draw through a loop,
keeping loop on right hand
needle, k3 sts; repeat from * to
last st, k1.
Row 4: *P3, p tog next st and loop;
repeat from * to last st, p1.

Diagonal Broken Rib

multiple of 6
Row 1: *K4, p2; repeat from * to
end of row.
Row 2 and foll alt rows: K the k sts
and p the p sts.
Row 3: *K4, p2; repeat from * to
end of row.
Rows 5 and 7: *K2, p2, k2; repeat
from * to end of row.
Rows 9 and 11: *P2, k4; repeat
from * to end of row.

Mock Kilting Pattern

multiple of 9
Row 1: *K8, p1; repeat from * to
end of row.
Row 2: *K2, p7; repeat from * to
end of row.
Row 3: *K6, p3; repeat from * to
end of row.
Row 4: *K4, p5; repeat from * to
end of row.
Row 5: as row 4.
Row 6: as row 3.
Row 7: as row 2.
Row 8: as row 1.

Chequered Pattern

multiple of 12 plus 1
Row 1: *K7, p5; repeat from * to last st, k1.
Row 2 and foll alt rows: K the k sts and p the p sts.
Rows 3 and 5: *K7, p5; repeat from * to last st, k1.
Rows 7, 9 and 11: K1, *p5, k7; repeat from * to end of row.

Diagonal Looped Stitch Pattern

multiple of 4 plus 2.
Row 1: *K1, p1; repeat from * to end of row.
Row 2 and foll alt rows: K the k sts and p the p sts.
Row 3: K1, p1, k1, p1, *put right hand needle under horizontal thread before next st and draw through a loop, k1, p1, k1, pass loop over these sts, p1; repeat from * to last 2 sts, k1, p1.
Row 5: K1, p1, *make loop as before, k1, p1, k1, pass loop over these sts, p1; repeat from * to end of row.
Repeat from row 2.

Nut Pattern

multiple of 4
Row 1: *P3, (k1, yon to m1, k1) into next st; repeat from * to end of row.
Rows 2 and 3: *P3, k3; repeat from * to end of row.
Row 4: *P3 tog, k3; repeat from * to end of row.
Row 5: Purl.
Row 6: Knit.
Row 7: *P1, (k1, yon to m1, k1) into next st, p2; repeat from * to end of row.
Row 8: K2, *p3, k3; repeat from * to last 4 sts, p3, k1.
Row 9: P1, *k3, p3; repeat from * to last 5 sts, k3, p2.
Row 10: K2, *p3 tog, k3; repeat from * to last 4 sts, p3 tog, k1.
Row 11: Purl.
Row 12: Knit.

Spur Stitch

multiple of 2 plus 2
Row 1: Knit.
Row 2: *P2 tog and then k tog those same 2 sts; repeat from * to end of row.
Row 3: Knit.
Row 4: P1, *p2 tog and then k tog these same 2 sts; repeat from * to last st, p1.

Broken V's Pattern

multiple of 13
Row 1: *K1, Tw2R, k2, Tw2R, k1, Tw2L, k3; repeat from * to end of row.
Row 2 and foll alt rows: Purl.
Row 3: *K4, Tw2R, k3, Tw2L, k2; repeat from * to end of row.
Row 5: *K3, Tw2R, k1, Tw2L, k2, Tw2L, k1;
Row 7: *K2, Tw2R, k3, Tw2L, k4; repeat from * to end of row.

Lozenge Pattern 2

multiple of 6 plus 2
Row 1: *Tw2R, k4; repeat from * to last 2 sts, Tw2R.
Row 2 and foll alt rows: Purl.
Row 3: K1, *Tw2L, k2, Tw2R; repeat from * to last st, k1.
Row 5: K2, *Tw2L, Tw2R, k2; repeat from * to end of row.
Row 7: K2, *k1, Tw2R, k3; repeat from * to end of row.
Row 9: K2, *Tw2R, Tw2L, k2; repeat from * to end of row.
Row 11: K1, *Tw2R, k2, Tw2L; repeat from * to last st, k1.

Tulip Pattern

multiple of 3.
Row 1: *K1 tbl, k2; repeat from * to end of row.
Row 2: *P2, p1 tbl; repeat from * to end of row.
Row 3: as row 1.
Row 4: as row 2.
Row 5: *K1 tbl, p1, k1 tbl; repeat from * to end of row.
Row 6: *P1 tbl, k1, p1 tbl; repeat from * to end of row.
Row 7: as row 5.
Row 8: as row 6.
Row 9: *P2, k1 tbl; repeat from * to end of row.
Row 10: *P1 tbl, k2; repeat from * to end of row.
Row 11: as row 9.
Row 12: as row 10.

Twisted V Stitch Pattern

multiple of 12 plus 2
Row 1 and foll alt rows: (wrong side)
K2, *p10, k2; repeat from * to end
of row.
Row 2: P2, *k3, RT, LT, k3, p2;

repeat from * to end of row.
Row 4: P2, *k2, RT, k2, LT, k2, p2;
repeat from * to end of row.
Row 6: P2, *k1, RT, k4, LT, k1, p2;
repeat from * to end of row.
Row 8: P2, *RT, k6, LT, p2; repeat
from * to end of row.

Diagonal Openwork Pattern

multiple of 2 plus 1
Row 1: K1, *yon to m1, k2; repeat
from * to end of row.
Row 2: P1, *p3, pass 3rd st over
1st 2 sts; repeat from * to end of
row.
Row 3: *K2, yon to m1; repeat
from * to last st, k1.
Row 4: *P3, pass 3rd st over 1st 2
sts; repeat from * to last st, p1.

Twisted Columns Pattern 2

multiple of 6
Row 1 and foll alt rows: (wrong side)
*P2, k1, p2, k1; repeat from * to
end of row.
Rows 2, 4, 6 and 8: *P1, k2, p1, **
yfwd, sl.1 purlwise, p1, yon to m1,
psso the p1 and m1**; repeat
from * to end of row.
Rows 10, 12, 14 and 16: *P1, ** to
** as in row 2, p1, k2; repeat
from * to end of row.

TEXTURED PATTERNS

Diagonal Fabric Stitch

multiple of 7
Row 1: ∗K3, Tw2R, Tw2L; repeat from ∗ to end of row.
Row 2 and foll alt rows: Purl.
Row 3: ∗K2, Tw2R, Tw2L, k1; repeat from ∗ to end of row.
Continue to move one st to the right finishing rows 5 and 9 with k1.

Diagonal Stitch

multiple of 2.
Row 1: Purl.
Row 2: ∗K2 tog leaving sts on left hand needle and k the first st again; repeat from ∗ to end of row.
Row 3: Purl.
Row 4: K1, ∗k2 tog leaving sts on left hand needle and k the first st again; repeat from ∗ to last st, k1.

Diagonal Cross Stitch

multiple of 2 plus 2
Row 1: ∗Sl.1 purlwise, k1, yon, psso the k1 and made st; repeat from ∗ to end of row.
Row 2 and foll alt rows: Purl.
Row 3: K1, ∗sl.1 purlwise, k1, yon, psso the k1 and made st; repeat from ∗ to last st, k1.
NOTE: this pattern has a tendency to slant and should not be used for large areas.

Slate Pattern

multiple of 4
Rows 1 and 2: ∗K2, p2; repeat from ∗ to end of row.
Row 3: ∗K2, p1, inc 1 by k into thread between p and next st, p1; repeat from ∗ to end of row.
Row 4: ∗K3, pass 1st st over other 2 sts, p2; repeat from ∗ to end of row.
Rows 5 and 6: ∗P2, k2; repeat from ∗ to end of row.
Row 7: ∗P1, inc 1 by k into thread between p and next st, p1, k2; repeat from ∗ to end of row.
Row 8: ∗P2, k3, pass 1st st over other 2 sts; repeat from ∗ to end of row.

Moss Stitch Diamond Pattern 2

multiple of 8
Row 1: *P1, k7; repeat from * to end of row.
Rows 2 and 8: *K1, p5, k1, p1; repeat from * to end of row.
Rows 3 and 7: *K2, p1, k3, p1, k1; repeat from * to end of row.
Rows 4 and 6: *P2, k1, p1, k1, p3; repeat from * to end of row.
Row 5: *K4, p1, k3; repeat from * to end of row.

Basket Stitch

multiple of 6
Rows 1 and 3: *K2, p4; repeat from * to end of row.
Rows 2 and 4: *K4, p2; repeat from * to end of row.
Rows 5 and 7: *P3, *k2, p4; repeat from * to last 3 sts, k2, p1.
Rows 6 and 8: K1, p2, *k4, p2; repeat from * to last 3 sts, k3.

Treble Cord Stitch

multiple of 9 plus 3
Row 1: *K3, (Tw2R) 3 times, repeat from * to last 3 sts, k3.
Row 2: Purl.

Smocked Rib Pattern

multiple of 16 plus 12
Row 1: K3, p6, *k2, p2, k2, p2, k2, p6; repeat from * to last 3 sts, k3.
Row 2 and foll alt rows: K the k sts and p the p sts.
Rows 3, 5 and 7: as row 1.
Row 9: K3, p2, k2, p2, * **sl next 10 sts on to a cable needle, wind yarn round needle 3 times back to front and on those 10 sts work k2, p6, k2**, p2, k2, p2; repeat from * to last 3 sts, k3.
Rows 11, 13, 15 and 17: K3, p2, k2, *p2, k2, p6, k2, p2, k2; repeat from * to last 5 sts, p2, k3.
Row 19: K1, *repeat from ** to **, p2, k2, p2; repeat from * to last 11 sts, ** to **, k1.

Basket Pattern 2

multiple of 18 plus 10
Row 1: *K11, p2, k2, p2, k1; repeat from * to last 10 sts, k10.
Row 2: P1, k8, p1, *p1, k2, p2, k2, p2, k8, p1; repeat from * to end of row.
Row 3: *K1, p8, k2, p2, k2, p2, k1; repeat from * to last 10 sts, k1, p8, k1.
Row 4: P10, *p1, k2, p2, k2, p11; repeat from * to end of row.
Row 5: as row 1.
Row 6: as row 2.
Row 7: as row 3.
Row 8: as row 4.
Row 9: Knit.
Row 10: P2, k2, p2, k2, p2, *p10, k2, p2, k2, p2; repeat from * to end of row.
Row 11: *K2, p2, k2, p2, k2, p8; repeat from * to last 10 sts, k2, p2, k2, p2, k2.
Row 12: P2, k2, p2, k2, p2, *k8, p2, k2, p2, k2, p2; repeat from * to end of row.
Row 13: *K2, p2, k2, p2, k10; repeat from * to last 10 sts, k2, p2, k2, p2, k2.
Row 14: as row 10.
Row 15: as row 11.
Row 16: as row 12.
Row 17: as row 13.
Row 18: Purl.

Raised Chevron Pattern

multiple of 8
Row 1: *P1, k3; repeat from * to end of row.
Row 2: *K1, p5, k1, p1; repeat from * to end of row.
Row 3: *K2, p1, k3, p1, k1; repeat from * to end of row.
Row 4: *P2, k1, p1, k1, p3; repeat from * to end of row.

Garter Stitch Check Pattern 1

multiple of 6.
Rows 1, 3 and 5: Knit.
Row 2 and foll alt rows: Purl.
Rows 7, 9 and 11: *K3, p3; repeat from * to end of row.
Rows 13, 15 and 17: as row 1.
Rows 19, 21 and 23: *P3, k3; repeat from * to end of row.

Garter Stitch Check Pattern 2

multiple of 6 plus 6
Rows 1 and 3: *P2, k4; repeat from * to end of row.
Row 2 and foll alt rows: Purl.
Rows 5 and 7: K3, *p2, k4; repeat from * to last 3 sts, p2, k1.

Elongated and Dice Check

multiple of 4
Rows 1, 2, 3 and 4: *P2, k2; repeat from * to end of row.
Rows 5 and 6: *K2, p2; repeat from * to end of row.
Rows 7 and 8: *P2, k2; repeat from * to end of row.
Rows 9 and 10: as rows 5 and 6.

Diagonal Grain Stitch

multiple of 4
Row 1 and foll alt rows: Knit.
Row 2: *Yon to m1, p2, pass m1 over p2, p2; repeat from * to end of row.
Row 4: *P2, m1, p2, pass m1 over p2; repeat from * to end of row.

Slip Stitch Diamond Pattern

multiple of 14 plus 2
Row 1: *RT, k12; repeat from * to last 2 sts, RT.
Row 2 and foll alt rows: Purl.
Row 3: K1, *LT, k10, RT; repeat from * to last st, k1.
Row 5: *K2, LT, k8, RT; repeat from * to last 2 sts, k2.
Continue working 2 sts less between crossed sts until the cross is made.

Chickens Foot Pattern

multiple of 4 plus 2
Row 1: Knit.
Row 2: *P2, yon to m1, k2, pass m1 over these 2 sts; repeat from * to end of row, p2.
Row 3: Knit.
Row 4: *Yon to m1, k2, pass m1 over these 2 sts, p2; repeat from * to last 2 sts, yon to m1, k2, pass m1 over these 2 sts.

Bowknot Pattern

multiple of 18 plus 9
Row 1: K9, *p9, k9; repeat from * to end of row.
Row 2: P9, *k9, p9; repeat from * to end of row.
Rows 3 and 5: Knit.
Rows 4 and 6: Purl.
Row 7: as row 1.
Row 8: as row 2.
Row 9: K13, *insert needle into the front of the next st 9 rows below and draw up a loop, sl the loop on to the left hand needle, k the loop and the next st tog, k17; repeat from * to last 13 sts, k13.
Row 10: Purl.
Row 11: as row 2.
Row 12: as row 1.
Rows 13 and 15: Knit.
Rows 14 and 16: Purl.
Row 17: as row 11.
Row 18: as row 12.
Row 19: K4, *pull up a loop from the next st 9 rows below, k the loop and next st tog, k17; repeat from * to last 4 sts, k4.
Row 20: Purl.

Tassel Stitch

multiple of 6 plus 1
Row 1: *K4, p2; repeat from * to last st, k1.
Row 2: P1, *k2, p4; repeat from * to end of row.
Row 3: as row 1.
Row 4: as row 2.
Row 5: *Put right hand needle between 4th and 5th sts and draw through loop, k1, p2, k3; repeat from * to last st, k1.
Row 6: P1, *p3, k2, p2 tog; repeat from * to end of row.
Row 7: K1, *p2, k4; repeat from * to end of row.
Row 8: *P4, k2; repeat from * to last st, p1.
Row 9: as row 7.
Row 10: as row 8.
Row 11: K3, *put right hand needle between 4th and 5th sts and draw through loop, k1, p2, k3; repeat from * to last 4 sts, k1, p2, k1.
Row 12: P1, k2, p1, *p3, k2, p2 tog; repeat from * to last 3 sts, p3.

Peanut Pattern

multiple of 12 plus 4
Row 1: (wrong side) *K1, Tw2R purlwise, k9; repeat from * to last 4 sts, k1, Tw2R purlwise, k1.
Row 2: Tw2R, Tw2L, *p8, Tw2R, Tw2L; repeat from * to end of row.
Row 3: *P4, k8; repeat from * to last 4 sts, p4.
Row 4: K4, *p8, k4; repeat from * to end of row.
Row 5: as row 3.
Row 6: Tw2L, Tw2R, *p8, Tw2L, Tw2R; repeat from * to end of row.
Row 7: as row 1.
Row 8: as row 2.
Row 9: as row 3.
Row 10: as row 4.
Row 11: as row 3.
Row 12: as row 6.
Row 13: as row 1.
Row 14: Purl.
Row 15: *K7, Tw2R purlwise, k3; repeat from * to last 4 sts, k4.
Row 16: P4, *p2, Tw2R, Tw2L, p6; repeat from * to end of row.
Row 17: *K6, p4, k2; repeat from * to last 4 sts, k4.
Row 18: P4, *p2, k4, p6; repeat from * to end of row.
Row 19: as row 17.
Row 20: P4, *p2, Tw2L, Tw2R, p6; repeat from * to end of row.
Row 21: as row 15.
Row 22: as row 16.
Row 23: as row 17.
Row 24: as row 18.
Row 25: as row 17.
Row 26: as row 20.
Row 27: as row 15.
Row 28: as row 14.

Darning Pattern

multiple of 4
Row 1: *K2, yfwd, sl 2 purlwise,
ybk; repeat from * to end of row.
Row 2 and foll alt rows: Purl.
Row 3: *K2, yfwd, sl 2 purlwise,
ybk; repeat from * to end of row.
Row 5: Knit.
Rows 7 and 9: *Yfwd, sl 2 purlwise,
ybk, k2; repeat from * to end of
row.

Valve Stitch

multiple of 3
Row 1: (wrong side) Knit.
Row 2: *K3 tog leaving sts on left
hand needle, k the 1st st, k next 2
sts tbl; repeat from * to end of
row.
Row 3: Purl.
Row 4: Knit.

Alternating Bell Pattern

multiple of 8
Rows 1 to 6: *K4, p4; repeat from *
to end of row.
Row 7: *Tw2L, Tw2R, k4; repeat
from * to end of row.
Rows 8 to 14: *P4, k4; repeat from
* to end of row.
Row 15: *K4, Tw2L, Tw2R; repeat
from * to end of row.
Row 16: *K4, p4; repeat from * to
end of row.

Broken Chevron Pattern

multiple of 18
Row 1: *K1, p2, k2, p2, k1, p1;
repeat from * to end of row.
Row 2: *K3, p2, k2, p2, k1, p2, k2,
p2, k2; repeat from * to end of
row.
Row 3: *P1, k2, p2, k2, p3, k2, p2,
k2, p2; repeat from * to end of
row.
Row 4: *K1, p2, k2, p2, k5, p2, k2,
p2; repeat from * to end of row.

Basket Check

multiple of 8
Rows 1, 2, 3 and 4: *K4, p4; repeat
from * to end of row.
Rows 5, 6, 7 and 8: *P4, k4; repeat
from * to end of row.

Ripple Stitch

multiple of 3
Row 1: *K2 tog, k the 1st st again,
k1; repeat from * to end of row.
Row 2 and foll alt rows: Purl.
Row 3: *K1, k2 tog, k the 1st st
again; repeat from * to end of
row.

Ridged Chevron Pattern 2

multiple of 10 plus 2
Row 1: K4, *RT, LT, k6; repeat
from * to last 4 sts, k4.
Rows 2, 4 and 6: Purl.
Row 3: K3, *RT, k2, LT, k4; repeat
from * to last 3 sts, k3.
Row 5: K2, *RT, k4, LT, k2; repeat
from * to end of row.
Row 7: K1, *RT, k6, LT; repeat
from * to last st, k1.
Row 8: K2, *p8, k2; repeat from *
to end of row.
Row 9: P2, *k8, p2; repeat from *
to end of row.
Row 10: Knit.

Row 11: as row 9.
Row 12: as row 10.
Row 13: as row 9.
Row 14: as row 8.
Row 15: K1, *LT, k6, RT; repeat
from * to last st, k1.
Rows 16, 18 and 20: Purl.
Row 17: K2, *LT, k4, RT, k2;
repeat from * to end of row.
Row 19: K3, *LT, k2, RT, k4;
repeat from * to last 3 sts, k3.
Row 21: K4, *LT, RT, k6; repeat
from * to last 4 sts, k4.
Row 22: P5, *k2, p8; repeat from *
to last 5 sts, p5.
Row 23: K5, *p2, k8; repeat from *
to last 5 sts, k5.
Row 24: Knit.
Row 25: as row 23.
Row 26: as row 24.
Row 27: as row 23.
Row 28: as row 22.

Dropped-stitch Patterns

*Dropped and lengthened stitches
worked with yarn overs
to make light, airy, openwork patterns*

Vertical Drop Stitch Pattern

multiple of 8 plus 4
Row 1: K1, *p2, k1, yon, k1, p2, k2; repeat from * to last 3 sts, p2, k1.
Rows 2 and 4: P1, *k2, p2, k2, p3; repeat from * to last 3 sts, k2, p1.
Rows 3 and 5: K1, *p2, k3, p2, k2; repeat from * to last 3 sts, p2, k1.
Row 6: as row 2.
Row 7: K1, *p2, k1, drop next st and unravel down to yon of 1st row, k1, p2, k1, yon, k1; repeat from * to last 3 sts, p2, k1.
Rows 8 and 10: P1, *k2, p3, k2, p2; repeat from * to last 3 sts, k2, p1.
Rows 9 and 11: K1, *p2, k2, p2, k3; repeat from * to last 3 sts, p2, k1.
Row 12: as row 8.
Row 13: K1, *p2, k1, yon, k1, p2, k1, drop next st and unravel to yon of 7th row, k1; repeat from * to last 3 sts, p2, k1.
Repeat from row 2.

Butterfly Pattern

multiple of 12 plus 4
Row 1: P2, *k4, k2 tog, yon, sl.1, k1, psso, k4; repeat from * to last 2 sts, p2.
Row 2: K2, *p3, p2 tog tbl, drop yo, y2on, p2 tog, p3; repeat from * to last 2 sts, k2.
Row 3: P2, *k2, k2 tog, drop yo, y3on, sl.1, k1, psso, k2; repeat from * to last 2 sts, p2.
Row 4: K2, *p1, p2 tog tbl, drop yo, y4on, p2 tog, p1; repeat from * to last 2 sts, k2.
Row 5: P2, *k2 tog, drop yo, cast on 4 sts on right hand needle, k1 under the 4 loose strands of yos, yon, k1 under the 4 loose strands, cast on 4 sts on right hand needle, sl.1, k1, psso; repeat from * to last 2 sts, p2.
Row 6: K2, *p5, p2 tog, p6; repeat from * to last 2 sts, k2.

*Sweater with neck cut straight across fastening with buttons, ribbed
deep yoke, knitted in elongated garter stitch in Jaeger Langora yarn*

Shell Stitch

multiple of 6 plus 2
Rows 1 and 2: Knit.
Row 3: K1, *y3on, k1; repeat from * to end of row.
Row 4: K1, *drop yo, k1; repeat from * to end of row.
Row 5: K1, *sl.3, k2 tog, p3sso, (k1, p1, k1, p1, k1) into next st; repeat from * to last st, k1.
Rows 6 to 8: Knit.
Row 9: as row 3.
Row 10: as row 4.
Row 11: K1, *(k1, p1, k1, p1, k1) into next st, sl.3, k2 tog, p3sso; repeat from * to last st, k1.
Row 12: Knit.

Cross Stitch

multiple of 8
Row 1: Knit.
Row 2: *(p1, y2on) 6 times, k2; repeat from * to end of row.
Row 3: *K2, sl 6 sts on to right hand needle dropping the loops, pass to left hand needle, lift last 3 sts over first 3 sts and k sts in sequence tbl; repeat from * to end of row.
Row 4: P4, *(p1 y2on) 6 times, k2; repeat from * to last 4 sts, p4.
Row 5: K4, *k2, put needle under first 3 sts, pull last 3 sts through and k sts in sequence; repeat from * to last 4 sts, k4.
Repeat from row 2.

Indian Cross Stitch

multiple of 8
Rows 1 to 4: Knit.
Row 5: K1, *with needle in next st, y4on and k the st; repeat from * to last st, k1.
Row 6: *Ybk, sl 8 sts letting loops drop, with left hand needle, pick up the first 4 sts and pass them over the second 4 sts, place the crossed sts on to the left hand needle and k the second 4 sts first, then the first 4 sts; repeat from * to end of row.
Rows 7 to 10: Knit.
Row 11: as row 5.
Row 12: Sl 4 sts dropping the loops, cross 2 over 2 and k these sts, *sl 8, cross and k as for row 6; repeat from * to last 4 sts, sl 4 sts, cross 2 over 2 and k.

Coral Loop Stitch

multiple of 2 plus 1
Row 1: Sl.1, *k2 tog; repeat from * to end of row.
Row 2: *Put needle knitwise into 1st st, wind yarn twice round needle point and draw through, put needle into loop between sts and k, wind yarn twice round needle and draw through; repeat from * to end of row.
Row 3: K1, *k 1st loop allowing 2nd loop to drop; repeat from * to end of row.
Row 4: Purl.

Clam Stitch

multiple of 6 plus 1
Row 1: Knit.
Row 2: *P1, (p1, y2on) 5 times;
repeat from * to last st, p1.
Row 3: K1, *sl 5 sts to right hand
needle, dropping the loops, pass
to left needle and work them thus,
k5 tog, y2on, p5 tog, y2on, k5 tog,
y2on, p5 tog, y2on, k5 tog, y2on,
k1; repeat from * to end of row.
Row 4: *P1, k5 dropping the loops;
repeat from * to last st, p1.
Row 5: Knit.
Row 6: P4, *(p1, y2on) 5 times, p1;
repeat from * to last 3 sts, p3.
Row 7: K3, *k1, work next 5 sts as
in row 3; repeat from * to last 4
sts, k4.
Row 8: P4, *k5 dropping the loops,
p1; repeat from * to last 3 sts, p3.

Dropped Stitch Triangle Pattern

multiple of 18 plus 6
Row 1: *P5, (k1, y2on, p1) 5 times,
p3; repeat from * to last 6 sts, p6.
Row 2: K the k sts, yfwd, sl the p
sts letting the yons drop.
Rows 3 and 7: P the p sts, ybk, sl
purlwise the k sts.
Rows 4 and 8: K the k sts, yfwd, sl
the p sts.
Row 5: *P5, k1, (p1, k1, y2on) 3
times, p1, k1, p4; repeat from * to
last 6 sts, p.6.
Rows 6 and 10: as row 2 but k the
first and last sl st of each triangle.
Row 9: *P7, k1, p1, k1, y2on, p1,
k1, p6; repeat from * to end of
row.
Row 11: as row 3.
Row 12: as row 4.
Row 13: P2, (k1, y2on, p1) twice,
*p3, k1, p4, (k1, y2on, p1) 5 times;
repeat from * to end of row.
Row 14: as row 2.
Row 15: as row 3.
Row 16: as row 4.
Row 17: P2, k1, y2on, p1, k1, *p9,
k1, p1, (k1, y2on, p1) three times,
k1; repeat from * to last st, p1.
Row 18: as row 6.
Row 19: as row 3.
Row 20: as row 4.
Row 21: P2, k1, p3, *p10, k1, p1,
k1, y2on, p1, k1, p3; repeat from *
to end of row.
Row 22: as row 6.
Row 23: as row 3.
Row 24: as row 4.

Moss Drop Stitch

multiple of 2 plus 1
Rows 1 to 6: *K1, p1; repeat from
* to last st, k1.
Row 7: Keeping in moss stitch,
work y2on each stitch.
Row 8: Keeping in moss stitch, let
loop drop from needle for each
stitch.

Hyacinth Stitch

multiple of 6 plus 2
Row 1: (wrong side) K1, *p5 tog,
(k1, p1, k1, p1, k1) into next st;
repeat from * to last st, k1.
Rows 2 and 4: Purl.
Row 3: K1, *(k1, p1, k1, p1, k1)
into next st, p5 tog; repeat from *
to last st, k1.
Row 5: K1, *(k1 y3on). six times;
repeat from * to last st, k1.
Row 6: P each st letting yons drop.

Wave Stitch

multiple of 10 plus 6
Rows 1 and 2: Knit.
Row 3: K6, *y2on, k1, y3on, k1,
y4on, k1, y3on, k1, y2on, k6;
repeat from * to end of row.
Row 4: K each st dropping yons
from needle.
Rows 5 and 6: Knit.
Row 7: *K1, y2on, k1, y3on, k1,
y4on, k1, y3on, k1, y2on, k5;
repeat from * to last 6 sts, k1,
y2on, k1, y3on, k1, y4on, k1,
y3on, k1, y2on, k1.
Row 8: as row 4.

Openwork Cross Stitch

multiple of 6
Row 1: Knit.
Row 2: *K1 y3on; repeat from * to
end of row.
Row 3: *Sl 6 sts to right hand
needle letting loops drop, sl to left
hand needle and k the 4th, then
the 5th and the 6th st, k the 1st,
2nd and 3rd sts; repeat from * to
end of row.
Row 4: Knit.

Simple Drop Stitch

multiple of any number of stitches
Row 1: *K1 y3on; repeat from * to
end of row.
Row 2: *P1 letting loops drop from
needle; repeat from * to end of
row.

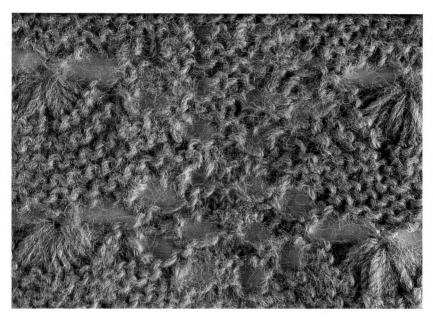

Garter Drop Stitch

multiple of any number of stitches
Rows 1 to 4: Knit.
Row 5: *K1, y2on; repeat from * to end of row.
Row 6: *K1 letting loop drop from needle; repeat from * to end of row.

Openwork Fan Pattern

multiple of 19
Rows 1 and 2: Knit.
Row 3: *K1, y2on, p2 tog tbl, k13, p2 tog, y2on, k1; repeat from * to end of row.
Row 4: *K1, k1 into 1st loop, p1 into 2nd loop, k15, p1 into 1st loop, k1 into 2nd loop, k1; repeat from * to end of row.
Rows 5 and 6: Knit.
Row 7: *K1, (y2on, p2 tog tbl) twice, k11, (p2 tog, y2on) twice, k1; repeat from * to end of row.
Row 8: *(K1, k1 into 1st loop, p1 into 2nd loop) twice, k13, (p1 into 1st loop, k1 into 2nd loop, k1) twice; repeat from * to end of row.
Row 9: Knit.
Row 10: *K6, (y2on, k1) 14 times, k5; repeat from * to end of row.
Row 11: *K1, (y2on, p2 tog tbl) twice, y2on, letting the extra loops of previous row drop, p15 tog, (y2on, p2 tog tbl) twice; y2on, k1; repeat from * to end of row.
Row 12: *(K1, p1 into 1st loop, k1 into 2nd loop) three times, k1, (k1, into 1st loop, p1 into 2nd loop, k1) three times; repeat from * to end of row.

Lace Patterns

Lace in its many and various forms: simple eyelets, old Shetland laces, laces based on patterns from nature

Alternating Leaf and Eyelet Pattern

multiple of 10 plus 2
Row 1: K1, *yon, sl.1, k1, psso, k8; repeat from * to last st, k1.
Row 2 and foll alt rows: Purl.
Row 3: K1, *k1, yon, sl.1, k1, psso, k5, k2 tog, yon; repeat from * to last st, k1.
Row 5: K1, *k2, yon, sl.1, k1, psso, k3, k2 tog, yon, k1; repeat from * to last st, k1.
Row 7: K1, *k5, yon, sl.1, k1, psso, k3; repeat from * to last st, k1.
Row 9: K1, *k3, k2 tog, yon, k1, yon, sl.1, k1, psso, k2; repeat from * to last st, k1.
Row 11: K1, *k2, k2 tog, yon, k3, yon, sl.1, k1, psso, k1; repeat from * to last st, k1.

Butterfly Eyelet Pattern

multiple of 10
Rows 1 and 3: *K2 tog, yon, k1, yon, sl.1, k1, psso, k5; repeat from * to end of row.
Rows 2 and 4: *P7, sl.1 purlwise, p2; repeat from * to end of row.
Row 5: Knit.

Row 6: Purl.
Rows 7 and 9: *K5, k2 tog, yon, k1, yon, sl.1, k1, psso; repeat from * to end of row.
Rows 8 and 10: *P2, sl.1 purlwise, p7; repeat from * to end of row.
Row 11: Knit.
Row 12: Purl.

Pearl Barred Scallop Pattern

multiple of 13 plus 2
Row 1: K2, *yon, k4, sl.1, k2 tog, psso, k4, yon, k2; repeat from * to end of row.
Rows 2, 4, 6, 8 and 10: Purl.
Rows 3, 5, 7 and 9: as row 1.
Row 11: Purl.
Row 12: Knit.

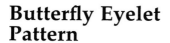

Easy fitting sweater with elbow length sleeves, ribbed at neck, cuffs and hem, knitted in an allover lacy leaf pattern in Sirdar Talisman DK

Alternating Feather Stitch

multiple of 6 plus 1.
Row 1: *K1, k2 tog, yon, k1, yon, sl.1, k1, psso; repeat from * to last st, k1.
Row 2 and foll alt rows: Purl.
Rows 3, 5, 7, 9 and 11: *K1, k2 tog, yon, k1, yon, sl.1, k1, psso; repeat from * to last st, k1.
Rows 13, 15, 17, 19, 21 and 23: *K1, yon, sl.1, k1, psso, k1, k2 tog, yon; repeat from * to last st, k1.

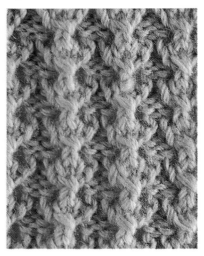

Simple Eyelet Rib

multiple of 3 plus 2
Row 1: *P2, yon, k1, yon; repeat from * to last 2 sts, p2.
Row 2: K2, *p3, k2; repeat from * to end of row.
Row 3: *P2, k3; repeat from * to last 2 sts, p2.
Row 4: K2, *p3 tog, k2; repeat from * to end of row.

Openwork Trellis Pattern

multiple of 7
Row 1: *K2, k2 tog, yon, k3; repeat from * to end of row.
Row 2: *P1, p2 tog tbl, yon, p1, yon, p2 tog, p1; repeat from * to end of row.
Row 3: *K2 tog, yon, k3, yon, sl.1, k1, psso; repeat from * to end of row.
Row 4: Purl.
Row 5: *Yon, sl.1, k1, psso, k5; repeat from * to end of row.
Row 6: *Yon, p2 tog, p2, p2 tog tbl, yon, p1; repeat from * to end of row.
Row 7: *K2, yon, sl.1, k1, psso, k2 tog, yon, k1; repeat from * to end of row.
Row 8: Purl.

Purse Stitch

multiple of 2 plus 2
Row 1 and foll rows: K1, *yon, p2 tog; repeat from * to last st, k1.

Little Leaf Panels

multiple of 9 plus 2
Row 1: *P2, sl.1, k1, psso, yon, k3, yon, k2 tog; repeat from * to last 2 sts, p2.
Rows 2 and 4: K2, *p7, k2; repeat from * to end of row.
Row 3: *P2, k2, yon, sl.1, k2 tog, psso, yon, k2; repeat from * to last 2 sts, p2.

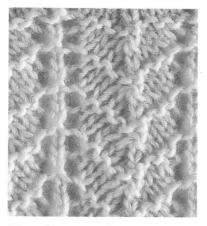

Eyelet and Chevron Pattern

multiple of 10
Rows 1 to 3: Knit.
Rows 4 and 6: *yon, k3, k3 tog, k3, yon, k1; repeat from * to end of row.
Row 5: Purl.
Row 7: Knit.
Repeat from row 4.

Snowdrop Lace Pattern 1

multiple of 8 plus 5
Rows 1 and 3: K1, *yon, k2 tbl and place st on left hand needle, pass next st over it and replace on right hand needle, yon, k5; repeat from * to last 4 sts, yon, k2 tbl and pass st over as before, yon, k1.
Row 2 and foll alt rows: Purl.
Row 5: K1, *k3, yon, sl.1, k1, psso, k1, k2 tog, yon; repeat from * to last 4 sts, k4.
Row 7: K1, *yon, k2 tbl and pass st over as before, yon, k1; repeat from * to last 4 sts, yon, k2 tbl and pass st over as before, yon, k1.

Little Leaf Pattern

multiple of 6 plus 3
Row 1: K1, p2, k3, *p3, k3; repeat from * to last 3 sts, p2, k1.
Rows 2 and 4: K3, *p3, k3; repeat from * to end of row.
Row 3: K1, p2, *yon, k3 tog, yon, p3; repeat from * to last 6 sts, yon, k3 tog, yon, p2, k1.

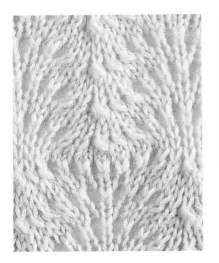

Ostrich Plume Pattern

multiple of 16 plus 1
Row 1 and foll alt rows: (wrong side) Purl.
Row 2: Knit.
Row 4: (K1, yon) three times, *
(sl.1, k1, psso) twice, sl 2, k1,
p2sso, (k2 tog) twice, (yon, k1) five
times, yon; repeat from * to last 3
sts, (yon, k1) three times.
Rows 6, 10, 14 and 18: Knit.
Rows 8, 12 and 16: as row 4.
Row 20: (K2 tog) three times, *
(yon, k1) five times, yon, (sl.1, k1
psso) twice, sl 2, k1, p2sso, (k2
tog) twice; repeat from * to last 11
sts, (yon, k1) five times, yon, (sl.1,
k1, psso) three times.
Rows 22, 26, 30: Knit.
Rows 24, 28 and 32: as row 20.

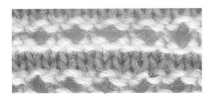

Ribbon Eyelet Pattern

An uneven number of stitches
Row 1: Knit.
Row 2: Purl.
Rows 3 and 4: Knit.
Row 5: *K2 tog, yon; repeat from
* to last st, k1.
Row 6: Knit.

Pine Trees Pattern 1

multiple of 16 plus 1
Row 1: K1, *k5, k2 tog, yon, k1,
yon, SSK, k6; repeat from * to end
of row.
Row 2 and foll alt rows: Purl.
Row 3: K1, *k4, k2 tog, yon, k3,
yon, SSK, k5; repeat from * to end
of row.
Row 5: K1, *k3, (k2 tog, yon)
twice, k1, (yon, SSK) twice, k4;
repeat from * to end of row.
Row 7: K1, *k2, (k2 tog, yon)
twice, k3, (yon, SSK) twice, k3;
repeat from * to end of row.
Row 9: K1, *k1, (k2 tog, yon) three
times, k1, (yon, SSK) three times,
k2; repeat from * to end of row.
Row 11: as row 7.
Row 13: as row 5.
Row 15: as row 3.
Row 17: as row 1.
Row 19: K1, *k6, k2 tog, yon, k8;
repeat from * to end of row.
Row 21: K1, *yon, SSK, k11, k2
tog, yon, k1; repeat from * to end
of row.
Row 23: K1, *k1, yon, SSK, k9, k2
tog, yon, k2; repeat from * to end
of row.
Row 25: K1, *(yon, SSK) twice, k7,
(k2 tog, yon) twice, k1; repeat from
* to end of row.
Row 27: K1, *k1 (yon, SSK) twice,
k5, (k2 tog, yon) twice, k2; repeat
from * to end of row.
Row 29: K1, *(yon, SSK) three
times, k3, (k2 tog, yon) three
times, k1; repeat from * to end of
row.
Row 31: as row 27.
Row 33: as row 25.
Row 35: as row 23.
Row 37: as row 21.
Row 39: K15, *k2 tog, yon, k14;
repeat from * to last 2 sts, k2.

Shell Pattern 1

multiple of 7 plus 4
Row 1: K2, *yon, sl.1, k1, psso, k5; repeat from * to last 2 sts, yon, k2 tog.
Row 2 and foll alt rows: Purl.
Row 3: K2, *yon, k1, sl.1, k1, psso, k4; repeat from * to last 2 sts, yon, k2 tog.
Row 5: K2, *yon, k2, sl.1, k1, psso, k3; repeat from * to last 2 sts, yon, k2 tog.
Row 7: K2, *yon, k3, sl.1, k1, psso, k2; repeat from * to last 2 sts, yon, k2 tog.
Row 9: K2, *yon, k4, sl.1, k1, psso, k1; repeat from * to last 2 sts, yon, k2 tog.
Row 11: K2, *yon, k5, sl.1, k1, psso; repeat from * to last 2 sts, yon, k2 tog.
NOTE this stitch should not be used for large areas of knitting because of its tendency to slant.

Faggot and Chevron Pattern

multiple of 7
Row 1: *K2, sl.1, k2 tog, psso, k2, yon; repeat from * to end of row.
Row 2: *P6, yon; repeat from * to end of row.

Mrs. Montague's Pattern

multiple of 16 plus 1
Row 1 and foll alt rows: (wrong side) Purl.
Row 2: K1, *k4, yon, k2 tog tbl, k3, k2 tog, yon, k5; repeat from * to end of row.
Row 4: K1, *yon, k2 tog tbl, k3, yon, k2 tog tbl, k1, k2 tog, yon, k3, k2 tog, yon, k1; repeat from * to end of row.
Row 6: K1, *k1, yon, k2 tog tbl, k3, yon, sl.1, k2 tog, psso, yon, k3, k2 tog, yon, k2; repeat from * to end of row.
Row 8: K1, *k2, yon, k2 tog tbl, k7, k2 tog, yon, k3; repeat from * to end of row.
Row 10: K1, *k1, k2 tog, yon, k9, yon, k2 tog tbl, k2; repeat from * to end of row.
Row 12: K1, *k2 tog, yon, k3, k2 tog, yon, k1, yon, k2 tog tbl, k3, yon, k2 tog tbl, k1; repeat from * to end of row.
Row 14: K2 tog, *yon, k3, k2 tog, yon, k3, yon, k2 tog tbl, k3, yon, sl.1, k2 tog, psso; repeat from * to last 2 sts, k2 tog tbl.
Row 16: K1, *k3, k2 tog, yon, k5, yon, k2 tog tbl, k4; repeat from * to end of row.

Bell Pattern

multiple of 5
Row 1: *K3, p2; repeat from * to end of row.
Row 2 and foll alt rows: *K2, p3; repeat from * to end of row.
Row 3: as row 1.
Row 5: *Yon, sl.1, k2 tog, psso, yon, p2; repeat from * to end of row.

Corded Ladder Stitch

multiple of 4
Row 1: *Yon, k4; repeat from * to end of row.
Rows 2, 4 and 6: Purl.
Rows 3 and 5: *Yon, k into 3rd st on left hand needle, k tog 1st and 2nd sts, from the back k the 2nd st tbl, k the 1st st.
Repeat from row 2.

Eyelet Check Pattern

multiple of 8 plus 5
Row 1: *K5, p3; repeat from * to last 5 sts, k5.
Row 2: P5, *k3, p5; repeat from * to end of row.
Row 3: *K5, p1, yon, p2 tog; repeat from * to last 5 sts, k5.
Row 4: as row 2.
Row 5: as row 1.
Row 6: Purl.
Row 7: *K1, p3, k4; repeat from * to last 5 sts, k1, p3, k1.
Row 8: P1, k3, p1, *p4, k3, p1; repeat from * to end of row.
Row 9: *K1, p1, yon, p2 tog, k4; repeat from * to last 5 sts, k1, p1, yon, p2 tog, k1.
Row 10: as row 8.
Row 11: as row 7.
Row 12: Purl.

Eyelet and Ridge Pattern

multiple of 7
Row 1: *P1, p2 tog, yon, k1, yon, p2 tog, p1; repeat from * to end of row.
Rows 2 and 4: Purl.
Row 3: Knit.

Diagonal Shell Lace Pattern

multiple of 6 plus 2
Row 1: K1, *k4, k2 tog, yon; repeat from * to last st, k1.
Row 2: P1, *yon, p1, p2 tog, p3; repeat from * to last st, p1.
Row 3: K1, *k2, k2 tog, k2, yon; repeat from * to last st, k1.
Row 4: P1, *yon, p3, p2 tog, p1; repeat from * to last st, p1.
Row 5: K1, *k2 tog, k4, yon; repeat from * to last st, k1.
Row 6: P2, *p4, yon, p2 tog; repeat from * to end of row.
Row 7: K1, *k1, yon, k3, k2 tog; repeat from * to last st, k1.
Row 8: P1, *p2 tog, p2, yon, p2; repeat from * to last st, p1.
Row 9: K1, *k3, yon, k1, k2 tog; repeat from * to last st, k1.
Row 10: P1, *p2 tog, yon, p4; repeat from * to last st, p1.

Ladder and Chevron Pattern

multiple of 8 plus 1
Row 1: *K1, yon, k2, sl.1, k2 tog, psso, k2, yon; repeat from * to last st, k1.
Rows 2 and 4: Purl.
Row 3: *K1, yon, k2, k3 tog purlwise, k2, yon; repeat from * to last st, k1.

Bell and Rope Pattern

multiple of 5
Row 1: P2, *k1 tbl, p4; repeat from * to last 3 sts, k1 tbl, p2.
Row 2: K2, p1 tbl, *k4, p1 tbl; repeat from * to last 2 sts, k2.
Row 3: P2, *k1 tbl, p2, cast on 8 sts, p2; repeat from * to last 3 sts, k1 tbl, p2.
Row 4: K2, p1 tbl, *k2, p8, k2, p1 tbl; repeat from * to last 2 sts, k2.
Row 5: P2, *k1 tbl, p2, k8, p2; repeat from * to last 3 sts, k1 tbl, p2.
Row 6: as row 4.
Row 7: P2, *k1 tbl, p2, sl.1, k1, psso, k4, k2 tog, p2; repeat from * to last 3 sts, k1 tbl, p2.
Row 8: K2, p1 tbl, *k2, p2 tog, p2, p1 and return st to left hand needle, pass next st over it and return to right hand needle, k2, p1 tbl; repeat from * to last 2 sts, k2.
Row 9: P2, *k1 tbl, p2, sl.1, k1, psso, k2 tog, p2; repeat from * to last three sts, k1 tbl, p2.
Row 10: K2, p1 tbl, *k1, (k2 tog) twice, k1, p1 tbl; repeat from * to last 2 sts, k2.

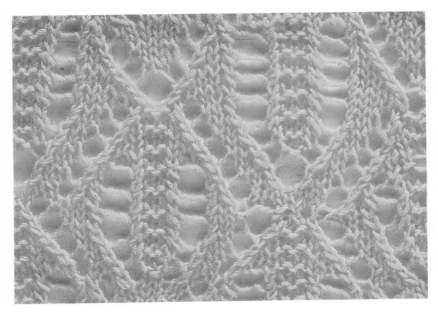

Diamond and Horseshoe Lace

multiple of 20 plus 4

Row 1: K2 tog, yon, *yon, SKPO, k3, k2 tog, y2on, SKPO, p2, k2 tog, y2on, SKPO, k3, k2 tog, yon; repeat from * to last 2 sts, yon, SKPO.

Row 2 and foll alt rows: Purl, working k1, p1 into each y2on.

Row 3: K2 tog, yon, *k1, yon, SKPO, k2, k2 tog, y2on, SKPO, p2, k2 tog, y2on, SKPO, k2, k2 tog, yon, k1; repeat from * to last 2 sts, yon, SKPO.

Row 5: K2 tog, yon, *k2, yon, SKPO, k1, k2 tog, y2on, SKPO, p2, k2 tog, y2on, SKPO, k1, k2 tog, yon, k2; repeat from * to last 2 sts, yon, SKPO.

Row 7: K2 tog, yon, *k3, yon, SKPO, k2 tog, y2on, SKPO, p2, k2 tog, y2on, SKPO, k2 tog, yon, k3; repeat from * to last 2 sts, yon, SKPO.

Row 9: K2 tog, yon, *(yon, SKPO, k2) twice, k1, p2, k1, (k2, k2 tog, yon) twice; repeat from * to last 2 sts, yon, SKPO.

Row 11: K2 tog, yon, *p1, (yon, SKPO, k2) twice, p2, (k2, k2 tog, yon) twice, p1; repeat from * to last 2 sts, yon, SKPO.

Row 13: K2 tog, yon, *p1, k1, yon, SKPO, k2, yon, SKPO, k1, p2, k1, k2 tog, yon, k2, k2 tog, yon, k1, p1; repeat from * to last 2 sts, yon, SKPO.

Row 15: K2 tog, yon, *p1, k2 tog, y2on, SKPO, k2, yon, SKPO, p2, k2 tog, yon, k2, k2 tog, y2on, SKPO, p1; repeat from * to last 2 sts, yon, SKPO.

Row 17: K2 tog, yon, *p1, k2 tog, y2on, SKPO, k3, yon, SKPO, k2 tog, yon, k3, k2 tog, y2on, SKPO, p1; repeat from * to last 2 sts, yon, SKPO.

Row 19: K2 tog, yon, *p1, k2 tog, y2on, SKPO, k1, k2 tog, yon, k4, yon, SKPO, k1, k2 tog, y2on, SKPO, p1; repeat from * to last 2 sts, yon, SKPO.

Row 21: K2 tog, yon, *p1, k2 tog, y2on, SKPO, k2 tog, yon, k6, yon, SKPO, k2 tog, y2on, SKPO, p1; repeat from * to last 2 sts, yon, SKPO.

Row 23: K2 tog, yon, *p1, (k2 tog, yon, k1) twice, k1, k2 tog, y2on, SKPO, k1, (k1, yon, SKPO) twice, p1; repeat from * to last 2 sts, yon, SKPO.

Row 25: K2 tog, yon, *p1, (k2, k2 tog, yon) twice, p2, (yon, SKPO, k2) twice, p1; repeat from * to last 2 sts, yon, SKPO.

Row 27: K2 tog, yon, *p1, (k1, k2 tog, yon, k1) twice, p2, (k1, yon, SKPO, k1) twice, p1; repeat from * to last 2 sts, yon, SKPO.

Row 29: K2 tog, yon, *p1, k2 tog, yon, k2, k2 tog, y2on, SKPO, p2, k2 tog, y2on, SKPO, k2, yon, SKPO, p1; repeat from * to last 2 sts, yon, SKPO.

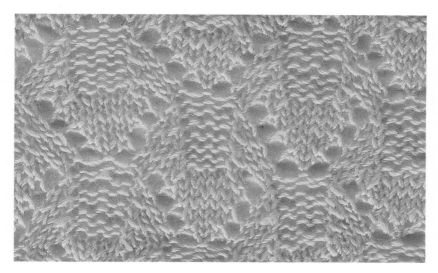

Filigree Pattern

multiple of 14 plus 2
Row 1: P1, *p2, k2 tog, k3, yon, k1, yon, k3, sl.1, k1, psso, p1; repeat from * to last st, p1.
Row 2 and foll alt rows: K the k sts and p the p sts.
Row 3: P1, *p2, k2 tog, k2, yon, k3, yon, k2, sl.1, k1, psso, p1; repeat from * to last st, p1.
Row 5: P1, *p2, k2 tog, k1, yon, k5, yon, k1, sl.1, k1, psso, p1; repeat from * to last st, p1.
Row 7: P1, *p2, k2 tog, yon, k7, yon, sl.1, k1, psso, p1; repeat from * to last st, p1.
*Row 9:*P1, *k1, yon, k3, sl.1, k1, psso, p3, k2 tog, k3, yon; repeat from * to last st, p1.
Row 11: P1, *k2, yon, k2, sl.1, k1, psso, p3, k2 tog, k2, yon, k1;

repeat from * to last st. p1.
Row 13: P1, *k3, yon, k1, sl.1, k1, psso, p3, k2 tog, k1, yon, k2; repeat from * to last st, p1.
Row 15: P1, *k4, yon, sl.1, k1, psso, p3, k2 tog, yon, k3; repeat from * to last st, p1.

Ridged Feather Stitch

multiple of 13
Row 1: *K4, (yon, k1) five times, yon, k4; repeat from * to end of row.
Row 2: Purl.
Row 3: *P2 tog three times, p7, p2 tog three times; repeat from * to end of row.
Rows 4 and 5: Knit.
Row 6: Purl.

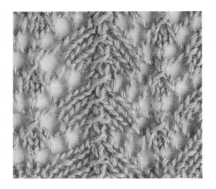

Horseshoe and Eyelet Pattern

multiple of 10 plus 3
Row 1: K1, *k1, yon, k3, sl.1, k2 tog, psso, k3, yon; repeat from * to last 2 sts, k2.
Row 2 and foll alt rows: Purl.
Row 3: K1, *k2, yon, k2, sl.1, k2 tog, psso, k2, yon, k1; repeat from * to last 2 sts, k2.
Row 5: K1, k2 tog, *yon, k1, yon, k1, sl.1, k2 tog, psso, k1, yon, k1, yon, sl.1, k2 tog, psso; repeat from * to last 3 sts, k2 tog, k1.

Fan Lace Pattern 1

multiple of 11
Row 1: *SSK, k3 tbl, yon, k1, yon, k3 tbl, k2 tog; repeat from * to end of row.
Row 2 and foll alt rows: Purl.
Row 3: *SSK, k2 tbl, yon, k1, yon, SSK, yon, k2 tbl, k2 tog; repeat from * to end of row.
Row 5: *SSK, k1 tbl, yon, k1, (yon, SSK) twice, yon, k1 tbl, k2 tog; repeat from * to end of row.
Row 7: *SSK, yon, k1, (yon, SSK) three times, yon, k2 tog; repeat from * to end of row.

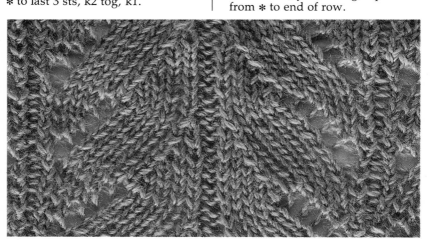

Spiral Lace Pattern

multiple of 25 plus 2
Row 1: *P2, k4, k2 tog, k4, yon, k1 tbl, p1, k1 tbl, yon, k4, SSK, k4; repeat from * to last 2 sts, p2.
Row 2 and foll alt rows: K2, *p11, k1, p11, k2; repeat from * to end of row.
Row 3: *P2, k3, k2 tog, k4, yon, k1, k1 tbl, p1, k1 tbl, k1, yon, k4, SSK, k3; repeat from * to last 2 sts, p2.

Row 5: *P2, k2, k2 tog, k4, yon, k2, k1 tbl, p1, k1 tbl, k2, yon, k4, SSK, k2; repeat from * to last 2 sts, p2.
Row 7: *P2, k1, k2 tog, k4, yon, k3, k1 tbl, p1, k1 tbl, k3, yon, k4, SSK, k1; repeat from * to last 2 sts, p2.
Row 9: *P2, k2 tog, k4, yon, k4, k1 tbl, p1, k1 tbl, k4, yon, k4, SSK; repeat from * to last 2 sts, p2.

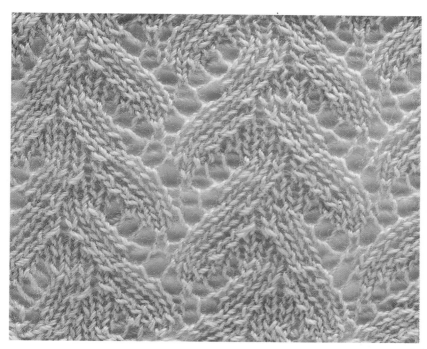

Curving Lattice Lace Pattern

multiple of 13 plus 2
Row 1: K1, *k2, sl.1, k1, psso, k4, k2 tog, k2, yon, k1, yon; repeat from * to last st, k1.
Row 2 and foll alt rows: Purl.
Row 3: K1, *yon, k2, sl.1, k1, psso, k2, k2 tog, k2, yon, k3; repeat from * to last st, k1.
Row 5: K1, *k1, yon, k2, sl.1, k1, psso, k2 tog, k2, yon, k4; repeat from * to last st, k1.
Row 7: K1, *yon, k1, yon, k2, sl.1, k1, psso, k4, k2 tog, k2; repeat from * to last st, k1.
Row 9: K1, *k3, yon, k2, sl.1, k1, psso, k2, k2 tog, k2, yon; repeat from * to last st, k1.
Row 11: K1, *k4, yon, k2, sl.1, k1, psso, k2 tog, k2, yon, k1; repeat from * to last st, k1.

Baby Fern Pattern

multiple of 9 plus 4
Row 1: (wrong side) Purl.
Row 2: K2, *k2 tog, k2, yon, k1, yon, k2, k2 tog; repeat from * to last 2 sts, k2.
Rows 3, 5 and 7: K1, purl across the row to last st, k1.

Row 4: K2, *k2 tog, k1, yon, k3, yon, k1, k2 tog; repeat from * to last 2 sts, k2.
Row 6: K2, *k2 tog, yon, k5, yon, k2 tog; repeat from * to last 2 sts, k2.
Repeat from row 2.

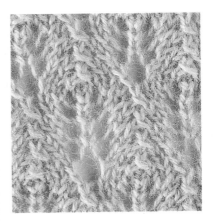

Fir Cone Pattern 1

multiple of 8 plus 1
Row 1: K1, *yon, sl.1, k1, psso, k6; repeat from * to end of row.
Row 2 and foll alt rows: Purl.
Rows 3, 5, 7 and 9: K1, *yon, k2, sl.1, k2 tog, psso, k2, yon, k1; repeat from * to last st.
Row 11: K4, *yon, sl.1, k1, psso, k6; repeat from * to last 5 sts, yon, sl.1, k1, psso, k3.
Rows 13, 15, 17 and 19: K1, k2 tog, *k2, yon, k1, yon, k2, sl.1, k2 tog, psso; repeat from * to last 2 sts, sl.1, k1, psso.

Chevron Lace 1

multiple of 8 plus 2
Row 1: K1, *k1, yon, sl.1, k1, psso, k3, k2 tog, yon; repeat from * to last st, k1.
Row 2 and foll alt rows: Purl.
Row 3: K1, *k2, yon, sl.1, k1, psso, k1, k2 tog, yon, k1; repeat from * to last st, k1.
Row 5: K1, *k1, yon, sl.1, k1, psso, yon, sl.1, k2 tog, psso, yon, k2 tog, yon; repeat from * to last st, k1.
Row 7: K1, *k2, yon, sl.1, k1, psso, k1, k2 tog, yon, k1; repeat from * to last st, k1.
Row 9: K1, *k3, yon, sl.1, k2 tog, psso, yon, k2; repeat from * to last st, k1.
Rows 11, 13 and 15: K1, *k1, k2 tog, k1, yon, k1, yon, k1, sl.1, k1, psso; repeat from * to last st, k1.
Row 17: K1, *k1, yon, sl.1, k1, psso, k3, k2 tog, yon; repeat from * to last st, k1.
Row 19: K1, *k2, yon, sl.1, k1, psso, k1, k2 tog, yon, k1; repeat from * to last st, k1.
Row 21: K1, *k1, yon, sl.1, k1, psso, yon, sl.1, k2 tog, psso, yon, k2 tog, yon; repeat from * to last st, k1.
Row 23: K1, *k2, yon, sl.1, k1, psso, k1, k2 tog, yon, k1; repeat from * to last st, k1.
Row 25: K1, *k3, yon, sl.1, k2 tog, psso, yon, k2; repeat from * to last st, k1.

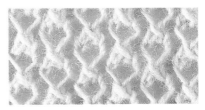

Allover Cross Stitch

multiple of 4 plus 3
Rows 1 and 3: Purl.
Row 2: K2, k into next st one row below, sl that st on to right hand needle, k2 tog, psso, *k into next st one row below, k the st and k into the row below to the left of the st (3 sts from 1 st), sl. 1, k2 tog, psso; repeat from * to last 2 sts, k into next st in row below, k the st, k1.
Row 4: K1, k2 tog, repeat from * of row 2 to the last 4 sts, k into the row below, then the st itself and into the row below to left of the st, sl. 1, k1, psso, k1.

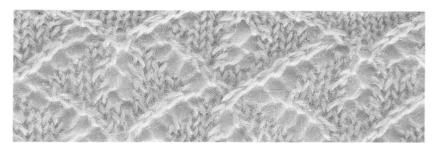

Openwork Diamond Pattern

multiple of 16
Row 1: *K5, k2 tog, yon, k2, yon, sl.1, k1, psso, k5; repeat from * to end of row.
Row 2: *P4, p2 tog, yon, p4, yon, p2 tog, p4; repeat from * to end of row.
Row 3: *K3, k2 tog, yon, k6, yon, sl.1, k1, psso, k3; repeat from * to end of row.
Row 4: *P2, p2 tog, yon, p4, yon, p2 tog, p2, yon, p2 tog, p2; repeat from * to end of row.
Row 5: *K1, k2 tog, yon, k5, yon, sl.1, k1, psso, k3, yon, sl.1, k1, psso, k1; repeat from * to end of row.
Row 6: *P2 tog, yon, p6, yon, p2 tog, p4, yon, p2 tog; repeat from * to end of row.
Row 7: *Sl.1 purlwise, k1, yon, sl.1, k1, psso, k4, yon, sl.1, k1, psso, k2, k2 tog, yon, k1, sl.1 purlwise; repeat from * to end of row.
Row 8: *P3, yon, p2 tog, p3, yon, p2 tog, p1, p2 tog, yon, p3; repeat from * to end of row.
Row 9: *Yon, sl.1, k1, psso, k2, yon, sl.1, k1, psso, k4, k2 tog, yon, k4.
Row 10: *Yon, p2 tog, p3, yon, p2 tog, p2, p2 tog, yon, p5; repeat from * to end of row.
Row 11: *Yon, sl.1, k1, psso, k4, yon, sl.1, k1, psso, k2 tog, yon, k6; repeat from * to end of row.
Row 12: *Yon, p2 tog, p2, p2 tog, yon, p1, sl.2 purlwise, p1, yon, p2 tog, p4; repeat from * to end of row.
Row 13: *Yon, sl.1, k1, psso, k1, k2 tog, yon, k2, Tw2R, k2, yon, sl.1, k1, psso, k3; repeat from * to end of row.
Row 14: *P2, p2 tog, yon, p4, yon, p2 tog, p2, yon, p2 tog, p2; repeat from * to end of row.
Row 15: *K1, k2 tog, yon, k5, yon, sl.1, k1, psso, k3, yon, sl.1, k1, psso, k1; repeat from * to end of row.
Row 16: *P2 tog, yon, p6, yon, p2 tog, p4, yon, p2 tog; repeat from * to end of row.
Repeat from row 7.

Eyelet Triangles Pattern

multiple of 11 plus 5
Row 1: *K3, (yon, sl.1, k1, psso) four times; repeat from * to last 5 sts, k5.
Row 2 and foll alt rows: Purl.
Row 3: *K4, (yon, sl.1, k1, psso) three times, K1; repeat from * to last 5 sts, k5.
Row 5: *K5, (yon, sl.1, k1, psso) twice, k2; repeat from * to last 5 sts, k5.
Row 7: *K6, yon, sl.1, k1, psso, k3; repeat from * to last 5 sts, k5.
Row 9: K5, *k3, (yon, sl.1, k1, psso) four times; repeat from * to end of row.
Row 11: K5, *k4, (yon, sl.1, k1, psso) three times, k1; repeat from * to end of row.
Row 13: K5, *k5, (yon, sl.1, k1, psso) twice, repeat from * to end of row.
Row 15: K5, *k6, yon, sl.1, k1, psso, k3; repeat from * to end of row.

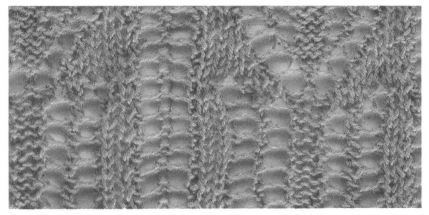

Lyre and Ladder Pattern

multiple of 20 plus 3
Row 1: K1, *k1, yon, k2 tog, p5, k2 tog, yon, k1, yon, k2 tog tbl, p5, k2 tog tbl, yon; repeat from * to last 2 sts, k2.
Row 2: P1, *p3, k5, p5, k5, p2; repeat from * to last 2 sts, p2.
Row 3: K1, *k1, yon, k2 tog, p4, k2 tog, yon, k3, k2 tog tbl, p4, k2 tog tbl, yon; repeat from * to last 2 sts, k2.
Row 4: P1, *p3, k4, p7, k4, p2; repeat from * to last 2 sts, p2.
Row 5: K1, *k1, yon, k2 tog, p3, k2 tog, yon, k5, yon, k2 tog tbl, p3, k2 tog tbl, yon; repeat from * to last 2 sts, k2.
Row 6: P1, *p3, k3, p9, k3, p2; repeat from * to last 2 sts, p2.
Row 7: K1, *k1, yon, k2 tog, p2, (k2 tog, yon) twice, k3, (yon, k2 tog tbl) twice, p2, k2 tog tbl, yon; repeat from * to last 2 sts, p2.
Row 8: P1, *p3, k2, p11, k2, p2; repeat from * to last 2 sts, p2.
Row 9: K1, *k1, yon, k2 tog, p2, k1, yon, k2 tog, yon, k2 tog tbl, k1, k2 tog, yon, k2 tog tbl, yon, k1, p2, k2 tog tbl, yon; repeat from * to last 2 sts, k2.
Row 10: P1, *p3, k2, p11, k2, p2; repeat from * to last 2 sts, p2.
Rows 11, 13, 15 and 17: as row 9.
Rows 12, 14, 16 and 18: as row 10.
Row 19: K1, *k1, yon, k2 tog, p1, k2 tog, yon, k1, p2, k3, p2, k1, yon, k2 tog tbl, p1, k2 tog tbl, yon; repeat from * to last 2 sts, k2.
Row 20: P1, *p3, k1, p3, k2, p3, k2, p3, k1, p2; repeat from * to last 2 sts, p2.

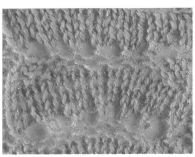

Embossed Shell Stitch Panel

multiple of 16 plus 3
Row 1: *P3, k1, p11, k1; repeat from * to last 3 sts, p3.
Row 2: *K3, p1, k11, p1; repeat from * to last 3 sts, k3.
Row 3: *P3, k4 tog, (yon, k1) five times, yon, k4 tog; repeat from * to last 3 sts, p3.
Rows 4, 6 and 8: K3, *p13, k3; repeat from * to end of row.
Rows 5 and 7: *P3, k13; repeat from * to last 3 sts, p3.

Ridged Eyelet Pattern

multiple of 2
Rows 1, 2 and 3: Purl.
Row 4: *Yon, sl.1, k1, psso.

Lotus Pattern

multiple of 10 plus 1
Rows 1 to 5: Knit.
Row 6: (wrong side) P1, *yon, p3, sl.2, p1, p2sso, p3, yon, p1; repeat from * to end of row.
Row 7: K2, *yon, k2, sl 2, k1, p2sso, k2, yon, k3; repeat from * to last 2 sts, k2.
Row 8: P3, *yon, p1, sl 2, p1, p2sso, p1, yon, p5; repeat from * to last 3 sts, p3.
Row 9: K4, *yon, sl 2, k1, p2sso, yon, k7; repeat from * to last 4 sts, k4.
Row 10: P2, *k2, p3; repeat from * to last 2 sts, p2.
Row 11: K1, *yon, sl.1, k1, psso, p1, yon, sl 2, k1, p2sso, yon, p1, k2 tog, yon, k1; repeat from * to end of row.
Row 12: P3, *k1, p3, k1, p5; repeat from * to last 3 sts, p3.
Row 13: K2, *yon, sl.1, k1, psso, yon, sl 2, k1, p2sso, yon, k2 tog, yon, k3; repeat from * to last 2 sts, k2.
Rows 14 and 16: P2, *k1, p5, k1, p3; repeat from * to last 2 sts, p2.
Row 15: K2, *p1, k1, yon, sl 2, k1, p2sso, yon, k1, p1, k3; repeat from * to last 2 sts, k2.

Swing Stitch

multiple of 12 plus 1
Row 1: *K10, SSK, yon; repeat from * to last st, k1.
Row 2 and foll alt rows: Purl.
Row 3: K9, *SSK, yon, k10; repeat from * to last 2 sts, k2.
Row 5: *K8, (SSK, yon) twice; repeat from * to last st, k1.
Row 7: K7, *(SSK, yon) twice, k8; repeat from * to last 2 sts, k2.
Row 9: *K6, (SSK, yon) three times; repeat from * to last st, k1.
Row 11: K5, *(SSK, yon) three times, k6; repeat from * to last 2 sts, k2.
Row 13: *K4, (SSK, yon) four times; repeat from * to last st, k1.
Row 15: K1, *yon, k2 tog, k10; repeat from * to end of row.
Row 17: K2, *yon, k2 tog, k10; repeat from * to last 9 sts, k9.
Row 19: K1, *(yon, k2 tog) twice, k8; repeat from * to end of row.
Row 21: K2, *(yon, k2 tog) twice, k8; repeat from * to last 7 sts, k7.
Row 23: K1, *(yon, k2 tog) three times, k6; repeat from * to end of row.
Row 25: K2, *(yon, k2 tog) three times, k6; repeat from * to last 5 sts, k5.
Row 27: K1, *(yon, k2 tog) four times, k4; repeat from * to end of row.

Flower Pattern

multiple of 13 plus 2
Row 1: Purl.
Row 2: Knit.
Row 3: P7, *(p1, k1, p1, k1, p1, k1) into next st, p12; repeat from * to last 8 sts, (p1, k1, p1, k1, p1, k1) into next st, p7.
Rows 4 and 6: K7, *p6, k12; repeat from * to last 13 sts, p6, k7.
Row 5: P7, *k6, p12; repeat from * to last 13 sts, k6, p7.
Row 7: P1, (p2 tog) twice, p2, *k2, yon, k2, yon, k2, p2, (p2 tog) 4 times, p2; repeat from * to last 13 sts, k2, yon, k2, yon, k2, p2, (p2 tog) twice, p1.
Row 8: K5, *p8, k8; repeat from * to last 13 sts, p8, k5.
Row 9: P1, (p2 tog) twice, *(k2 tog, yon, k1, yon) twice, k2 tog, (p2 tog) 4 times; repeat from * to last 5 sts, (p2 tog) twice, p1.
Row 10: K3, *p9, k4; repeat from * to last 3 sts, k3.

Wave and Steps Pattern

multiple of 9 plus 2
Row 1: *K2, yon, k1, yon, k2, k2 tog tbl, k2 tog; repeat from * to last 2 sts, k2.
Row 2 and foll alt rows: Purl.
Rows 3, 5, 7 and 9: as row 1.
Rows 11, 13, 15, 17 and 19: *K2, k2 tog tbl, k2 tog, k2, yon, k1, yon; repeat from * to last 2 sts, k2.

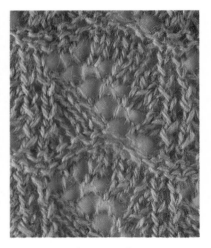

Curved Leaf Lace 1

multiple of 9 plus 2
Row 1: Purl.
Row 2: Knit.
Row 3: K1, *SSK, yon, k1, yon, k4, k2 tog; repeat from * to last st, k1.
Row 4 and foll alt rows: Purl.
Row 5: K1, *SSK, (k1, yon) twice, k3, k2 tog; repeat from * to last st, k1.
Row 7: K1, *SSK, k2, yon, k1, yon, k2, k2 tog; repeat from * to last st, k1.
Row 9: K1, *SSK, k3, (yon, k1) twice, k2 tog; repeat from * to last st, k1.
Row 11: K1, *SSK, k4, yon, k1, yon, k2 tog; repeat from * to last st, k1.

Bird's Eye Pattern

multiple of 4
Row 1: *K2 tog, y2on, k2 tog; repeat from * to end of row.
Row 2: *K1, (k1, p1) into the y2on of row 1, k1; repeat from * to end of row.
Row 3: K2, *k2 tog, y2on, k2 tog; repeat from * to last 2 sts, k2.
Row 4: K2, *K1 (k1, p1) into the y2on of row 3, k1; repeat from * to last 2 sts, k2.

Garter Stitch Lozenge Pattern

multiple of 16

Row 1: *K6, k2 tog, yon, k1, yon, k2 tog, k5; repeat from * to end of row.

Row 2 and foll alt rows: Knit.

Row 3: *K5, k2 tog, yon, k3, yon, k2 tog, k4; repeat from * to end of row.

Row 5: *K4, k2 tog, yon, k5, yon, k2 tog, k3; repeat from * to end of row.

Row 7: *K3, k2 tog, yon, k7, yon, k2 tog, k2; repeat from * to end of row.

Row 9: *K2, k2 tog, yon, k9, yon, k2 tog, k1; repeat from * to end of row.

Rows 11 and 13: *K1, k2 tog, yon, k11, yon, k2 tog, yon; repeat from * to end of row.

Row 15: as row 9.
Row 17: as row 7.
Row 19: as row 5.
Row 21: as row 3.

Little Bell Pattern

multiple of 14

Row 1: *P2, k3 tbl, p4, k3 tbl, p2; repeat from * to end of row.

Row 2: *K2, p3 tbl, k4, p3 tbl, k2; repeat from * to end of row.

Row 3: *P2, k3 tbl, p4, yon, sl. 1, k2 tog, psso, yon, p2; repeat from * to end of row.

Row 4: *K2, p1, p1 tbl, p1, k4, p3 tbl, k2; repeat from * to end of row.

Row 5: as row 1.
Row 6: as row 2.

Row 7: *P2, yon, sl. 1, k2 tog, psso, yon, p4, k3 tbl, p2; repeat from * to end of row.

Row 8: *K2, p3 tbl, k4, p1, p1 tbl, p1, k2; repeat from * to end of row.

Dimple Eyelet Pattern

multiple of 2
Row 1: Knit.
Row 2: Purl.
Row 3: P1, *yon, p2 tog; repeat from * to last st, p1.
Row 4: Purl, purling all yon sts tbl.
Row 5: Knit.
Row 6: Purl.
Row 7: P2, *yon, p2 tog; repeat from * to end of row.
Row 8: Purl, purling all yon sts tbl.

Vine Lace

multiple of 9 plus 2
Row 1: K1, *k1, yon, k2, sl.1, k1, psso, k2 tog, k2, yon; repeat from * to last st, k1.
Row 2: Purl.
Row 3: K1, * yon, k2, sl.1, k1, psso, k2 tog, k2, yon, k1; repeat from * to last st, k1.
Row 4: Purl.

Chevron and Eyelet Pattern

multiple of 9
Row 1: *K4, yon, sl.1, k1, psso, k3; repeat from * to end of row.
Row 2 and foll alt rows: Purl.
Row 3: *K2, k2 tog, yon, k1, yon, sl.1, k1, psso, k2; repeat from * to end of row.
Row 5: *K1, k2 tog, yon, k3, yon, sl.1, k1, psso, k1; repeat from * to end of row.
Row 7: *K2 tog, yon, k5, yon, sl.1, k1, psso; repeat from * to end of row.

Plain and Eyelet Diamond Pattern

multiple of 8 plus 3
Row 1: K1, k2 tog, *yon, k1, (yon, sl.1, k1, psso) twice, yon, sl.1, k2 tog, psso; repeat from * to end of row.
Row 2 and foll alt rows: Purl.
Row 3: K2, *k1, (yon, sl.1, k1, psso) three times, k1; repeat from * to last st, k1.
Row 5: K2, *k2, (yon, sl.1, k1, psso) twice, k2, repeat from * to last st, k1.
Row 7: K2, *k3, yon, sl.1, k1, psso, k3; repeat from * to last st, k1.
Row 9: K2, *k1, k2 tog, yon, k1, yon, sl.1, k1, psso, k2; repeat from * to last st, k1.
Row 11: K2, *k2 tog, yon, k1, (yon, sl.1, k1, psso) twice, k1; repeat from * to last st, k1.

Feather Faggot Pattern

multiple of 4
Row 1 and foll rows: *K1, yon, p2 tog, k1; repeat from * to end of row.

Flower and Stem Pattern

multiple of 11
Row 1: *K1, yon, sl.1, k1, psso, k8; repeat from * to end of row.
Row 2 and foll alt rows: Purl.
Row 3: *K2, yon, sl.1, k1, psso, k7; repeat from * to end of row.
Row 5: *K3, yon, sl.1, k1, psso, k6; repeat from * to end of row.
Row 7: *K1, k2 tog, yon, k1, yon, sl.1, k1, psso, k5; repeat from * to end of row.
Row 9: *K2 tog, yon, k3, yon, sl.1, k1, psso, k4; repeat from * to end of row.
Row 11: *K1, k2 tog, yon, k1, yon, sl.1, k1, psso, k5; repeat from * to end of row.
Row 13: *K2 tog, yon, k3, yon, sl.1, k1, psso, k4; repeat from * to end of row.
Row 15: *K2, yon, sl.1, k2 tog, psso, yon, k6; repeat from * to end of row.
Continue in pattern by starting the stem of the design on the 3rd and 4th sts between the previous design.

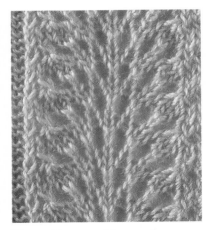

Fan Lace Panel

panel of 16 sts plus 1
Row 1: P1, *k1 tbl, k4 tog, (yon, k1) five times, yon, k4 tog, k1 tbl, p1.
Rows 2 and 4: K1, *p15, k1.
Row 3: P1, *k1 tbl, k13, k1 tbl, p1.

Banded Lozenge Pattern

multiple of 8
Rows 1 and 2: Purl.
Row 3: Knit.
Rows 4 and 5: Purl.
Row 6: *K3, yon, sl.1, k1, psso, k3; repeat from * to end of row.
Row 7 and foll alt rows: Purl.
Row 8: *K2, (yon, sl.1, k1, psso) twice, k2; repeat from * to end of row.
Row 10: *K1, (yon, sl.1, k1, psso) three times, k1; repeat from * to end of row.
Row 12: as row 8.

Diamond Eyelet Pattern 1

multiple of 10 plus 4
Row 1: K2, yon, SSK, *k1, k2 tog, y2on, SSK; repeat from * to last 5 sts, k1, k2 tog, yon, k2.
Row 2 and foll alt rows: Purl, purling into the front and back of each y2on.
Row 3: K2, *k2 tog, yon, k6, yon, SSK; repeat from * to last 2 sts, k2.
Row 5: K3, *k2 tog, yon, k4, yon, SSK, k2; repeat from * to last st, k1.
Row 7: K4, *k2 tog, yon, k2, yon, SSK, k4; repeat from * to end of row.
Row 9: K2, yon, SSK, *k1, k2 tog, y2on, SSK; repeat from * to last 5 sts, k1, k2 tog, yon, k2.
Row 11: K5, *yon, SSK, k2 tog, yon, k6; repeat from * to last 5 sts, k5.
Row 13: K4, *yon, SSK, k2, k2 tog, yon, k4; repeat from * to end of row.
Row 15: K3, *yon, SSK, k4, k2 tog, yon, k2; repeat from * to last st, k1.

Lace Check Pattern

multiple of 16
Row 1 and foll alt rows: (wrong side) Purl.
Rows 2, 4, 6 and 8: *K8, (yon, sl.1, k1, psso) 4 times; repeat from * to end of row.
Rows 10, 12, 14 and 16: *(Yon, sl.1, k1, psso) 4 times, k8; repeat from * to end of row.

Eyelet Lace Panel

Panel of 18 sts.
Row 1: K2, k2 tog, yon, k1, yon, sl 1, k1, psso, k4, k2 tog, yon, k1, yon, sl.1, k1, psso, k2.
Row 2 and foll alt rows: Purl.
Row 3: K1, k2 tog, yon, k3, yon, sl.1, k1, psso, k2, k2 tog, yon, k3, yon, sl.1, k1, psso, k1.
Row 5: K2 tog, yon, k14, yon, sl.1, k1, psso.
Row 7: K1, yon, sl.1, k1, psso, k12, k2 tog, yon, k1.
Row 9: K2, yon, sl.1, k1, psso, k10, k2 tog, yon, k2.
Row 11: K3, yon, sl.1, k1, psso, k8, k2 tog, yon, k3.
Row 13: K4, yon, sl.1, k1, psso, k6, k2 tog, yon, k4.

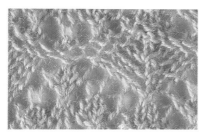

Fan Mesh Stitch

multiple of 10 plus 1
Row 1: K2 tog, *k3, (yon, k1) twice, k2, k3 tog; repeat from * to last 2 sts, k2 tog.
Rows 2, 4, 6, 8 and 10: Purl.
Row 3: K2 tog, *k2, yon, k3, yon, k2, k3 tog; repeat from * to last 2 sts, k2 tog.
Row 5: K2 tog, *(k1, yon) twice, k3 tog, (yon, k1) twice, k3 tog; repeat from * to last 2 sts, k2 tog.
Row 7: K2 tog, *yon, k7, yon, k3 tog; repeat from * to last 2 sts, k2 tog.
Row 9: *K1, (k1, yon, k3 tog, yon) twice, k1; repeat from * to last st, k1.
Row 11: Purl.
Row 12: Knit.

Slip Stitch Mesh

multiple of 2 plus 2
Row 1: Purl.
Row 2: Knit.
Row 3: K2, *sl.1, k1; repeat from * to end of row.
Row 4: *K1, yfwd, sl.1; repeat from * to last 2 sts, k2.
Row 5: K1, *yon, k2 tog; repeat from * to last st, k1.
Row 6: Purl.

Lozenge Stitch

multiple of 10 plus 2
Row 1: K1, *yon, sl.1, k1, psso, k5, k2 tog, yon, k1; repeat from * to last st, k1.
Row 2 and foll alt rows: Purl.
Row 3: K1, *k1, yon, sl.1, k1, psso, k3, k2 tog, yon, k2; repeat from * to last st, k1.
Row 5: K1, *k2, yon, sl.1, k1, psso, k1, k2 tog, yon, k3; repeat from * to last st, k1.
Row 7: K1, *k3, yon, sl.1, k2 tog, psso, yon, k4; repeat from * to last st, k1.
Row 9: K1, *k2, k2 tog, yon, k1, yon, sl.1, k1, psso, k3; repeat from * to last st, k1.
Row 11: K1, *k1, k2 tog, yon, k3, yon, sl.1, k1, psso, k2; repeat from * to last st, k1.
Row 13: K1, *k2 tog, yon, k5, yon, sl.1, k1, psso, k1; repeat from * to last st, k1.
Row 15: K1, *yon, k7, yon, sl.1, k2 tog, psso; repeat from * to last st, k1.

Barred Flagon Stitch

multiple of 6 plus 2
Rows 1, 3, 5 and 7: K1, *yon, sl.1, k2 tog, psso, yon, k3; repeat from * to last st, k1.
Row 2 and foll alt rows: Purl.
Rows 9, 11, 13 and 15: K1, *k3, yon, sl.1, k2 tog, psso, yon; repeat from * to last st, k1.

Linked Chevron Lace Pattern

multiple of 9 plus 1
Row 1: *K4, yon, sl.1, k1, psso, k3; repeat from * to last st, k1.
Row 2 and foll alt rows: Purl.
Rows 3 and 5: as row 1.
Row 7: *K2, k2 tog, yon, k1, yon, sl.1, k1, psso, k2; repeat from * to last st, k1.
Row 9: *K1, k2 tog, yon, k3, yon, sl.1, k1, psso, k1; repeat from * to last st, k1.
Rows 11, 13, and 15: *K2 tog, yon, k5, yon, sl.1, k1, psso; repeat from * to last st, k1.

Trellis Shell Pattern

multiple of 13 plus 1
Row 1 and foll alt rows: (wrong side) Purl.
Row 2: K2 tog, *k5, yon, k2 tog, yon, k1, yon, k2, sl.1, k2 tog, psso; repeat from * to last 2 sts, k2 tog.
Row 4: K2 tog, *k4, yon, k2 tog, yon, k3, yon, k1, sl.1, k2 tog, psso; repeat from * to last 2 sts, k2 tog.

Row 6: K2 tog, *k3, yon, k2 tog, yon, k5, yon, sl.1, k2 tog, psso; repeat from * to last 2 sts, k2 tog.
Row 8: K2 tog, *k2, yon, k1, yon, SSK, yon, k5, sl.1, k2 tog, psso; repeat from * to last 2 sts, k2 tog.
Row 10: K2 tog, *k1, yon, k3, yon, SSK, yon, k4, sl.1, k2 tog, psso; repeat from * to last 2 sts, k2 tog.
Row 12: K2 tog, *yon, k5, yon, SSK, yon, k3, sl.1, k2 tog, psso; repeat from * to last 2 sts, k2 tog.

Zig Zag Lace Pattern

multiple of 2
Row 1 and foll alt rows: (wrong side) Purl.
Rows 2, 4 and 6: K1, *yon, k2 tog; repeat from * to last st, k1.
Rows 8, 10 and 12: K1, *sl.1, k1, psso, yon; repeat from * to last st, k1.

Crest of the Wave Pattern

multiple of 12 plus 1
Rows 1 to 4: Knit.
Row 5: K1, *k2 tog twice, (yon, k1) three times, yon, (ssk twice); repeat from * to end of row.
Row 6: Purl.
Rows 7, 9 and 11: as row 5.
Rows 8, 10 and 12: as row 6.

Eyelet Flower Pattern

multiple of 16 plus 8
Row 1: K10, *k2 tog, y2on, SSK, k12; repeat from * to last 14 sts, k2 tog, y2on, SSK, k10.
Row 2 and foll alt rows: Purl, knitting the first loop of the yon and purling the second loop.
Row 3: K8, *(k2 tog, y2on, SSK) twice, k8; repeat from * to end of row.
Row 5: as row 1.
Row 7: as row 3.
Row 9: as row 1.
Row 11: K2, *k2 tog, y2on, SSK, k12; repeat from * to last 6 sts, k2 tog, y2on, SSK, k2.
Row 13: *(K2 tog, y2on, SSK) twice, k8; repeat from * to last 8 sts, (k2 tog, y2on, SSK) twice.
Rows 15 and 19: as row 11.
Row 17: as row 13.

Ridged Feather Pattern

multiple of 11
Row 1: Knit.
Rows 2 and 4: Purl.
Row 3: *(P2 tog) twice, (inc 1 through loop between sts, k1) three times, inc 1, (p2 tog) twice; repeat from * to end of row.

Diamond Eyelet Pattern 2

multiple of 8
Row 1: Knit.
Row 2 and foll alt rows: Purl.
Row 3: K3, *yon, SSK, k6; repeat from * to last 3 sts, k3.
Row 5: K1, *k2 tog, yon, k1, yon, SSK, k3; repeat from * to last 2 sts, k2.
Row 7: as row 3.
Row 9: Knit.
Row 11: K7, *yon, SSK, k6; repeat from * to last st, k1.
Row 13: K5, *k2 tog, yon, k1, yon, SSK, k3; repeat from * to last 3 sts, k3.
Row 15: as row 11.

Hexagon Eyelet and Split Leaf Pattern

multiple of 11
Rows 1, 3 and 5: ∗K2 tog, k3, yon, k1, yon, k3, sl.1, k1, psso; repeat from ∗ to end of row.
Row 2 and foll alt rows: Purl.
Row 7: ∗K2 tog, k2, yon, k3, yon, k2, sl.1, k1, psso; repeat from ∗ to end of row.
Row 9: ∗K2 tog, k1, yon, k5, yon, k1, sl.1, k1, psso; repeat from ∗ to end of row.
Rows 11 and 13: ∗K2 tog, yon, k1, k2 tog, yon, k1, yon, sl.1, k1, psso, k1, yon, sl.1, k1, psso; repeat from ∗ to end of row.
Row 15: ∗K2 tog, k1, yon, k5, yon, k1, sl.1, k1, psso; repeat from ∗ to end of row.
Row 17: ∗K2 tog, k2, yon, k3, yon, k2, sl.1, k1, psso; repeat from ∗ to end of row.

Feather and Fan Panel

panel of 9 sts
Row 1: P1, SSK, (yon, k1) three times, yon, k2 tog, p1.
Row 2: K1, p9, k1.
Row 3: P1, SSK, k5, k2 tog, p1.
Row 4: K1, p7, k1.

Lace Wings Pattern

multiple of 7
Row 1: Purl.
Row 2: ∗K1, k2 tog, yon, k1, yon, sl.1, k1, psso, k1; repeat from ∗ to end of row.
Row 3: Purl.
Row 4: ∗K2 tog, yon, k3, yon, sl.1, k1, psso; repeat from ∗ to end of row.

Faggot Stitch

multiple of 2 plus 2
Row 1 and foll rows: K1, ∗yon, sl.1, k1, psso; repeat from ∗ to last st, k1.

Diagonal Trellis Lace

multiple of 15 plus 5
Row 1: K2, *k3, (yon, SSK) three times, (k2 tog, yon) three times; repeat from * to last 3 sts, k3.
Row 2 and foll alt rows: Purl.
Row 3: K2, *k4, (yon, SSK) three times, (k2 tog, yon) twice, k1; repeat from * to last 3 sts, k3.
Row 5: K2, *K5, (yon, SSK) three times, k2 tog, yon, k2; repeat from * to last 3 sts, k3.
Row 7: K2, *k6, (yon, SSK) three times, k3; repeat from * to last 3 sts, k3.
Row 9: K2, *k4, k2 tog, yon, k1, (yon, SSK) three times, k2; repeat from * to last 3 sts, k3.
Row 11: K2, *k3, (k2 tog, yon) twice, k1, (yon, SSK) three times, k1; repeat from * to last 3 sts, k3.
Row 13: K2, *k2, (k2 tog, yon) three times, k1, (yon, SSK) three times; rep from * to last 3 sts, k3.

Row 15: K1, yon, *SSK, (k2 tog, yon) three times, k3, (yon, SSK) twice, yon; repeat from * to last 4 sts, SSK, yon, k2.
Row 17: K2, *(k2, tog, yon) three times, k5, (yon, SSK) twice; repeat from * to last 3 sts, k3.
Row 19: K1, *(k2 tog, yon) three times, k7, yon, SSK; repeat from * to last 4 sts, k2 tog, yon, k2.
Row 21: K1, *(k2 tog, yon) twice, k9, k2 tog, yon; repeat from * to last 3 sts, k2 tog, yon, k1.
Row 23: K1, k2 tog, *yon, k2 tog, yon, k1, yon, SSK, k6, k2 tog, yon, k2 tog; repeat from * to last 2 sts, yon, k2.
Row 25: K2, k2 tog, yon, *k1, (yon, SSK) twice, k4, (k2 tog, yon) three times; repeat from * to last st, k1.
Row 27: K1, k2 tog, yon, *k1, (yon, SSK) three times, k2, (k2 tog, yon) three times; repeat from * to last 2 sts, k2.

Travelling Eyelet Pattern

multiple of 6 plus 8
Row 1: K1, yon, sl. 1, k1, psso, k2, *k2 tog, yon, sl. 1, k1, psso, k2; repeat from * to last 3 sts, k2 tog, yon, k1.
Row 2: K1, p1, *p4, p into front and back of yo; repeat from * to last 6 sts, p5, k1.
Row 3: K2, *k2 tog, yon, sl. 1, k1, psso, k2; repeat from * to end of row.
Row 4: K1, p2, *p into front and back of next st, p4; repeat from * to last 4 sts, p into front and back of next st, p2, k1.

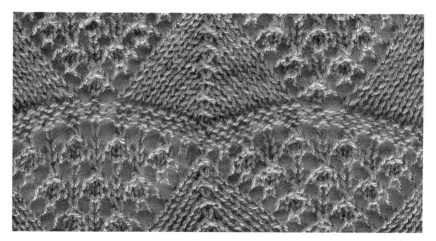

Madeira Cascade Pattern

multiple of 20 plus 5
Row 1: Purl.
Row 2: Knit
Row 3: K2, *k1, yon, k8, sl.1, k2 tog, psso, k8, yon; repeat from * to last 3 sts, k3.
Rows 4, 6, 8, 10, 12, 14, 16 and 18: Purl.
Row 5: K2, *k2, yon, k7, sl.1, k2 tog, psso, k7, yon, k1; repeat from * to last 3 sts, k3.
Row 7: K2, k2 tog, *yon, k1, yon, k6, sl.1, k2 tog, psso, k6, yon, k1, yon, sl.1, k2 tog, psso; repeat from * to last 4 sts, yon, k2 tog tbl, k2.
Row 9: K2, *k4, yon, k5, sl.1, k2 tog, psso, k5, yon, k3; repeat from * to last 3 sts, k3.
Row 11: K2, *k1, yon, sl.1, k2 tog, psso, yon, k1, yon, k4, sl.1, k2 tog, psso, k4, yon, k1, yon, sl.1, k2 tog, psso, yon; repeat from * to last 3 sts, k3.
Row 13: K2, *k6, yon, k3, sl.1, k2 tog, psso, k3, yon, k5; repeat from * to last 3 sts, k3.
Row 15: K2, k2 tog, *yon, k1, yon, sl.1, k2 tog, psso, yon, k1, yon, k2, sl.1, k2 tog, psso, k2, (yon, k1, yon, sl.1, k2 tog, psso) twice; repeat from * to last 4 sts, yon, k2 tog tbl, k2.
Row 17: K2, *k8, yon, k1, sl.1, k2 tog, psso, k1, yon, k7; repeat from * to last 3 sts, k3.
Row 19: K2, *(k1, yon, sl.1, k2 tog, psso, yon) five times; repeat from * to last 3 sts, k3.
Row 20: Knit.

Snowflake Lace Pattern

multiple of 8 plus 5
Row 1 and foll alt rows: (wrong side) Purl.
Row 2: K4, *SSK, yon, k1, yon, k2 tog, k3; repeat from * to last st, k1.
Row 4: K5, *yon, sl 2, k1, p2sso, yon, k5; repeat from * to end of row.
Row 6: as row 2.
Row 8: SSK, yon, k1, yon, k2 tog, *k3, SSK, yon, k1, yon, k2 tog; repeat from * to end of row.
Row 10: K1, *yon, sl 2, k1, p2sso, yon, k5; repeat from * to last st, k1.
Row 12: as row 8.

Snowdrop Lace Pattern 2

multiple of 8 plus 5
Rows 1 and 3: K1, *yon, sl.1 purlwise, k2 tog, psso, yon, k5; repeat from * to last 4 sts, yon, sl.1, k2 tog, psso, yon, k1.
Row 2 and foll alt rows: Purl.
Row 5: K1, *k3, yon, sl.1, k1, psso, k1, k2 tog, yon; repeat from * to last 4 sts, k4.
Row 7: K1, *yon, sl.1, k2 tog, psso, yon, k1; repeat from * to last 4 sts, yon, sl.1, k2 tog, psso, yon, k1.

Laburnum Stitch

multiple of 5 plus 2
Row 1: P2, *yfwd, sl.1, ybk, k2 tog, psso, y2on, p2; repeat from * to end of row.
Row 2: K2, *p into back of 1st yon and then into front of 2nd yon, p1, k2; repeat from * to end of row.
Row 3: P2, *k3, p2; repeat from * to end of row.
Row 4: K2, *p3, k2; repeat from * to end of row.

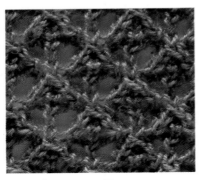

Leaf Lace Pattern

multiple of 6 plus 1
Row 1: K1, *yon, SSK, k1, k2 tog, yon, k1; repeat from * to end of row.
Row 2 and foll alt rows: Purl.
Row 3: K1, *yon, k1, sl.1, k2 tog, psso, k1, yon, k1; repeat from * to end of row.
Row 5: K1, *k2 tog, yon, k1, yon, SSK, k1; repeat from * to end of row.
Row 7: K2 tog, *(k1, yon) twice, k1, sl.1, k2 tog, psso; repeat from * to last 5 sts, (k1, yon) twice, k1, SSK.

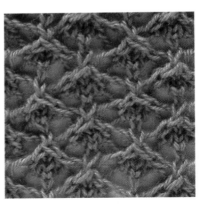

Miniature Leaf Pattern 1

multiple of 6 plus 3
Row 1: K1, *k1, yon, SSK, k1, k2 tog, yon; repeat from * to last 2 sts, k2.
Row 2: K1, *p2, yon, p3 tog, yon, p1; repeat from * to last 2 sts, p1, k1.
Row 3: Knit.
Row 4: K1, *p1, p2 tog tbl, yon, p1, yon, p2 tog; repeat from * to last 2 sts, p1, k1.
Row 5: K1, k2 tog, *yon, k3, yon, sl.1, k2 tog, psso; repeat from * to last 6 sts, yon, k3, yon, SSK, k1.
Row 6: Purl.

Clustered Leaf Pattern

multiple of 12 plus 3
Row 1: K1 *k1, yon, k4, sl.1, k2 tog, psso, k4, yon; repeat from * to last 2 sts, k2.
Row 2 and foll alt rows: Purl.
Row 3: K3, *yon, k3, sl.1, k2 tog, psso, k3, yon, k3; repeat from * to end of row.
Row 5: K4, *yon, **place right hand needle between 7th and 8th sts drawing up a long loop and k loop and 1st st tog, k1, sl.1, k2 tog, psso, k2, **yon, k5; repeat from * to last 4 sts, k4.
Row 7: K1, k2 tog, *k4, yon, k1, yon, k4, sl.1, k2 tog, psso; repeat from * to last 3 sts, k2 tog, k1.
Row 9: K1, k2 tog, *k3, yon, k3, yon, k3, sl.1, k2 tog, psso; repeat from * to last 3 sts, k2 tog, k1.
Row 11: K1, k2 tog, k2, *yon, k5, yon, place right hand needle between 7th and 8th sts and work from ** to ** of row 5; repeat from * to last 10 sts, yon, k5, yon, k2, k2 tog, k1.

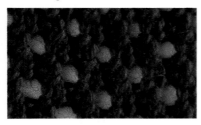

Cat's Eye Pattern

multiple of 4
Row 1: K4, *y2on, k4; repeat from *to end of row.
Row 2: P2, *p2 tog, p1 into 1st yo, k1 into 2nd yo, p2 tog; repeat from * to last 2 sts, p2.
Row 3: K2, yon, *k4, y2on; repeat from * to last 6 sts, k4, yon, k2.
Row 4: P3, *(p2 tog) twice, p1 into 1st yo, k1 into 2nd yo; repeat from * to last 7 sts, (p2 tog) twice, p3.

Grand Eyelet Lace Pattern

multiple of 4 plus 4
Row 1: P2, *yon, p4 tog; repeat from * to last 2 sts, p2.
Row 2: K2, *k1, (k1, p1, k1) into yon of previous row; repeat from * to last 2 sts, k2.
Row 3: Knit.
Note: row 3 should be worked loosely.

Rosebud Mesh Pattern

multiple of 10 plus 1
Row 1 and foll alt rows: (wrong side) Purl.
Row 2: K2 tog, *yon, k3, yon, k into front and back of next st, yon, k3, yon, sl.1, k2 tog, psso; repeat from * to last 2 sts, sl.1, k1, psso.
Row 4: Sl.1, k1, psso, *yon, sl.2, k1, p2sso, yon, k2 tog, yon, sl.1, k1, psso, (yon, sl.2, k1, p2sso) twice; repeat from * to last 2 sts, k2 tog.
Row 6: K2, *k2 tog, yon, k3, yon, sl.1, k1, psso, k3; repeat from * to last 2 sts, k2.
Row 8: K1, *k2 tog, yon, k1 tbl, yon, sl.1, k2 tog, psso, yon, k1 tbl, yon, sl.1, k1, psso, k1; repeat from * to end of row.

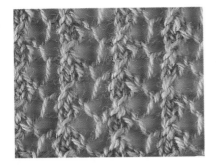

Miniature Leaf Pattern 2

multiple of 6 plus 2
Row 1: K1, *k3, yon, k3 tog, yon;
repeat from * to last st, k1.
Rows 2 and 4: Purl.
Row 3: K1, *yon, k3 tog, yon, k3;
repeat from * to last st, k1.

Fuchsia Pattern 1

multiple of 8 plus 1
Row 1: *P7, k1, yon; repeat from *
to last st, p1.
Row 2: P1, *p2, k7; repeat from *
to end of row.
Row 3: *P7, k2, yon; repeat from *
to last st, p1.
Row 4: P1, *p3, k7; repeat from *
to end of row.
Row 5: *P7, k3, yon; repeat from *
to last st, p1.
Row 6: P1, *p4, k7; repeat from *
to end of row.
Row 7: *P7, k4, yon; repeat from *
to last st, p1.
Row 8: P1, *p5, k7; repeat from *
to end of row.
Row 9: *P7, k5, yon; repeat from *
to last st, p1.
Row 10: P1, *p6, k7; repeat from *
to end of row.
Row 11: *P7, k6, yon; repeat from
* to last st, p1.
Row 12: P1, *p7, k7; repeat from *
to end of row.
Row 13: *P7, k5, k2 tog; repeat
from * to last st, p1.
Row 14: P1, *p2 tog, p4, k7; repeat
from * to end of row.
Row 15: *P7, k3, k2 tog; repeat
from * to last st, p1.
Row 16: P1, *p2 tog, p2, k7; repeat
from * to end of row.
Row 17: *P7, k1, k2 tog; repeat
from * to last st, p1.
Row 18: P1, *p2 tog, k7; repeat

from * to end of row.
Row 19: *P3, k1, yon, p4; repeat
from * to last st, p1.
Row 20: P1, *k4, p2, k3; repeat
from * to end of row.
Row 21: *P3, k2, yon, p4; repeat
from * to last st, p1.
Row 22: P1, *k4, p3, k3; repeat
from * to end of row.
Row 23: *P3, k3, yon, p4; repeat
from * to last st, p1.
Row 24: P1, *k4, p4, k3; repeat
from * to end of row.
Row 25: *P3, k4, yon, p4; repeat
from * to last st, p1.
Row 26: P1, *k4, p5, k3; repeat
from * to end of row.
Row 27: *P3, k5, yon, p4; repeat
from * to last st, p1.
Row 28: P1, *k4, p6, k3; repeat
from * to end of row.
Row 29: *P3, k6, yon, p4; repeat
from * to last st, p1.
Row 30: P1, *k4, p7, k3; repeat
from * to end of row.
Row 31: *P3, k5, k2 tog, p4; repeat
from * to last st, p1.
Row 32: P1, *k4, p2 tog, p4, k3;
repeat from * to end of row.
Row 33: *P3, k3, k2 tog, p4; repeat
from * to last st, p1.
Row 34: P1, *k4, p2 tog, p2, k3;
repeat from * to end of row.
Row 35: *P3, k1, k2 tog, p4; repeat
from * to last st, p1.
Row 36: P1, *k4, p2 tog, k3.

Fuchsia Pattern 2

multiple of 6
Row 1: ∗P2, k2, yon, p2; repeat from ∗ to end of row.
Row 2: ∗K2, p3, k2; repeat from ∗ to end of row.
Row 3: ∗P2, k3, yon, p2; repeat from ∗ to end of row.
Row 4: ∗K2, p4, k2; repeat from ∗ to end of row.
Row 5: ∗P2, k4, yon, p2; repeat from ∗ to end of row.
Row 6: ∗K2, p5, k2; repeat from ∗ to end of row.
Row 7: ∗P2, k3, k2 tog, p2; repeat from ∗ to end of row.
Row 8: as row 4.
Row 9: ∗P2, k2, k2 tog, p2; repeat from ∗ to end of row.
Row 10: as row 2.
Row 11: ∗P2, k1, k2 tog, p2; repeat from ∗ to end of row.
Row 12: ∗K2, p2, k2; repeat from ∗ to end of row.

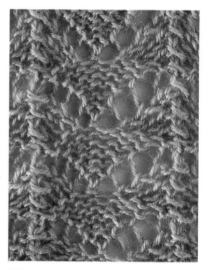

Fan Lace Pattern 2

multiple of 10 plus 1
Row 1: Knit.
Row 2: P1, ∗yon, k3, sl.1, k2 tog, psso, k3, yon, p1; repeat from ∗ to end of row.
Row 3: K1, ∗p9, k1; repeat from ∗ to end of row.
Row 4: P1, ∗p1, yon, k2, sl.1, k2 tog, psso, k2, yon, p2; repeat from ∗ to end of row.
Row 5: K1, ∗k1, p7, k2; repeat from ∗ to end of row.
Row 6: P1, ∗p2, yon, k1, sl.1, k2 tog, psso, k1, yon, p3; repeat from ∗ to end of row.
Row 7: K1, ∗k2, p5, k3; repeat from ∗ to end of row.
Row 8: P1, ∗p3, yon, sl.1, k2 tog, psso, yon, p4; repeat from ∗ to end of row.

Horseshoe Lace

multiple of 10 plus 1
Row 1 and foll alt rows: (wrong side) Purl.
Row 2: K1, ∗yon, k3, sl.1, k2 tog, psso, k3, yon, k1; repeat from ∗ to end of row.
Row 4: P1, ∗k1, yon, k2, sl.1, k2 tog, psso, k2, yon, k1, p1; repeat from ∗ to end of row.
Row 6: P1, ∗k2, yon, k1, sl.1, k2 tog, psso, k1, yon, k2, p1; repeat from ∗ to end of row.
Row 8: P1, ∗k3, yon, sl.1, k2 tog, psso, yon, k3, p1; repeat from ∗ to end of row.

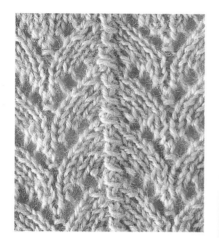

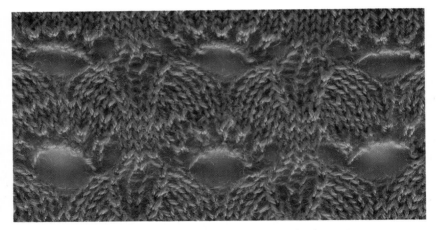

Crown of Glory Pattern

multiple of 14 plus 5
Row 1: K3, *sl.1, k1, psso, k9, k2 tog, k1; repeat from * to last 2 sts, k2.
Row 2: P2, *p1, p2 tog, p7, p2 tog tbl; repeat from * to last 3 sts, p3.
Row 3: K3, *sl.1, k1, psso, k2, y3on, k3, k2 tog, k1; repeat from * to last 2 sts, k2.
Row 4: P2, *p1, p2 tog, p2, (k1, p1, k1, p1, k1) into yo, p1, p2 tog tbl; repeat from * to last 3 sts, p3.
Row 5: K3, *sl.1, k1, psso, k6, k2 tog, k1; repeat from * to last 2 sts, k2.
Row 6: P2, *p1, p2 tog, p6; repeat from * to last 3 sts, p3.
Row 7: K3, *k1, (yon, k1) six times, k1; repeat from * to last 2 sts, k2.
Rows 8, 10 and 12: Purl.
Rows 9 and 11: Knit.

Eye of the Lynx Pattern

multiple of 8 plus 6
Rows 1 and 3: Purl.
Row 2: Knit.
Row 4: P5, *p1, sl 2 purlwise, p5; repeat from * to last st, p1.
Row 5: K1, *k5, sl 2 purlwise, k1; repeat from * to last 5 sts, k5.
Row 6: P5, *p1, sl 2, p5; repeat from * to last st, p1.
Row 7: K1, *sl.1, k1, psso, yon, k2 tog, k1, sl 2 purlwise, k1; repeat from * to last 5 sts, sl.1, k1, psso, yon, k2 tog, k1.
Row 8: P2, p into front and back of yo, p1, *p1, sl 2 purlwise, p2, p into front and back of yo, p1; repeat from * to last st, p1.
Row 9: K1, *k5, sl 2 purlwise, k1; repeat from * to last 5 sts, k5.
Rows 10 and 12: Knit.
Row 11: Purl.
Rows 13 and 15: K1, *k1, sl 2 purlwise, k5; repeat from * to last 5 sts, k1, sl 2 purlwise, k2.
Row 14: P2, sl 2 purlwise, p1, *p5, sl 2 purlwise, p1; repeat from * to last st, p1.
Row 16: P2, sl 2 purlwise, p1, *p2 tog, yon, p1 and return st to left hand needle, pass next st over it and replace on right hand needle, p1, sl 2 purlwise, p1; repeat from * to last st, p1.
Row 17: K1, *k1, sl 2 purlwise, k2, k into front and back of yo, k1; repeat from * to last 5 sts, k1, sl 2 purlwise, k2.
Row 18: as row 14.

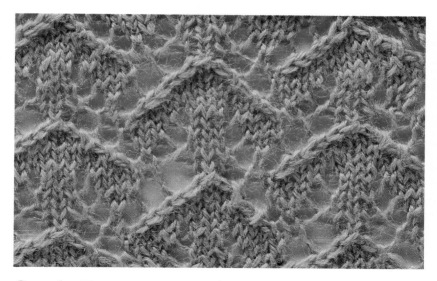

Spade Pattern

multiple of 18 plus 1
Row 1: K2, *yon, k1, yon, SSK, k9, k2 tog, yon, k1, yon, k3; repeat from * to last 2 sts, k2.
Row 2: P5, *p2 tog, p7, p2 tog tbl, p9; repeat from * to last 5 sts, p5.
Row 3: K2, *yon, k3, yon, SSK, k5, k2 tog, (yon, k3) twice; repeat from * to last 2 sts, k2.
Row 4: P7, *p2 tog, p3, p2 tog tbl, p13; repeat from * to last 7 sts, p7.
Row 5: K2, *yon, k5, yon, SSK, k1, k2 tog, yon, k5, yon, k3; repeat from * to last 2 sts, k2.
Row 6: P9, *p3 tog, p17; repeat from * to last 9 sts, p9.
Row 7: K5, *k2 tog, yon, k1, yon, k3, yon, k1, yon, SSK, k9; repeat from * to last 5 sts, k5.
Row 8: P4, *p2 tog tbl, p9, p2 tog, p7; repeat from * to last 4 sts, p4.
Row 9: K3, *k2 tog, (yon, k3) three times, yon, SSK, k5; repeat from * to last 3 sts, k3.
Row 10: P2, *p2 tog tbl, p13, p2 tog, p3; repeat from * to last 2 sts, p2.
Row 11: K1, *k2 tog, yon, k5, yon, k3, yon, k5, yon, SSK, k1; repeat from * to end of row.
Row 12: P2 tog, *p17, p3 tog; repeat from * to last 2 sts, p2 tog.

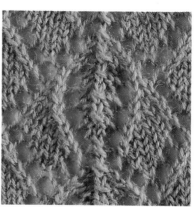

Branched Eyelet Panel

panel of 19 sts
Row 1: K2, yon, k4, k2 tog, yon, sl 2, k1, p2sso, yon, SSK, k4, yon, k2.
Row 2 and foll alt rows: Purl.
Row 3: K3, yon, k2, k3 tog, yon, k3, yon, sl.1, k2 tog, psso, k2, yon, k3.
Row 5: K4, yon, k1, k2 tog, yon, k1, sl 2, k1, p2sso, k1, yon, SSK, k1, yon, k4.
Row 7: K5, yon, k2 tog, yon, k1, sl 2, k1, p2sso, k1, yon, SSK, yon, k5.
Row 9: K3, k2 tog, yon, k1, yon, k2, sl 2, k1, p2sso, k2, yon, k1, yon, SSK, k3.
Row 11: K2, k2 tog, yon, k3, yon, k1, sl 2, k1, p2sso, k1, yon, k3, yon, SSK, k2.
Row 13: K1, k2 tog, yon, k5, yon, sl 2, k1, p2sso, yon, k5, yon, SSK, k1.

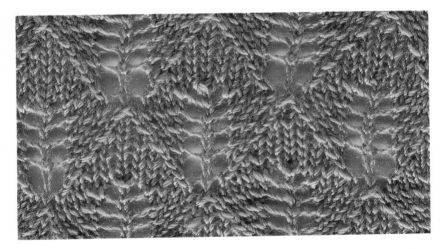

Fern Stitch Pattern

multiple of 12 plus 6
Row 1: *K1, yon, sl.1, k1, psso, k7, k2 tog, yon; repeat from * to last 6 sts, k1, yon, sl.1, k1, psso, k3.
Row 2 and foll alt rows: Purl.
Row 3: *K1, yon, k1, sl.1, k1, psso, k5, k2 tog, k1, yon; repeat from * to last 6 sts, k1, yon, k1, sl.1, k1, psso, k2.
Row 5: *K1, yon, k2, sl.1, k1, psso, k3, k2 tog, k2, yon; repeat from * to last 6 sts, k1, yon, k2, sl.1, k1, psso, k1.
Row 7: *K1, yon, k3, sl.1, k1, psso, k2 tog, k3, yon; repeat from * to last 6 sts, k1, yon, k3, sl.1, k1, psso.
Row 9: *K1, yon, k4, sl.1, k2 tog, psso, k4, yon; repeat from * to last 6 sts, k1, yon, k5.
Row 11: *K4, k2 tog, yon, k1, yon, sl.1, k1, psso, k3; repeat from * to last 7 sts, k4, k2 tog, yon, k1.
Row 13: *K3, k2 tog, (k1, yon) twice, k1, sl.1, k1, psso, k2; repeat from * to last 7 sts, k3, k2 tog, k1, yon, k1.
Row 15: *K2, k2 tog, k2, yon, k1, yon, k2, sl.1, k1, psso, k1; repeat from * to last 7 sts, k2, k2 tog, k2, yon, k1.
Row 17: *K1, k2 tog, k3, yon, k1, yon, k3, sl.1, k1, psso; repeat from * to last 7 sts, k1, k2 tog, k3, yon, k1.
Row 19: Sl.1, k1, psso, k4, yon, k1, *yon, k4, sl.1, k2 tog, psso, k4, yon, k1; repeat from * to end of row.

Crochet Knit Shell Pattern

multiple of 6 plus 3
Row 1: K1, *yon, k1; repeat from * to last st, k1.
Row 2: Knit dropping all yons off needle.
Row 3: K1, k3 tog, *y2on, k1, y2on, sl.2, k3 tog, p2sso; repeat from * to last 5 sts, y2on, k1, y2on, k3 tog, k1.
Row 4: K1, *k1, k into front and back of yon; repeat from * to last 2 sts, k2.
Row 5: as row 1.
Row 6: as row 2.
Row 7: K1, *k1, y2on, sl 2, k3 tog, p2sso, y2on; repeat from * to last 2 sts, k2.
Row 8: as row 4.

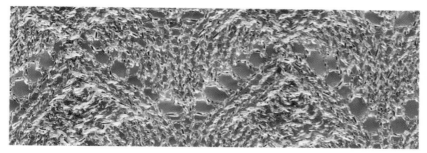

Pine Trees Pattern 2

multiple of 14 plus 1
Row 1: K1, *yon, k2, p3, p3 tog, p3, k2, yon, k1; repeat from * to end of row.
Row 2: *P4, k7, p3; repeat from * to last st, p1.
Row 3: K1, *k1, yon, k2, p2, p3 tog, p2, k2, yon, k2; repeat from * to end of row.
Row 4: *P5, k5, p4; repeat from * to last st. p1.
Row 5: K1, *k2, yon, k2, p1, p3 tog, p1, k2, yon, k3; repeat from *
to end of row.
Row 6: *P6, k3, p5; repeat from * to last st, p1.
Row 7: K1, *k3, yon, k2, p3 tog, k2, yon, k4; repeat from * to end of row.
Row 8: *P7, k1, p6; repeat from * to last st. p1.
Row 9: K1, *k4, yon, k1, sl.1, k2 tog, psso, k1, yon, k5; repeat from * to end of row.
Rows 10 and 12: Purl.
Row 11: K1, *k5, yon, sl.1, k2 tog, psso, yon, k6; repeat from * to end of row.

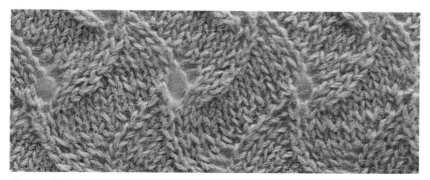

Scroll Pattern

multiple of 10 plus 2
Row 1: K1, *yon, k8, k2 tog; repeat from * to last st, k1.
Row 2: P1, *p2 tog, p7, yon, p1; repeat from * to last st, p1.
Row 3: K1, *k2, yon, k6, k2 tog; repeat from * to last st, k1.
Row 4: P1, *p2 tog, p5, yon, p3; repeat from * to last st, p1.
Row 5: K1, *k4, yon, k4, k2 tog; repeat from * to last st, k1.
Row 6: P1, *p2 tog, p3, yon, p5; repeat from * to last st, p1.
Row 7: K1, *k6, yon, k2, k2 tog; repeat from * to last st, k1.
Row 8: P1, *p2 tog, p1, yon, p7; repeat from * to last st, p1.
Row 9: K1, *k8, yon, k2 tog; repeat from * to last st, k1.
Row 10: P1, *yon, p8, p2 tog tbl; repeat from * to last st, p1.
Row 11: K1, *sl.1, k1, psso, k7, yon, k1; repeat from * to last st, k1.
Row 12: P1, *p2, yon, p6, p2 tog tbl; repeat from * to last st, p1.
Row 13: K1, *sl.1, k1, psso, k5, yon, k3; repeat from * to last st, k1.
Row 14: P1, *p4, yon, p4, p2 tog tbl; repeat from * to last st, p1.
Row 15: K1, *sl.1, k1, psso, k3, yon, k5; repeat from * to last st, k1.
Row 16: P1, *p6, yon, p2, p2 tog tbl; repeat from * to last st, p1.
Row 17: K1, *sl.1, k1, psso, k1, yon, k7; repeat from * to last st, k1.
Row 18: P1, *p8, yon, p2 tog tbl; repeat from * to last st, p1.

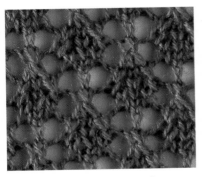

Miniature Leaf Pattern 3

multiple of 6 plus 1
Row 1 and foll alt rows: (wrong side) Purl.
Row 2: K1, *k2 tog, yon, k1, yon, sl.1, k1, psso, k1; repeat from * to end of row.
Row 4: K2 tog, *yon, k3, yon, sl 2, k1, p2sso; repeat from * to end of row.
Row 6: K1, *yon, sl.1, k1, psso, k1, k2 tog, yon, k1; repeat from * to end of row.
Row 8: K2, *yon, sl 2, k1, p2sso, yon, k3; repeat from * to last 2 sts, k2.

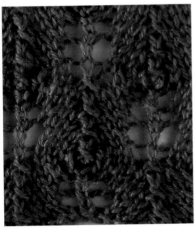

Fir Cone Pattern 2

multiple of 10 plus 1
Row 1 and foll alt rows: Purl.
Rows 2, 4, 6 and 8: K1, *yon, k3, sl.1, k2 tog, psso, k3, yon, k1; repeat from * to end of row.
Rows 10, 12, 14 and 16: K2 tog, * k3, yon, k1, yon, k3, sl.1, k2 tog, psso; repeat from * to last 9 sts, k3, yon, k1, yon, k3, sl.1, k1, psso.

Curved Leaf Lace 2

multiple of 10 plus 5
Row 1: K1, k2 tog, *yon, k3, yon, k into front and back of next st, yon, k3, yon, sl.1, k2 tog, psso; repeat from * to last 3 sts, sl.1, k1, psso, k1.
Row 2 and foll alt rows: Purl.
Row 3: K1, k2 tog, *yon, k3 tog, yon, k2 tog, yon, sl.1, k1, psso, yon, sl.2 sts on to right hand needle, k1 and pass 2 sl sts over this st, yon, sl.1, k2 tog, psso; repeat from * to last 3 sts, sl.1, k1, psso, k1.
Row 5: K4, *k2 tog, yon, k1, yon, sl.1, k1, psso, k5; repeat from * to last 4 sts, k4.
Row 7: K3, *k2 tog, yon, k3, yon, sl.1, k1, psso, k3; repeat from * to last 3 sts, k3.
Row 9: K1, k3 tog, *yon, k1, yon, k3, yon, k1, yon, sl next 2 sts knitwise, k1, p2sso, sl this st on to left hand needle and pass next 2 sts over it then return it to right hand needle; repeat from * to last 8 sts, yon, k1, yon, k3, yon, sl.2, k1, p2sso, k1.
Row 11: K2, *k2 tog, yon, k1, yon, sl.1, k2 tog, psso, yon, k1, yon, sl.1, k1, psso, k1; repeat from * to last st, k1.

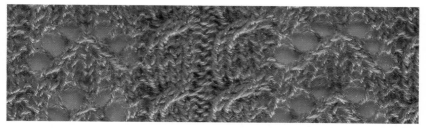

Lace Cable Pattern

multiple of 19 plus 2
Row 1: *P2, k4 tbl, k1, yon, k2 tog tbl, k3, k2 tog, yon, k1, k4 tbl; repeat from * to last 2 sts, p2.
Rows 2, 4, 6 and 8: *K2, p4 tbl, k1, p7, k1, p4 tbl; repeat from * to last 2 sts, k2.

Row 3: *P2, k4 tbl, k2, yon, k2 tog tbl, k1, k2 tog, yon, k2, k4 tbl; repeat from * to last 2 sts, p2.
Row 5: *P2, k4 tbl, k3, yon, sl.1, k2 tog, psso, yon, k3, k4 tbl; repeat from * to last 2 sts, p2.
Row 7: *P2, k4 tbl, k9, k4 tbl; repeat from * to last 2 sts, p2.

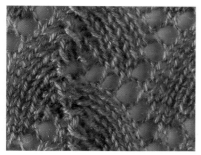

Shell Lace 2

multiple of 11 plus 1
Row 1 and foll alt rows: (wrong side) Purl.
Row 2: K2 tog, *k5, yon, k1, yon, k2, sl.1, k2 tog, psso; repeat from * to last 10 sts, k5, yon, k1, yon, k2, k2 tog tbl.
Row 4: K2 tog, *k4, yon, k3, yon, k1, sl.1, k2 tog, psso; repeat from * to last 10 sts, k4, yon, k3, yon, k1, k2 tog tbl.
Row 6: K2 tog, *k3, yon, k5, yon, sl.1, k2 tog, psso; repeat from * to last 10 sts, k3, yon, k5, yon, k2 tog tbl.
Row 8: K2 tog, *k2, yon, k1, yon, k5, sl.1, k2 tog, psso; repeat from * to last 10 sts, k2, yon, k1, yon, k5, k2 tog tbl.
Row 10: K2 tog, *k1, yon, k3, yon, k4, sl.1, k2 tog, psso; repeat from * to last 10 sts, k1, yon, k3, yon, k4, k2 tog tbl.
Row 12: K2 tog, *yon, k5, yon, k3, sl.1, k2 tog, psso; repeat from * to last 10 sts, yon, k5, yon, k3, k2 tog tbl.

Lace Butterfly Pattern

multiple of 14 plus 4
Rows 1 and 3: *P1, sl the second st then the 1st st on left hand needle, taking both off together, p1, k3, k2 tog, y2on, k2 tog tbl, k3; repeat from * to last 4 sts, p1, sl 2 sts as before, p1.
Rows 2 and 4: *K1, p2, k1, p4, k into back and front of yo, p4; repeat from * to last 4 sts, k1, p2, k1.
Rows 5 and 7: *P1, sl 2 sts as before, p1, k1, k2 tog, y2on, k2 tog tbl, k2 tog, y2on, k2 tog tbl, k1; repeat from * to last 4 sts, p1, sl.2 as before, p1.
Rows 6 and 8: *K1, p2, k1, p2, k into back and front of yo, p2, k into back and front of yo, p2; repeat from * to last 4 sts, k1, p2, k1.

Herringbone Eyelet Pattern

multiple of 6 plus 2
Row 1 and foll alt rows: (wrong side) Purl.
Rows 2, 4 and 6: *Sl.1, k1, psso, k2, yon, k2; repeat from * to last 2 sts, k2.
Rows 8, 10 and 12: K1, *k2, yon, k2, k2 tog; repeat from * to last st, k1.

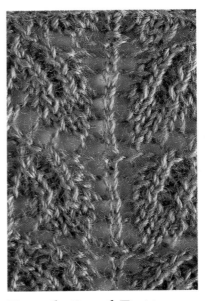

Beech Leaf Pattern

multiple of 14 plus 1
Row 1: *K1, yon, k5, yon, sl.1, k2 tog, psso, yon, k5, yon; repeat from * to last st, k1.
Row 2: Purl.
Row 3: *K1, yon, k1, k2 tog, p1, sl.1, k1, psso, k1, yon, p1, yon, k1, k2 tog, p1, sl.1, k1, psso, k1, yon; repeat from * to last st, k1.
Row 4: P1, *p3, (k1, p3) twice, k1, p4; repeat from * to end of row.
Row 5: *K1, yon, k1, k2 tog, p1, sl.1, k1, psso, k1, p1, k1, k2 tog, p1, sl.1, k1, psso, k1, yon; repeat from * to last st, k1.
Row 6: P1, *p3, (k1, p2) twice, k1, p4; repeat from * to end of row.
Row 7: *(K1, yon) twice, k2 tog, p1, sl.1, k1, psso, p1, k2 tog, p1, sl.1, k1, psso, yon, k1, yon; repeat from * to last st, k1.
Row 8: P1, *p4, k1, (p1, k1) twice, p5; repeat from * to end of row.
Row 9: *K1, yon, k3, yon, sl.1, k2 tog, psso, p1, k3 tog, yon, k3, yon; repeat from * to last st, k1.
Row 10: Purl.

Banded Chevron Pattern

multiple of 8 plus 1
Rows 1 to 8: Work in moss stitch.
Row 9: *K1, yon, sl.1, k1, psso, k3, k2 tog, yon; repeat from * to last st, k1.
Rows 10, 12 and 14: Purl.
Row 11: *K2, yon, sl.1, k1, psso, k1, k2 tog, yon, k1; repeat from * to last st, k1.
Row 13: *K3, yon, sl.1, k2 tog, psso, yon, k2; repeat from * to last st, k1.

Openwork Diamond Pattern 2

multiple of 10 plus 2
Row 1: K1, *k1, yon, sl.1, k1, psso, k5, k2 tog, yon; repeat from * to last st, k1.
Row 2 and foll alt rows: Purl.
Row 3: K1, *k2, yon, sl.1, k1, psso, k3, k2 tog, yon, k1; repeat from * to last st, k1.
Row 5: K1, *k1, yon, sl.1, k1, psso, yon, sl.1, k1, psso, k1, k2 tog, yon, k2 tog, yon; repeat from * to last st, k1.
Row 7: K1, *k2, yon, sl.1, k1, psso, yon, sl.1, k2 tog, psso, yon, k2 tog, yon, k1; repeat from * to last st, k1.
Row 9: K1, *k3, k2 tog, yon, k1, yon, sl.1, k1, psso, k2; repeat from * to last st, k1.
Row 11: K1, *k2, k2 tog, yon, k3, yon, sl.1, k1, psso, k1; repeat from * to last st, k1.
Row 13: K1, *k1, k2 tog, yon, k2 tog, yon, k1, yon, sl.1, k1, psso, yon, sl.1, k1, psso; repeat from * to last st, k1.
Row 15: K2 tog, *yon, k2 tog, yon, k3, yon, sl.1, k1, psso, yon, sl.1, k2 tog, psso; repeat from * to last 2 sts, k2.

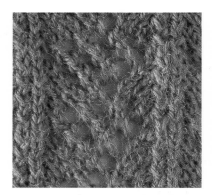

Cascade Mesh Stitch

multiple of 11
Row 1: *K2 tog tbl, k3, yon, k1, yon, k3, k2 tog; repeat from * to end of row.
Row 2 and foll alt rows: Purl.
Row 3: *K2 tog tbl, k2, yon, k1, yon, k2 tog tbl, yon, k2, k2 tog; repeat from * to end of row.
Row 5: *K2 tog tbl, (k1, yon) twice, (k2 tog tbl, yon) twice, k1, k2 tog; repeat from * to end of row.
Row 7: *K2 tog tbl, yon, k1, (yon, k2 tog tbl) three times, yon, k2 tog; repeat from * to end of row.

Dewdrop Pattern

multiple of 6 plus 1
Row 1: K2, *p3, k3; repeat from * to last 5 sts, p3, k2.
Row 2: P2, *k3, p3; repeat from * to last 5 sts, k3, p2.
Row 3: as row 1.
Row 4: K2, *yon, sl.1, k2 tog, psso, yon, k3; repeat from * to last 5 sts, yon, sl.1, k2 tog, psso, yon, k2.
Rows 5 and 7: as row 2.
Row 6: as row 1.
Row 8: K2 tog, *yon, k3, yon,sl.1, k2 tog, psso; repeat from * to last 5 sts, yon, k3, yon, sl.1, k1, psso.

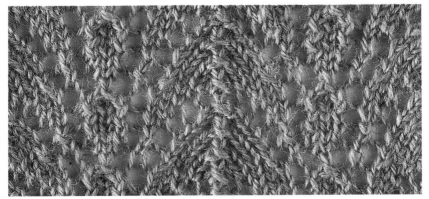

Fountain Lace Pattern

multiple of 16 plus 1
Row 1: SSK, *yon, k2, k2 tog, yon, k1, yon, sl.1, k2 tog, psso, yon, k1, yon, SSK, k2, yon, sl.1, k2 tog, psso; repeat from * to last 2 sts, k2 tog.
Row 2 and foll alt rows: Purl.
Row 3: SSK, *k3, yon, k2 tog, yon, k3, yon, SSK, yon, k3, sl.1, k2 tog, psso; repeat from * to last 2 sts, k2 tog.
Row 5: SSK, *(k2, yon) twice, k2 tog, k1, SSK, (yon, k2) twice, sl.1, k2 tog, psso; repeat from * to last 2 sts, k2 tog.
Row 7: SSK, *k1, yon, k3, yon, k2 tog, k1, SSK, yon, k3, yon, k1, sl.1, k2 tog, psso; repeat from * to last 2 sts, k2 tog.

Arched Lace Pattern

multiple of 12 plus 1
Rows 1, 3 and 5: P1, *SSK, k3, yon, p1, yon, k3, k2 tog, p1; repeat from * to end of row.
Rows 2, 4 and 6: K1, *p5, k1; repeat from * to end of row.
Row 7: P1, *yon, k3, k2 tog, p1, SSK, k3, yon, p1; repeat from * to end of row.
Row 8: As row 2.
Row 9: P2, *yon, k2, k2 tog, p1, SSK, k2, yon, p3; repeat from * to last 2 sts, p2.
Row 10: K2, *p4, k1, p4, k3; repeat from * to last 2 sts, k2.
Row 11: P3, *yon, k1, k2 tog, p1, SSK, k1, yon, p5; repeat from * to last 3 sts, p3.

Row 12: K3, *p3, k1, p3, k5; repeat from * to last 3 sts, k3.
Row 13: P4, *yon, k2 tog, p1, SSK, yon, p7; repeat from * to last 4 sts, p4.
Row 14: K4, *p2, k1, p2, k7; repeat from * to last 4 sts, k4.
Rows 15, 17 and 19: as row 7.
Rows 16, 18 and 20: as row 2.
Row 21: as row 1.
Row 22: as row 2.
Row 23: P1, *SSK, k2, yon, p3, yon, k2, k2 tog, p1; repeat from * to end of row.
Row 24: K1, *p4, k3, p4, k1; repeat from * to end of row.
Row 25: P1, *SSK, k1, yon, p5, yon, k1, k2 tog, p1; repeat from * to end of row.
Row 26: K1, *p3, k5, p3, k1; repeat from * to end of row.
Row 27: P1, *SSK, yon, p7, yon, k2 tog, p1; repeat from * to end of row.
Row 28: K1, *p2, k7, p2, k1; repeat from * to end of row.

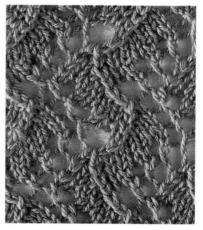

Chevron Lace 2

multiple of 10 plus 2
Row 1: K1, *k1, yon, k2 tog, k5, sl.1, k1, psso, yon; repeat from * to last st, k1.
Row 2 and foll alt rows: Purl.
Rows 3 and 5: as row 1.
Row 7: K1, *k1, yon, k3, sl.1, k2 tog, psso, k3, yon; repeat from * to last st, k1.
Row 9: K1, *k2, yon, k2, sl.1, k2 tog, psso, k2, yon, k1; repeat from * to last st, k1.
Row 11: K1, *k3, yon, k1, sl.1, k2 tog, psso, k1, yon, k2; repeat from * to last st, k1.
Row 13: K1, *k4, yon, sl.1, k2 tog, psso, yon, k3; repeat from * to last st, k1.

Travelling Vine Pattern

multiple of 8
Row 1: *Yon, k1 tbl, yon, sl.1, k1, psso, k5; repeat from * to end of row.
Row 2: *P4, p2 tog tbl, p3; repeat from * to end of row.
Row 3: *Yon, k1 tbl, yon, k2, sl.1, k1, psso, k3; repeat from * to end of row.
Row 4: *P2, p2 tog tbl, p5; repeat from * to end of row.
Row 5: *K1 tbl, yon, k4, sl.1, k1, psso, k1, yon; repeat from * to end of row.
Row 6: *P1, p2 tog tbl, p6; repeat from * to end of row.
Row 7: *K5, k2 tog, yon, k1 tbl, yon; repeat from * to end of row.
Row 8: *P3, p2 tog, p4; repeat from * to end of row.
Row 9: *K3, k2 tog, k2, yon, k1 tbl, yon; repeat from * to end of row.

Row 10: *P5, p2 tog, p2; repeat from * to end of row.
Row 11: *Yon, k1, k2 tog, k4, yon, k1 tbl; repeat from * to end of row.
Row 12: *P6, p2 tog, p1; repeat from * to end of row.

Chevron Lace 3

multiple of 10 plus 1
Row 1 and foll alt rows: (wrong side) Purl.
Rows 2, 4 and 6: *K1, yon, sl.1, k1, psso, k2 tog, yon, k1, yon, sl.1, k1, psso, k2 tog, yon; repeat from * to last st, k1.
Row 8: *K1, yon, sl.1, k1, psso, k5, k2 tog, yon; repeat from * to last st, k1.
Row 10: *K2, yon, sl.1, k1, psso, k3, k2 tog, yon, k1; repeat from * to last st, k1.
Row 12: *K3, yon, sl.1, k1, psso, k1, k2 tog, yon, k2; repeat from * to last st, k1.
Row 14: *K4, yon, sl.1, k2 tog, psso, yon, k3; repeat from * to last st, k1.

Shell Pattern 2

multiple of 9 plus 3
Row 1: K2, *yon, k8, yon, k1;
repeat from * to last st, k1.
Row 2: K3, *p8, k3; repeat from *
to end of row.
Row 3: K3, *yon, k8, yon, k3;
repeat from * to end of row.

Row 4: K4, *p8, k5; repeat from *
to last 4 sts, k4.
Row 5: K4, *yon, k8, yon, k5;
repeat from * to last 4 sts, k4.
Row 6: K5, *p8, k7; repeat from *
to last 5 sts, k5.
Row 7: K5, *k4 tog tbl, k4 tog, k7;
repeat from * to last 5 sts, k5.
Row 8: Knit.

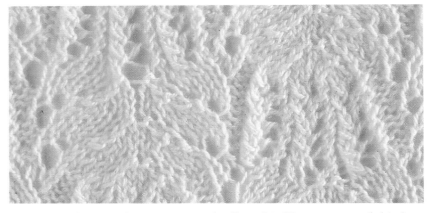

Frost Flowers Pattern

multiple of 34 plus 2
Row 1: K1, *k3, k2 tog, k4, yon,
p2, (k2, yon, SSK) three times, p2,
yon, k4, SSK, k3; repeat from * to
last st, k1.
Row 2: K1, *p2, p2 tog tbl, p4,
yon, p1, k2, (p2, yon, p2 tog) three
times, k2, p1, yon, p4, p2 tog, p2;
repeat from * to last st, k1.
Row 3: K1, *k1, k2 tog, k4, yon,
k2, p2, (k2, yon, SSK) three times,
p2, k2, yon, k4, SSK, k1; repeat
from * to last st, k1.
Row 4: K1, *p2 tog tbl, p4, yon,
p3, k2, (p2, yon, p2 tog) three
times, k2, p3, yon, p4, p2 tog;
repeat from * to last st, k1.

Rows 5 to 12: repeat rows 1-4 twice.
Row 13: K1, *yon, SSK, k2, yon,
SSK, p2, yon, k4, SSK, k6, k2 tog,
k4, yon, p2, k2, yon, SSK, k2;
repeat from * to last st, k1.
Row 14: K1, *yon, p2 tog, p2, yon,
p2 tog, k2, p1, yon, p4, p2 tog, p4,
p2 tog tbl, p4, yon, p1, k2, p2,
yon, p2 tog, p2; repeat from * to
last st, k1.
Row 15: K1 *yon, SSK, k2, yon,
SSK, p2, k2, yon, k4, SSK, k2, k2
tog, k4, yon, k2, p2, k2, yon, SSK,
k2; repeat from * to last st, k1.
Row 16: K1, *yon, p2 tog, p2, yon,
p2 tog, k2, p3, yon, p4, p2 tog, p2
tog tbl, p4, yon, p3, k2, p2, yon,
p2 tog, p2; repeat from * to last st,
k1.
Rows 17 to 24: repeat rows 13-16
twice.

Trellis Framed Leaf Pattern

multiple of 19 plus 2

Rows 1, 3, 5 and 7: K1, *sl.1, k1, psso, k3, (yon, sl.1, k1, psso) twice, yon, k1, yon, (k2 tog, yon) twice, k3, k2 tog; repeat from * to last st, k1.

Row 2 and foll alt rows: Purl.

Row 9: K1, *sl.1, k1, psso, k2, (yon, k2 tog) twice, yon, k3, yon, (sl.1, k1, psso, yon) twice, k2, k2 tog; repeat from * to last st, k1.

Row 11: K1, *sl.1, k1, psso, k1, (yon, k2 tog) twice, yon, k5, yon, (sl.1, k1, psso, yon) twice, k1, k2 tog; repeat from * to last st, k1.

Row 13: K1, *sl.1, k1, psso (yon, k2 tog) twice, yon, k7, yon, (sl.1, k1, psso, yon) twice, k2 tog; repeat from * to last st, inc 1, k1.

Row 15: *Sl.1, k1, psso, (yon, k2 tog) twice, yon, k3, k2 tog, k4, yon, (sl.1, k1, psso, yon) twice; repeat from * to last 2 sts, sl.1, k1, psso, k1.

Rows 17, 19, 21 and 23: K1, *(yon, k2 tog) twice, yon, k3, k2 tog, sl.1, k1, psso, k3, yon, (sl.1, k1, psso, yon) twice, k1; repeat from * to last st, k1.

Row 25: K1, *k1, (yon, sl.1, k1, psso) twice, yon, k2, k2 tog, sl.1, k1, psso, k2 (yon, k2 tog) twice, yon, k2; repeat fom * to last st, k1.

Row 27: K1, *k2, (yon, sl.1, k1, psso) twice, yon, k1, k2 tog, sl.1, k1, psso, k1, yon, (k2 tog, yon) twice, k3; repeat from * to last st, k1.

Row 29: K1, *k3, (yon, sl.1, k1, psso) twice, yon, k2 tog, sl.1, k1, psso, yon, (k2 tog, yon) twice, k4; repeat from * to last st, k1.

Row 31: K1, *k4, (yon, sl.1, k1, psso) twice, yon, sl.1, k1, psso, yon, (k2 tog, yon) twice, k3, k2 tog; repeat from * to last st, k1.

Tortoise Stitch

multiple of 6 plus 1

Row 1: *K1, yon, sl.1, k1, psso, k1, k2 tog, yon; repeat from * to last st, k1.

Row 2 and foll alt rows: Purl.

Row 3: *K2, yon, k3, yon, k1; repeat from * to last st, k1.

Row 5: K2 tog, *yon, sl.1, k1, psso, k1, k2 tog, yon, sl.1, k2 tog, psso; repeat from * to last 2 sts, sl.1, k1, psso.

Row 7: *K1, k2 tog, yon, k1, yon, sl.1, k1, psso; repeat from * to last st, k1.

Row 9: as row 3.

Row 11: *K1, k2 tog, yon, sl.1, k2 tog, psso, yon, sl.1, k1, psso; repeat from * to last st, k1.

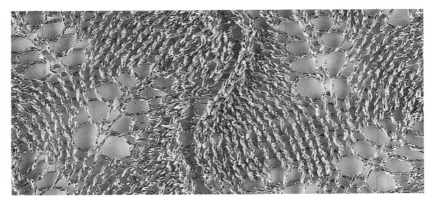

Curved Leaf Pattern

multiple of 18 plus 1
Row 1: P1, *k9, yon, k1, yon, k4, k3 tog, p1; repeat from * to end of row.
Row 2 and foll alt rows: K1, *p17, k1; repeat from * to end of row.
Row 3: P1, *k10, yon, k1, yon, k3, k3 tog, p1; repeat from * to end of row.
Row 5: P1, *k11, yon, k1, yon, k2, k3 tog, p1; repeat from * to end of row.
Row 7: P1, *k3 tog, k5, yon, k1, yon, k3, yon, k1, yon, k1, k3 tog, p1; repeat from * to end of row.
Row 9: P1, *k3 tog, k4, yon, k1, yon, k9, p1; repeat from * to end of row.
Row 11: P1, *k3 tog, k3, yon, k1, yon, k10, p1; repeat from * to end of row.
Row 13: P1, *k3 tog, k2, yon, k1, yon, k11, p1; repeat from * to end of row.
Row 15: P1, *k3 tog, (k1, yon) twice, k3, (yon, k1) twice, k4, k3 tog, p1; repeat from * to end of row.

Split Leaf Pattern

multiple of 12 plus 1
Row 1: P1, *k2 tog, k3, yon, k1, yon, k3, SSK, p1; repeat from * to end of row.
Rows 2, 4, 6 and 8: K1, *p11, k1; repeat from * to end of row.
Row 3: P1, *k2 tog, k2, yon, k3, yon, k2, SSK, p1; repeat from * to end of row.
Row 5: P1, *k2 tog, k1, yon, k5, yon, k1, SSK, p1; repeat from * to end of row.
Row 7: P1, *k2 tog, yon, k7, yon, SSK, p1; repeat from * to end of row.
Row 9: K1, *yon, k3, SSK, p1, k2 tog, k3, yon, k1; repeat from * to end of row.
Rows 10, 12, 14 and 16: P6, *k1, p11; repeat from * to last 7 sts, k1, p6.
Row 11: K2, *yon, k2, SSK, p1, k2 tog, k2, yon, k3; repeat from * to last 2 sts, k2.
Row 13: K3, *yon, k1, SSK, p1, k2 tog, k1, yon, k5; repeat from * to last 3 sts, k3.
Row 15: K4, *yon, SSK, p1, k2 tog, yon, k7; repeat from * to last 4 sts, k4.

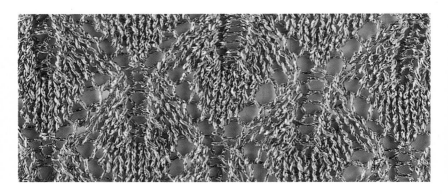

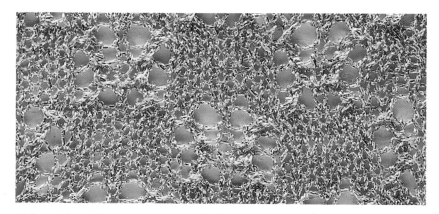

Checked Florette Pattern

multiple of 12 plus 5
Row 1: K2, *k4, p2 tog, yon, k1, yon, p2 tog, k3; repeat from * to last 3 sts, k3.
Row 2 and foll alt rows: Purl.
Row 3: K2, *k4, yon, p2 tog, k1, p2 tog, yon, k3; repeat from * to last 3 sts, k3.
Row 5: as row 3.
Row 7: as row 1.
Row 9: K2, *k1, yon, p2 tog, k7, p2 tog, yon; repeat from * to last 3 sts, k3.
Row 11: K2, *k1, p2 tog, yon, k7, yon, p2 tog; repeat from * to last 3 sts, k3.
Row 13: as row 11.
Row 15: as row 9.

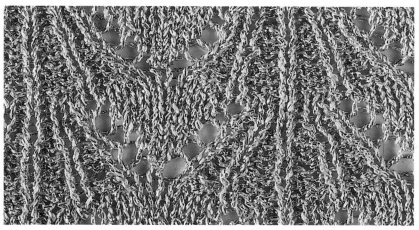

Umbrella Pattern

multiple of 18 plus 1
Row 1: *P1, (p1, k3) four times, p1; repeat from * to last st, p1.
Row 2: *K1, yon, k1, p2 tog, p1, (k1, p3) twice, k1, p1, p2 tog, k1, yon; repeat from * to last st, k1.
Row 3: *P3, k2, (p1, k3) twice, p1, k2, p2; repeat from * to last st, p1.
Row 4: *K2, yon, k1, p2, (k1, p1, p2 tog) twice, k1, p2, k1, yon, k1; repeat from * to last st, k1.
Row 5: *P3, (p1, k2) four times, p3; repeat from * to last st, p1.
Row 6: *K3, yon, k1, p2 tog, (k1, p2) twice, k1, p2 tog, k1, yon, k2; repeat from * to last st, k1.
Row 7: *P5, k1, (p1, k2) twice, p1, k1, p4; repeat from * to last st, p1.
Row 8: *K4, yon, k1, p1, (k1, p2 tog) twice, k1, p1, k1, yon, k3; repeat from * to last st, k1.
Row 9: *P5, (p1, k1) four times, p5; repeat from * to last st, p1.
Row 10: *K5, yon, SSK, (k1, p1) twice, k1, k2 tog, yon, k4; repeat from * to last st, k1.
Row 11: *P8, k1, p1, k1, p7; repeat from * to last st, p1.
Row 12: *K8, p1, k1, p1, k7; repeat from * to last st, k1.

Cable and Aran

A mixture of cable, Aran and bobble patterns to use on their own or as part of a multi-patterned design

Clover Pattern

multiple of 8 plus 5
Row 1: K4, ∗ ∗∗k into front, back and front of next st, turn and k the 3 sts, turn and p the 3 sts, turn and k the 3 sts, turn and pass the 2nd st over the 1st st, pass the 3rd st over the 1st ∗∗, k1, work from ∗∗ to ∗∗ again, k5; repeat from ∗ to last st, k1.
Row 2 and foll alt rows: Purl.
Row 3: K5, ∗ work from ∗∗ to ∗∗ of row 1, k7; repeat from ∗ to end of row.
Row 5: Knit.
Row 7: ∗ work from ∗∗ to ∗∗, k1, work from ∗∗ to ∗∗, k5; repeat from ∗ to last 5 sts, work from ∗∗ to ∗∗, k1, work from ∗∗ to ∗∗, k2.
Row 9: ∗K1, work from ∗∗ to ∗∗, k7; repeat from ∗ to last 5 sts, k1, work from ∗∗ to ∗∗, k3.
Row 11: Knit.

Diagonal Bobble Stitch

multiple of 6
Row 1: ∗k2, (k into front and back of st) three times, take 2nd, 3rd, 4th, 5th and 6th sts over 1st st, p3; repeat from ∗ to end of row.
Rows 2 and foll alt rows: ∗K3, p3; repeat from ∗ to end of row.
Row 3: ∗P1, k2, (k into front and back of st) three times, take 2nd, 3rd, 4th, 5th and 6th sts over 1st st, p2; repeat from ∗ to end of row.
Row 5: ∗P2, k2, (k into front and back of st) three times, take 2nd, 3rd, 4th, 5th and 6th sts over 1st st, p1; repeat from ∗ to end of row.
Row 7: ∗P3, k2, (k into front and back of st) three times, take 2nd, 3rd, 4th, 5th and 6th sts over 1st st; repeat from ∗ to end of row.

Loose fitting Aran style sweater with set in sleeves, using panels of moss stitch, Jacob's ladder and cables, knitted in Lister Motoravia DK

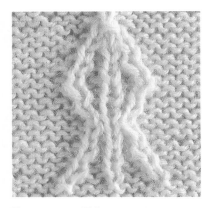

Lovers Knot Pattern

worked over 9 sts
Row 1: (wrong side) (P1, k3) twice, p1.
Row 2: C2f, p2, k1, p2, C2b.
Row 3 and foll alt rows: K the k sts and p the p sts.
Row 4: P1, C2f, p1, k1, p1, C2b, p1.
Row 6: P2, C2f, k1, C2b, p2.
Row 8: P2, C2b, k1, C2f, p2.
Row 10: P1, C2b, p1, k1, p1, C2f, p1.
Row 12: as row 4.
Row 14: as row 6.
Row 16: P3, p1 into loop before next st, sl.1, k2 tog, psso, p1 into loop before next st, p3.
Rows 17 and 19: Knit.
Rows 18 and 20: Purl.

Travelling Cable Rib

multiple of 7 plus 3
Rows 1 and 3: *P3, k4; repeat from * to last 3 sts, p3.
Row 2 and foll alt rows: *K3, p4; repeat from * to last 3 sts, k3.
Row 5: *P3, C4B; repeat from * to last 3 sts, p3.
Rows 7 and 9: *P3, k4; repeat from * to last 3 sts, p3.
Row 11: *P3, C4F; repeat from * to last 3 sts, p3.

Simple Cable

worked over 6 sts
Rows 1 and 3: K6.
Rows 2 and 4: P6.
Row 5: C6F.
Row 6: P6.

Corded Cable Rib

multiple of 9 plus 3
Rows 1 and 3: *P3, k6; repeat from * to last 3 sts, p3.
Rows 2 and 4: *K3, p6; repeat from * to last 3 sts, k3.
Row 5: *P3, C6B; repeat from * to last 3 sts, p3.
Row 6: *K3, p6; repeat from * to last 3 sts, k3.

Wishbone Cable

multiple of 12 plus 4
Rows 1, 3 and 5: P4, *k2, p4; repeat from * to end of row.
Rows 2 and 4: K4, *p2, k4; repeat from * to end of row.
Row 6: K4, *yfwd, sl 2 purlwise, yb, k4; repeat from * to end of row.
Row 7: P4, *sl 2 on to cable needle and leave at front of work, p2, yon, k2 tog tbl from cable needle, sl 2 on to cable needle and leave at back of work, k2 tog, yon, p2 from cable needle, p4; repeat from * to end of row.
Row 8: K4, *p2, k1 tbl, p2, k1 tbl, p2, k4; repeat from * to end of row.

V Patterned Cable

worked over 12 sts
Row 1: P4, C4F, p4.
Row 2 and foll alt rows: K the k sts and p the p sts.
Row 3: P3, C3b, C3f, p3.
Row 5: P2, C3b, p2, C3f, p2.
Row 7: P1, C3b, p4, C3f, p1.
Row 9: C3b, p1, C4F, p1, C3f.
Repeat from row 3.

Stemmed Berry Pattern

multiple of 6 plus 5
Row 1: *P2, (k1 into front and back) twice into next st, p2, ybk, sl.1 purlwise, yfwd; repeat from * to last 2 sts, p2.
Rows 2 and 4: K2, (k1 y2on) four times, k2, p1; repeat from * to last 2 sts, k2.
Rows 3 and 5: *P2, k4 dropping the yons, p2, ybk, sl.1 purlwise, yfwd; repeat from * to last 2 sts, p2.
Row 6: *K2, p4 tog, k2, p1; repeat from * to last 2 sts, k2.
Row 7: *P2, ybk, sl.1 purlwise, yfwd, p2, (k1 into front and back) twice into next st; repeat from * to last 2 sts, p2.
Rows 8 and 10: *K2, p1, k2, (k1 y2on) four times; repeat from * to last 2 sts, k2.
Rows 9 and 11: *P2, ybk, sl.1 purlwise, yfwd, p2, k4 dropping the yons; repeat from * to last 2 sts, k2.
Row 12: *K2, p1, k2, p4 tog; repeat from * to last 2 sts, k2.

Tyrolean Cable

worked over 19 sts
Row 1: (wrong side) K2, p15 tbl, k2.
Row 2: P2, C6F tbl, k3 tbl, C6B tbl, p2.
Rows 3 and 5: K2, p15 tbl, k2.
Rows 4 and 6: P2, k15 tbl, p2.
Row 7: K2, p15 tbl, k2.
Row 8: P2, C6B tbl, k3 tbl, C6F tbl, p2.
Rows 9 and 13: as row 3.
Rows 10 and 14: as row 4.
Rows 11 and 15: as row 5.
Rows 12 and 16: as row 6.

Ladder of Life with Cables

worked over 15 sts
Row 1: (wrong side) P4, k1, p5, k1, p4.
Row 2: C4F, p1, k5, p1, C4B.
Rows 3 and 5: P4, k1, p5, k1, p4.
Row 4: K4, p1, k5, p1, k4.
Row 6: K4, p7, k4.

Wavy Cable

worked over 15 sts with two cable needles
Rows 1 and 3: P3, k9, p3.
Row 2 and foll alt rows: K3, p9, k3.
Row 5: P3, sl 3 sts on to first cable needle and leave at back, slip next 3 sts on to second cable needle and leave at front, k3, k3 from second cable needle, k3 from first cable needle, p3.
Rows 7, 9, 11, 13, 15, 17 and 19: P3, k9, p3.
Row 21: P3, sl 3 sts on to first cable needle and leave at back, slip next 3 sts on to second cable needle and leave at back, k3, k3 from second cable needle, k3 from first cable needle, p3.
Rows 23, 25, 27, 29, 31, 33 and 35: P3, k9, p3.
Repeat from row 5.

Twisted Cable Rib

multiple of 8 plus 3
Row 1: *P3, k5; repeat from * to last 3 sts, p3.
Row 2 and foll alt rows: *K3, p5; repeat from * to last 3 sts, k3.
Row 3: *P3, k1, (C2B) twice; repeat from * to last 3 sts, p3.
Row 5: *P3, (C2B) twice, k1; repeat from * to last 3 sts, p3.
Repeat from row 2.

Knotted Cable

multiple of 9 plus 3
Rows 1 and 3: P3, *k2, p2, k2, p3; repeat from * to end of row.
Rows 2 and 4: *K3, p2, k2, p2; repeat from * to last 3 sts, k3.
Row 5: P3, *sl 2 sts on to cable needle and leave at back of work, sl 2 sts on to cable needle and leave at front of work, p2 tog, k2 from cable needle at front, p2 tog from cable needle at back, p3; repeat from * to end of row.
Row 6: K4, *p2, k5; repeat from * to last 4 sts, k4.
Row 7: P4, *p5, k2; repeat from * to last 4 sts, p4.
Row 8: *K3, sl. 1 st on to cable needle and leave at front of work, sl 2 sts on to cable needle and leave at back of work, p into front and back of next st, k the 2 sts from cable needle at back, p into front and back of st on cable needle at front; repeat from * to last 3 sts, k3.
Rows 9, 11, 13 and 15: as row 1.
Rows 10, 12, 14 and 16: as row 2.

Banana Tree Pattern

worked over 20 sts
Row 1: (wrong side) K3, p3, k3, p4, C2bp, k5.
Row 2: P4, C2B, k1, C2b, k2, p3, C2f, k1, p3.
Row 3: K3, p2, k4, p2, k1, p3, C2bp, k3.
Row 4: P3, k3, C2b, p1, k1, C2F,

p3, C2f, p3.
Row 5: K7, C2fp, p2, k2, p4, k3.
Row 6: P3, k2, C2b, p2, k1, C2F twice, p6.
Row 7: K5, C2fp, p4, k3, p3, k3.
Row 8: P3, k1, C2b, p3, k2, C2f, k1, C2F, p4.
Row 9: K3, C2fp, p3, k1, p2, k4, p2, k3.
Row 10: P3, C2b, p3, C2B, k1, p1, C2f, k3, p3.
Row 11: K3, p4, k2, p2, C2bp, k7.
Row 12: P6, C2B twice, k1, p2, C2f, k2, p3.

Gull Stitch with Twisted Rib

multiple of 12
Row 1: (wrong side) *K2, p6, k2, Tw2L purlwise; repeat from * to end of row.
Row 2: *Tw2L, p2, k2, sl 2, k2, p2; repeat from * to end of row.
Row 3: *K2, p2, sl 2, p2, k2, Tw2L purlwise; repeat from * to end of row.
Row 4: *Tw2L, p2, C3bk, C3fk, p2; repeat from * to end of row.

Zigzag with Bobble Cable

worked over 14 sts
Row 1: P3, k2, p9.
Row 2 and foll alt rows: K the k sts and p the p sts.
Row 3: P3, C3f, p8.
Row 5: P4, C3f, p7.
Row 7: P5, C3f, p6.
Row 9: P6, C3f, p5.
Row 11: P7, C3f, p4.
Row 13: P5, *(p1 but before dropping st from needle k1 yfwd, k1 ybk, k1 yfwd, k1 ybk) into st *, p2, C3f, p3.
Row 14: K3, p2, k3, p5, k5.
Row 15: P5, *ybk, sl 5 sts knitwise, yon, pass the sl sts one by one over yon*, p2, C3b, p3.
Row 17: P7, C3b, p4.
Row 19: P6, C3b, p5.
Row 21: P5, C3b, p6.
Row 23: P4, C3b, p7.
Row 25: P3, C3b, p2, work next st * to * as in row 13, p5.
Row 27: P3, C3f, p2, work next sts * to * as in row 15, p5.
Repeat from row 5.

Twisted Diamond Pattern

multiple of 14 plus 2
Row 1: Knit.
Row 2: Purl.
Row 3: K2, *p12, k2; repeat from *

to end of row.
Row 4: P2, *k12, p2; repeat from * to end of row.
Row 5: K2, *p5, k2 tbl, p5, k2; repeat from * to end of row.
Row 6: P2, *k5, p2 tbl, k5, p2; repeat from * to end of row.
Row 7: K2, *p4, k4 tbl, p4, k2; repeat from * to end of row.
Row 8: P2, *k4, p4 tbl, k4, p2; repeat from * to end of row.
Row 9: K2, *p3, k6 tbl, p3, k2; repeat from * to end of row.
Row 10: P2, *k3, p6 tbl, k3, p2; repeat from * to end of row.
Row 11: K2, *p2, k1 tbl, C6B tbl, k1 tbl, p2, k2; repeat from * to end of row.
Row 12: P2, *k2, p8 tbl, k2, p2; repeat from * to end of row.
Rows 13 and 14: as rows 9 and 10.
Rows 15 and 16: as rows 7 and 8.
Rows 17 and 18: as rows 5 and 6.
Rows 19 and 20: as rows 3 and 4.

Knot Stitch 1

multiple of 4
Rows 1 and 3: Knit.
Rows 2 and 4: Purl.
Row 5: *K2, yon, pass 1st st over 2nd st and yon, yon, pass 2nd st over the 2 yons, k2; repeat from * to end of row.
Row 6: Purl.

Knotted Cord Stitch

multiple of 4 plus 1
Row 1: *P3, k1; repeat from * to last st, p1.
Row 2: K1, *p1, k3; repeat from * to end of row.
Row 3: *P3, k into front, back and front of next st; repeat from * to last st, p1.
Row 4: K1, *p3 tog, k3; repeat from * to end of row.

Curling Cable

worked over 12 sts
Rows 1 and 3: K2, p2, k4, p2, k2.
Row 2: P2, k2, p4, k2, p2.
Row 4: P2, C4f, C4b, p2.
Row 5: K4, p4, k4.
Row 6: P4, C4f, p4.
Row 7: K4, p2, k6.

Row 8: P6, C3f, p3.
Row 9: K3, p2, k7.
Row 10: P7, C3f, p2.
Rows 11 and 13: K2, p2, k8.
Row 12: P3, *(k1, p1, k1, p1, k1, p1, k1) into next st, lifting each st sep lift the 2nd st over the 1st st then the 3rd, 4th, 5th, 6th and 7th sts, * p4, k2, p2.
Row 14: P7, C3b, p2.
Row 15: K3, p2, k7.
Row 16: P6, C3b, p3.
Row 17: K4, p2, k6.
Row 18: P4, C4B, p4.
Row 19: K4, p4, k4.
Row 20: P2, C4b, C4f, p2.
Rows 21 to 25: as rows 1 to 5.
Row 26: P4, C4b, p4.
Row 27: K6, p2, k4.
Row 28: P3, C3b, p6.
Row 29: K7, p2, k3.
Row 30: P2, C3b, p7.
Row 31: K8, p2, k2.
Row 32: P2, k2, p4, work from * to * of row 12, p3.
Row 33: K8, p2. k2.
Row 34: P2, C3f, p7.
Row 35: K7, p2, k3.
Row 36: P3, C3f, p6.
Row 37: K6, p2, k4.
Row 38: P4, C4F, p4.
Row 39: K4, p4, k4.
Row 40: P2, C4b, C4f, p2.

Cabled Heart Pattern

worked over 16 sts
Rows 1 and 3: (wrong side) K6, p4, k6.
Row 2: P6, C4F, p6.
Row 4: P5, C3b, C3f, p5.
Row 5: K5, p2, k2, p2, k5.
Row 6: P4, C3b, p2, C3f, p4.
Row 7: K4, p2, k4, p2, k4.
Row 8: P3, C3b, p4, C3f, p3.
Row 9: K3, p2, k6, p2, k3.
Row 10: P2, C3b twice, C3f twice, p2.
Row 11: K2, (p2, k1, p2, k2) twice.
Row 12: P1, C3b twice, p2, C3f twice, p1.
Row 13: (K1, p2) twice, k4, (p2, k1) twice.
Row 14: P1, k1, C2f, C3f, p2, C3b, C2b, k1, p1.
Row 15: (K1, p1) twice, k1, p2, k2, p2, k1, (p1, k1) twice.
Row 16: P1, k1, p1, C2f, C3f, C3b, C2b, p1, k1, p1.
Row 17: K1, p1, k2, p1, k1, p4, k1, p1, k2, p1, k1.
Row 18: P1, C2f, C2b, p1, C4F, p1, C2f, C2b, p1.
Row 19: K2, C2B, k2, p4, k2, C2F, k2.
Repeat from row 4.

Bramble Stitch

multiple of 4
Row 1: (wrong side) k2, *(k1, p1, k1) into next st, p3 tog; repeat from * to last 2 sts, k2.
Rows 2 and 4: Purl.
Row 3: K2, *p3 tog, (k1, p1, k1) into next st; repeat from * to last 2 sts, k2.

Knot Stitch 2

multiple of 8 plus 5
Rows 1, 3 and 5: Knit.
Rows 2, 4 and 6: Purl.
Row 7: K5, *(p3 tog, k3 tog, p3 tog) into next 3 sts, k5; repeat from * to end of row.
Rows 8, 10, 12 and 14: Purl.
Rows 9, 11 and 13: Knit.
Row 15: K1, *(p3 tog, k3 tog, p3 tog) into next 3 sts, k5; repeat from * to last st, k1.
Row 16: Purl.

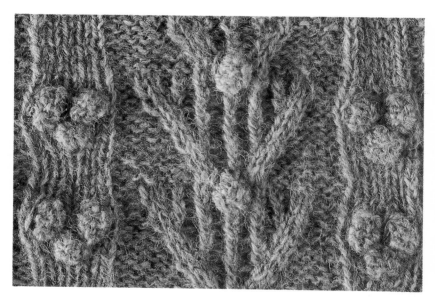

Half Diamond Cable with Bobbles 1

worked over 29 sts
Row 1: K5, p7, k2, *(p1, k1, p1, k1, p1) in next st, turn, k5, turn, p5, lift 2nd, 3rd, 4th and 5th sts over 1st st)*, k2, p7, k5.
Row 2: P5, k7, p2, p1 tbl, p2, k7, p5.
Row 3: K5, p6, C3b, k1 tbl, C3f, p6, k5.
Row 4: P5, k6, p2, k1, p1 tbl, k1, p2, k6, p5.
Row 5: K5, p5, C3Btbl, p1, k1 tbl, p1, C3Ftbl, p5, k5.
Row 6: P5, k5, p2, (p1 tbl, k1) twice, p1 tbl, p2, k5, p5.
Row 7: K2, work from * to * of row 1, k2, p4, C3b, (k1 tbl, p1) twice, k1 tbl, C3f, p4, k2, work from * to *, k2.
Row 8: P5, k4, p2, (k1, p1 tbl) three times, k1, p2, k4, p5.
Row 9: K1, (work from * to * of row 1, k1) twice, p3, C3B tbl, (p1, k1 tbl) three times, p1, C3F tbl, p3, k1, (work from * to *, k1) twice.
Row 10: P5, k3, p2, (p1 tbl, k1) four times, p1 tbl, p2, k3, p5.
Row 11: K5, p2, C3b, (k1 tbl, p1) four times, k1 tbl, C3f, p2, k5.
Row 12: P5, k2, p2, (k1, p1 tbl) five times, k1, p2, k2, p5.

Knot Stitch 3

multiple of 4 plus 3
Row 1: P2, *k1, p1, k1, p1; repeat from * to last st, p1.
Row 2: K2, *p1, k1, p1, k1; repeat from * to last st, k1.
Row 3: P2, *k into front, back and front of next st, p1, k1, p1; repeat from * to last st, p1.
Row 4: K2, *p1, k1, p3 tog, k1; repeat from * to last st, k1.
Row 5: P2, *k1, p1, k into front, back and front of next st, p1; repeat from * to last st, p1.
Row 6: K2, *p3 tog, k1, p1, k1; repeat from * to last st, k1.
Repeat from row 3.

Cable and Rope Pattern

worked over 20 sts
Row 1: P7, C6F, p7.
Row 2: K7, p6, k7.
Row 3: P7, k6, p7.
Row 4: P5, k2, p6, k2, p5.
Row 5: K5, p2, k6, p2, k5.
Row 6: P5, k2, p6, k2, p5.

Rope and Lattice Cable

worked over 21 sts
Row 1: P1, k2, p2, k2, p7, k2, p2, k2, p1.
Row 2: K1, Yp2, k2, Yp2, k7, Yp2, k2, Yp2, k1.
Row 3: P1, k2, p2, k2, p3, pick up loop between sts and work into back of it, (k1, p1, k1) in next st, pick up loop between sts and work into back of it, p3, k2, p2, k2, p1.
Row 4: K1, Yp2, k2, Yp2, k3, p2, k1, p2, k3, Yp2, k2, Yp2, k1.
Row 5: P1, k2, p2, C3f, C4b, p1, C4f, C3b, p2, k2, p1.
Rows 6 and 8: K1, Yp2, k3, p4, k5, p4, k3, Yp2, k1.
Row 7: P1, k2, p3, C4B, p5, C4B, p3, k2, p1.
Row 9: P1, C3f, C4b, C4f, p1, C4b, C4f, C3b, p1.
Rows 10 and 12: K2, p4, k4, p2, k1, p2, k4, p4, k2.
Row 11: P2, C4F, p4, *sl 3 sts on to cable needle and leave at front, k2, sl last st on cable needle to left

hand needle and p it, k2 from cable needle*, p4, C4F, p2.
Row 13: C4b, C4f, C4b, p1, C4f, C4b, C4f.
Rows 14 and 16: P2, k4, p4, k5, p4, k4, p2.
Row 15: K2, p4, C4B, p5, C4B, p4, k2.
Row 17: C4f, C4b, C4f, p1, C4b, C4f, C4b.
Rows 18 and 20: as row 10.
Row 19: P2, C4F, p4, work from * to * of row 11, p4, C4F, p2.
Row 21: P1, C3b, C4f, C4b, p1, C4f, C4b, C3f, p1.
Rows 22 and 24: as row 6.
Row 23: as row 7.
Row 25: P1, k2, p2, C3b, C4f, p1, C4b, C3f, p2, k2, p1.
Row 26: K1, Yp2, k2, Yp2, k3, sl. 1 purlwise, p1, psso, p3 tog, pass last p st over p3 tog, k3, Yp2, k2, Yp2, k1.
Rows 27, 29 and 31: as row 1.
Rows 28, 30 and 32: as row 2.

Braided Cable

worked over 14 sts
Rows 1 and 3: K2, p2, k2, p2, k2,
p2, k2.
Rows 2 and 4: P2, k2, p2, k2, p2,
k2, p2.
Row 5: *sl 4 sts on to cable needle
and leave at front of work, k2, p
the 2 p sts on cable needle, k the 2
k sts *, p2, work from * to * once
more.
Rows 6, 8 and 10: P2, k2, p2, k2, p2,
k2, p2.
Rows 7 and 9: K2, p2, k2, p2, k2,
p2, k2.
Row 11: K2, p2, sl 4 sts on to cable
needle and leave at back of work,
k2, p the 2 p sts on cable needle, k
the 2 k sts, p2, k2.
Row 12: P2, k2, p2, k2, p2, k2, p2.

Bishop's Mitre Pattern

worked over 18 sts
Row 1: P5, Tw2R, p1, Tw2R, p1,
Tw2L, p5.
Row 2: K5, p2 tbl, (k1, p2 tbl)
twice, k5.
Row 3: P4, Tw2R, k1, p1, Tw2R,
p1, k1, Tw2L, p4.

Row 4: K4, (p1 tbl, k1) twice, p2
tbl, (k1, p1 tbl) twice, k4.
Row 5: P3, Tw2R twice, p1, Tw2R,
p1, Tw2L twice, p3.
Row 6: K3, p1 tbl, (k1, p2 tbl) three
times, k1, p1 tbl, k3.
Row 7: P2, Tw2R twice, k1, p1,
Tw2R, p1, k1, Tw2L twice, p2.
Row 8: K2, (p1 tbl, k1) three times,
p2 tbl, (k1, p1 tbl) three times, k2.
Row 9: P1, Tw2R three times, p1,
Tw2R, p1, Tw2L three times, p1.
Row 10: K1, (p1 tbl, k1) twice, (p2
tbl, k1) three times, (p1 tbl, k1)
twice.
Row 11: Tw2R three times, k1, p1,
Tw2R, p1, k1, Tw2L three times.
Row 12: (P1 tbl, k1) four times, p2
tbl, (k1, p1 tbl) four times.
Row 13: as row 9.
Row 14: as row 10.
Row 15: as row 7.
Row 16: as row 8.
Row 17: as row 5.
Row 18: as row 6.
Row 19: as row 3.
Row 20: as Row 4.
Row 21: as row 1.
Row 22: as row 2.
Row 23: P6, k1, p1, Tw2R, p1, k1,
p6.
Row 24: K6, p1 tbl, k1, p2 tbl, k1,
p1 tbl, k6.
Row 25: P8, Tw2R, P8.
Row 26: K8, p2 tbl, k8.
Row 27: Purl.
Row 28: Knit.

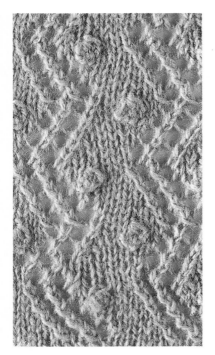

Eyelet and Bobble Pattern

multiple of 9 plus 4
Row 1: K1, *yon, sl.1, k1, psso, yon, sl.1, k1, psso, k5; repeat from * to last 3 sts, k3.
Row 2 and foll alt rows: Purl.
Row 3: K2, *yon, sl.1, k1, psso, yon, sl.1, k1, psso, k5; repeat from * to last 2 sts, k2.
Row 5: K3, *yon, sl.1, k1, psso, yon, sl.1, k1, psso, k5; repeat from * to last st, k1.
Row 7: K4, *yon, sl.1, k1, psso, yon, sl.1, k1, psso, k2, ** k into front and back of st twice, p4, k4, pass 2nd st over 1st st then 3rd and 4th sts **, k2; repeat from * to end of row.
Row 9: K3, *k2 tog, yon, k2 tog, yon, k5; repeat from * to last st, k1.
Row 11: K2, *k2 tog, yon, k2 tog, yon, k5; repeat from * to last 2 sts, k2.
Row 13: K1, *k2 tog, yon, k2 tog, yon, k5; repeat from * to last 3 sts, k3.
Row 15: *K2 tog, yon, k2 tog, yon, k2, work from ** to **, k2; repeat from * to last 4 sts, k4.

Bobble Stitch 1

multiple of 6 plus 1
Row 1: *K3, **k into front, back and front of next st, turn and k the 3 sts, turn and p the 3 sts, turn and k the 3 sts, turn and pass the 2nd st over the 1st st, pass the 3rd st over the 1st st **, k2, repeat from * to last st, k1.
Row 2, 4 and 6: Purl.
Rows 3 and 5: Knit.
Row 7: *Work from ** to ** of row 1, k5; repeat from * to last st, work from ** to **.
Rows 8, 10 and 12: Purl.
Rows 9 and 11: Knit.

Lattice Cable

multiple of 6
Row 1: *K4, p2; repeat from * to end of row.
Row 2 and foll alt rows: K the k sts and p the p sts.
Row 3: *C4B, p2; repeat from * to end of row.
Row 5: P2, *k2, C4b; repeat from * to last 4 sts, k4.
Row 7: *P2, C4F; repeat from * to end of row.
Row 9: K4, *C4f, k2; repeat from * to last 2 sts, p2.
Repeat from row 3.

Blackberry Stitch

multiple of 4
Row 1: (wrong side) *(K1, yon, k1) into next st, p3 tog; repeat from * to end of row.
Row 2: *K1, p3; repeat from * to end of row.
Row 3: *K3, p1; repeat from * to end of row.
Row 4: *P1, k3; repeat from * to end of row.
Row 5: *P3 tog, (k1, yon, k1) into next st; rep from * to end of row.
Row 6: *P3, k1; repeat from * to end of row.
Row 7: *P1, k3; repeat from * to end of row.
Row 8: *K3, p1; repeat from * to end of row.

Latticed Diamond Cable

worked over 22 sts
Rows 1 and 3: (wrong side) K8, p6, k8.
Row 2: P8, C6B, p8.
Row 4: P7, sl 3 sts to cable needle and hold at back, k3, p1 from cable needle, slip 1 st to cable needle and hold at front, p1, k3 from cable needle, p7.
Rows 5, 7, 9 and 11: K the k sts and p the p sts.
Row 6: P6, sl 1 st to cable needle and hold at back, k3, p1 from cable needle, p2, sl 3 sts to cable needle and hold at front, p1, k3 from cable needle, p6.
Row 8: P5, C3b, k1, p4, k1, C3f, p5.
Row 10: P4, C3b, p1, C2f, p2, C2b, p1, C3f, p4.
Row 12: P3, C2b, k1, p3, C2f, C2b, p3, k1, C2f, p3.
Row 13: K3, p1, k1, p1, k4, C2fp, k4, p1, k1, p1, k3.

Row 14: P2, C2b, p1, C2f, p2, C2b, C2f, p2, C2b, p1, C2f, p2.
Rows 15 and 19: as row 5.
Row 16: P2, k1, p3, C2f, C2b, p2, C2f, C2b, p3, k1, p2.
Row 17: K2, p1, (k4, C2bp) twice, k4, p1, k2.
Row 18: P2, k1, p3, C2b, C2f, p2, C2b, C2f, p3, k1, p2.
Row 20: P2, C2f, p1, C2b, p2, C2f, C2b, p2, C2f, p1, C2b, p2.
Row 21: as row 13.
Row 22: P3, C2f, k1, p3, C2b, C2f, p3, k1, C2b, p3.
Rows 23, 25, 27 and 29: as row 5.
Row 24: P4, C3f, p1, C2b, p2, C2f, p1, C3b, p4.
Row 26: P5, C3f, k1, p4, k1, C3b, p5.
Row 28: P6, C4f, p2, C4b, p6.
Row 30: P7, sl 3 sts to cable needle and hold at front, p1, k3 from cable needle, sl 1 st to cable needle and hold at back, k3, p1 from cable needle, p7.

Open Plaited Cable

worked over 18 sts
Row 1: K6, p6, k6.
Row 2: P6, k2, C4F, p6.
Row 3 and foll alt rows: K the k sts and p the p sts.
Row 4: P6, C4B, k2, p6.
Row 6: P6, k2, C4F, p6.
Row 8: P6, C4B, k2, p6.
Row 10: P6, k2, C4F, p6.
Row 12: P6, C4B, k2, p6.
Row 14: P5, C3b, k2, C3f, p5.
Row 16: P4, C3b, p1, k2, p1, C3f, p4.
Row 18: P3, C3b, p2, k2, p2, C3f, p3.
Row 20: P3, C3f, p2, k2, p2, C3b, p3.
Row 22: P4, C3f, p1, k2, p1, C3b, p4.
Row 24: P5, C3f, k2, C3b, p5.

Tree of Life Pattern

worked over 17 sts
Row 1: P6, k3 tbl, p8.
Row 2: K6, p3 tbl, k8.
Row 3: P5, C2b tbl, C2f tbl, p7.
Row 4: K5, p1 tbl, k1, p1 tbl, k1, p1 tbl, k7.
Row 5: P4, C2b tbl, p1, k1 tbl, p1, C2f tbl, p6.
Row 6: K4, p1 tbl, k2, p1 tbl, k2, p1 tbl, k6.
Row 7: P3, C2b tbl, p2, k1 tbl, p2, C2f tbl, p5.
Row 8: K3, p1 tbl, k3, p1 tbl, k3, p1

tbl, k5.
Row 9: P2, C2b tbl, p3, k1 tbl, p3, C2f tbl, p4.
Row 10: K2, p1 tbl, k4, p1 tbl, k4, p1 tbl, k4.
Row 11: P1, C2b tbl, p4, k1 tbl, p4, C2f tbl, p3.
Row 12: K1, p1 tbl, k5, p1 tbl, k5, p1 tbl, k3.
Row 13: C2b tbl, p5, k1 tbl, p5, C2f tbl, p2.
Row 14: P1 tbl, k6, p1 tbl, k6, p1 tbl, k2.

Elongated Bobble Stitch

multiple of 6
Rows 1 and 3: Knit.
Row 2: Purl.
Row 4: *P4, p2 (turn, sl.1, k1, turn, sl.1, p1) three times; repeat from * to end of row.
Rows 5 and 7: Knit.
Row 6: Purl.
Row 8: *P1, p2 (turn, sl.1, k1, turn, sl.1, p1) three times, p3; repeat from * to end of row.

Chain and Moss Stitch Cable

worked over 18 sts
Rows 1 and 3: P3, k3, work 6 sts in moss st, k3, p3.
Rows 2 and 4: K3, p3, work 6 sts in moss st, p3, k3.
Row 5: P3, sl 3 sts to cable needle and hold at back of work, work next 3 sts in moss st, k the 3 sts from cable needle, sl 3 sts to cable needle and hold at front of work, k3, work next 3 sts in moss st, p3.
Rows 6, 8, 10, 12 and 14: K3, work 3 sts in moss st, p6, work 3 sts in moss st, k3.
Rows 7, 9, 11 and 13: P3, work 3 sts in moss st, k6, work 3 sts in moss st, p3.
Row 15: P3, sl 3 sts to cable needle and hold at front of work, k3, work 3 sts on cable needle in moss st, sl 3 sts to cable needle and hold at back of work, work next 3 sts in moss st, k3 from cable needle, p3.
Rows 16, 18, 20, 22, 24, 26 and 28: K3, p3, work 6 sts in moss st, p3, k3.
Rows 17, 19, 21, 23, 25, 27: P3, k3, work 6 sts in moss st, k3, p3.
Repeat from row 5.

Bobble Stitch 2

multiple of 6 plus 5
Rows 1 to 5: Knit.
Row 6: K5, *(yon, k1) three times in next st, turn and sl 1 st, p5, turn and sl 1st, k5, turn and p2 tog three times, turn and sl 1 st, k2 tog, psso, k5*; repeat from * to end of row.
Row 7: K5, *p1 tbl, k5; repeat from * to end of row.
Rows 8 to 11: Knit.
Row 12: K8, *work from * to * of row 6; repeat from * to last 3 sts, k3.
Row 13: K8, *p1 tbl, k5; repeat from * to last 3 sts, k3.
Repeat from row 2.

Rope Cable

worked over 13 sts
Row 1: P2, k9, p2.
Row 2 and foll alt rows: K2, p9, k2.
Row 3: P2, k9, p2.
Row 5: P2, k3, C6F, p2.
Row 7: P2, k9, p2.
Row 9: P2, k9, p2.
Row 11: P2, C6B, k3, p2.

Small Honeycomb Pattern

multiple of 4
Row 1: *Tw2R, Tw2L; repeat from * to end of row.
Rows 2 and 4: Purl.
Row 3: *Tw2L, Tw2R; repeat from * to end of row.

Cord and Knots Pattern

multiple of 16 plus 1
Rows 1, 3 and 5: P8 *k1, p15; repeat from * to last 9 sts, k1, p8.
Row 2 and foll alt rows: K the k sts and p the p sts.
Row 7: P8, *k into front, back and front of next st, p15; repeat from * to last 8 sts, p8.
Row 9: P8, *k3, p15; repeat from * to last 11 sts, k3, p8.
Row 11: P8, *k3 tog, p15; repeat

from * to last 8 sts, p8.
Row 13: P7, k into front, back and front of next st, *p1, k into front, back and front of next st, p13, k into front, back and front of next st; repeat from * to last 7 sts, p7.
Row 15: P7, k3, *p1, k3, p13, k3; repeat from * to last 7 sts, p7.
Row 17: P7, k3 tog, *p1, k3 tog, p13, k3 tog; repeat from * to last 7 sts, p7.
Rows 19, 21, 23: as row 1.
Row 24: K the k sts and p the p sts.

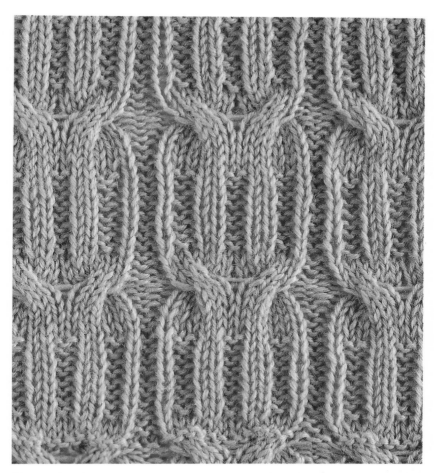

Banded Cable

multiple of 14 plus 2
Rows 1 and 3: P2, *k12, p2; repeat
from * to end of row.
Rows 2 and 4: K2, *p12, k2; repeat
from * to end of row.
Row 5: P2, *C6B, C6F, p2; repeat
from * to end of row.
Rows 6 and 8: as row 2.
Rows 7 and 9: as row 1.
Rows 10 and 12: K2, *k5, p2, k7;
repeat from * to end of row.
Row 11: P2, *p5, k2, p7; repeat
from * to end of row.
Rows 13, 15 and 17: as row 1.
Rows 14, 16, 18 and 20: as row 2.
Row 19: P2, C6F, C6B, p2; repeat
from * to end of row.

Wheat Ear Cable and Twist

worked over 19 sts
Row 1: P2, k6, Tw3R, k6, p2.
Rows 2 and 4: K2, p15, k2.
Row 3: P2, C6B, k3, C6F, p2.

Alternating Cable Rib

multiple of 9 plus 3
Row 1: *P3, k6; repeat from * to last 3 sts, p3.
Row 2 and foll alt rows: *K3, p6; repeat from * to last 3 sts, k3.
Row 3: *P3, C4B, k2; repeat from * to last 3 sts, p3.
Row 5: *P3, k2, C4F; repeat from * to last 3 sts, p3.
Repeat from row 3.

Arrowhead Cable

worked over 18 sts
Row 1: P8, C2B tbl, p8.
Row 2: K8, p2 tbl, k8.
Row 3: P7, C2B tbl, C2F tbl, p7.
Row 4: K7, p4 tbl, k7.
Row 5: P6, C2b tbl, k2 tbl, C2f tbl, p6.
Row 6: K6, p1 tbl, k1, p2 tbl, k1, p1 tbl, k6.
Row 7: P5, C2B tbl, p1, k2 tbl, p1, C2F tbl, p5.
Row 8: K5, (p2 tbl, k1) twice, p2 tbl, k5.
Row 9: P4, C2b tbl, k1 tbl, p1, k2 tbl, p1, k1 tbl, C2f tbl, p4.
Row 10: K4, (p1 tbl, k1) twice, p2 tbl, (k1, p1 tbl) twice, k4.
Row 11: P3, C2B tbl, p1, k1 tbl, p1, k2 tbl, p1, k1 tbl, p1, C2F tbl, p3.
Row 12: K3, (p2 tbl, k1, p1 tbl, k1) twice, p2 tbl, k3.
Row 13: P2, C2b tbl, k1 tbl, p1, k1 tbl, C2B tbl, C2F tbl, k1 tbl, p1, k1 tbl, C2f tbl, p2.
Row 14: K2, (p1 tbl, k1) twice, p6 tbl, (k1, p1 tbl) twice, k2.
Row 15: P2, (k1 tbl, p1) twice, C2b tbl, k2 tbl, C2f tbl, (p1, k1 tbl)

twice, p2.
Row 16: K2, (P1 tbl, k1) three times, p2 tbl, (k1, p1 tbl) three times, k2.
Row 17: P2, k1 tbl, p1, k1 tbl, C2b tbl, p2, C2b tbl, p1, C2f tbl, k1 tbl, p1, k1 tbl, p2.
Row 18: K2, p1 tbl, k1, (p2 tbl, k2) twice, p2 tbl, k1, p1 tbl, k2.
Row 19: P2, k1 tbl, p1, C2b tbl, p2, k2 tbl, p2, C2f tbl, p1, k1 tbl, p2.
Row 20: K2, p1 tbl, k1, p1 tbl, k3, p2 tbl, k3, p1 tbl, k1, p1 tbl, k2.
Row 21: P2, k1 tbl, C2b tbl, p3, C2b tbl, p3, C2f tbl, k1 tbl, p2.
Row 22: K2, (p2 tbl, k4) twice, p2 tbl, k2.
Row 23: P2, C2b tbl, p4, k2 tbl, p4, C2f tbl, p2.
Row 24: K2, p1 tbl, k5, p2 tbl, k5, p1 tbl, k2.

Double Cable 1

worked over 12 sts
Rows 1, 3, 5 and 7: K2, p8, k2.
Row 2: P2, C4B, C4F, p2.
Rows 4, 6 and 8: P2, k8, p2.

Elongated Chain Cable

worked over 12 sts
Rows 1, 3 and 5: K12.
Rows 2, 4, 6 and 8: P12.
Row 7: C6B, C6F.
Rows 9 to 16: as rows 1 to 8.
Rows 17, 19 and 21: K12.
Rows 18, 20 and 22: P12.
Row 23: C6F, C6B.
Row 24: P12.

Plaited Cable 1

worked over 16 sts
Rows 1 and 3: Knit.
Rows 2 and 4: Purl.
Row 5: C8F twice.
Rows 6, 8 and 10: Purl.
Rows 7 and 9: Knit.
Row 11: K4, C8B, k4.
Row 12: Purl.

Linked Lattice Cable

worked over 14 sts
Row 1: K1, p3, k2, p2, k2, p3, k1.
Row 2: P1, k3, p2, k2, p2, k3, p1.
Rows 3 and 5: as row 1.
Rows 4, 6 and 8: as row 2.

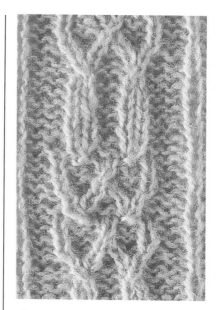

Row 7: K1, p3, Tw2R, p2, Tw2L, p3, k1.
Row 9: K1, p2, C2b, C2f, C2b, C2f, p2, k1.
Row 10: (P1, k2) twice, p1, (p1, k2) twice, p1.
Row 11: (K1, p2) twice, Tw2R, (p2, k1) twice.
Row 12: (P1, k2) twice, p2, (k2, p1) twice.
Rows 13 and 19: as row 7.
Rows 14 and 20: as row 8.
Row 15: as row 9.
Row 16: as row 10.
Row 17: as row 11.
Row 18: as row 12.

Chain Cable

worked over 12 sts
Row 1: K2, p8, k2.
Row 2: P2, C4B, C4F, p2.
Rows 3, 5 and 7: K2, p8, k2.
Row 4: P2, k8, p2.
Row 6: P2, C4F, C4B, p2.
Row 8: P2, k8, p2.

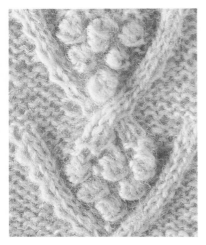

Half Diamond Cable with Bobbles 2

worked over 19 sts
Rows 1 and 3: K7, p2, k1, p2, k7.
Row 2: P7, C5B, p7.
Row 4: P6, C3b, p1, C3f, p6.
Row 5 and foll alt rows: K all the k
sts and p all the p sts.
Row 6: P5, C3b, p1, *(k1, p1, k1,
p1, k1, p1, k1) into next st, lift 2nd
st on right hand needle over 1st
then separately over the 3rd, 4th,
5th, 6th and 7th sts*, p1, C3f, p5.
Row 8: P4, C3b, (p1, work from *
to * of row 6) twice, p1, C3f, p5.
Row 10: P3, C3b, (p1, from * to *
of row 6) three times, p1, C3f, p3.
Row 12: P2, C3b, p2, k2, p1, k2,
p2, C3f, p2.
Row 14: P1, C3b, p3, k2, p1, k2,
p3, C3f, p1.

Clove Stitch

multiple of 4
Row 1: (wrong side) *(K1, yon, k1)
into next st, p3 tog; repeat from *
to end of row.
Row 2: *P1, k3; repeat from * to
end of row.
Row 3: *P3 tog, (k1, yon, k1) into
next st; repeat from * to end of
row.
Row 4: *K3, p1; repeat from * to
end of row.

Lace Berry Pattern

multiple of 6 plus 1
Row 1: P3, *k1, p5; repeat from *
to last 4 sts, k1, p3.
Row 2: K3 tog, *yon, (k1, yon, k1)
in next st, yon, k2 tog tbl, k3 tog,
pass 2nd st over last st; repeat
from * to last 3 sts, k3 tog tbl.
Rows 3 and 5: K1, *p5, k1; repeat
from * to end of row.
Row 4: P1, *k5, p1; repeat from *
to end of row.
Row 6: K twice into 1st st, *yon, k2
tog tbl, k3 tog, pass 2nd st over
last st, yon, (k1, yon, k1) in next
st; repeat from * to last st, k twice
into last st.
Row 7: as row 1.
Row 8: K3, *p1, k5; repeat from *
to last 4 sts, p1, k3.

Vertical Bobble Stitch

multiple of 8 plus 3
Row 1: *K3, p2, (p1, k1) twice into
next st, pass 2nd, 3rd and 4th sts
over first st, p2; repeat from * to
last 3 sts, k3.
Rows 2 and 4: P3, *k5, p3; repeat
from * to end of row.
Row 3: *K3, p5; repeat from * to
last 3 sts, k3.

Cable and Bobble Pattern

worked over 19 sts
Row 1: C8B, *k into front, back and front of next st, turn, k3, turn, p3, turn k3, turn and pass 2nd st over 1st st, 3rd st over 1st st*, k1, work from * to *, C8F.
Rows 2 and 4: Purl.
Row 3: K9, work from * to * of row 1, k9.

Interlaced Flower and Stem Pattern

worked over 17 sts
Row 1: K5, p1, k1, p2, k2, p1, k5.
Row 2: P5, LT, p1, LT, RT, p5.
Row 3: K6, p2, k2, p1, k6.
Row 4: P4, (k1, yon, k1) in next st, turn and p3, turn and (k1, y2on) three times, p1, LT, p1, RT, p6.
Row 5: K6, p2, k1, p1, k2, sl 3 dropping yons, sl to left hand needle and p3 tog tbl, k4.
Row 6: P4, LT, p1, k1 tbl, RT, LT, p5.
Row 7: K5, p1, k2, p2, k1, p1, k5.
Row 8: P5, LT, RT, p1, RT, p5.
Row 9: K6, p1, k2, p2, k6.
Row 10: P6, LT, p1, RT, p1, (k1, yon, k1) in next st, turn and p3, turn and (k1, y2on) three times, p4.
Row 11: K4, sl 3 dropping yons, sl

to left hand needle and p3 tog, k2, p1, k1, p2, k6.
Row 12: P5, RT, LT, k1 tbl, p1, RT, p4.

Ribbed Cable

worked over 18 sts
Rows 1, 3 and 5: P1, k1, (p2, k2) three times, p2, k1, p1.
Rows 2, 4 and 6: K1, p1, k2 (p2, k2) three times, p1, k1.
Row 7: P1, slip next 4 sts on to a cable needle and leave at back of work, k1, p2, k1, (k1, p2, k1) from cable needle, slip 4 sts on to a cable needle and leave at front of work, k1, p2, k1, (k1, p2, k1) from cable needle, p1.
Rows 8 and 10: K1, p1, k2, (p2, k2) three times, p1, k1.
Row 9: P1, k1, (p2, k2) three times, p2, k1, p1.

Acorn Pattern

multiple of 10 plus 2
Row 1: K1, p3, k4, *p6, k4; repeat
from * to last 4 sts, p3, k1.
Row 2: K4, p4, *k6, p4; repeat
from * to last 4 sts, k4.
Row 3: K1, p1, *C4b, (k1, p1) into
loop before next st, C4f, p2; repeat
from * to last 2 sts, p1, k1.
Row 4: K2, *p2, k2; repeat from *
to end of row.
Row 5: K1, p1, *k2, p2; repeat
from * to last 4 sts, k2, p1, k1.
Row 6: as row 4.
Row 7: K2, *sl.1, k1, psso, p6, k2
tog, k2; repeat from * to end of
row.
Row 8: K1, p2, k6, *p4, k6; repeat
from * to last 3 sts, p2, k1.
Row 9: K1, k1 into loop before next
st, *C4f, p2, C4b, (k1, p1) into
loop before next st; repeat from *
to last st, k1 into loop before next
st, k1.
Row 10: K1, p1, *k2, p2; repeat
from * to last 4 sts, k2, p1, k1.
Row 11: K2, *p2, k2; repeat from *
to end of row.
Row 12: as row 10.
Row 13: K1, p3, *k2 tog, k2, sl.1,
k1, psso, p6; repeat from * to last
4 sts, p3, k1
Repeat from row 2.

Shadow Cable

multiple of 12 plus 2
Row 1: Knit.
Row 2 and foll alt rows: Purl.
Row 3: K1, *C6F, k6; repeat from
* to last st, k1.
Row 5: Knit.
Row 7: K1, *k6, C6B; repeat from
* to last st, k1.

Reverse Wheat Ear Cable

worked over 9 sts
Row 1: K9
Row 2: P9.
Row 3: C4F, k1, C4B.
Row 4: P9.

Knot Stitch 4

multiple of 12 plus 3
Rows 1, 3 and 5: Knit.
Rows 2, 4 and 6: Purl.
Row 7: ∗K9, ∗∗ into next 3 sts, p3 tog, k3 tog, p3 tog ∗∗; repeat from ∗ to last 3 sts, k3.
Rows 8, 10, 12 and 14: Purl.
Rows 9, 11 and 13: Knit.
Row 15: K3, ∗ work from ∗∗ to ∗∗ of row 7, k9; repeat from ∗ to end of row.
Row 16: Purl.

Diamond and Moss Stitch Cable 1

worked over 19 sts.
Rows 1 and 3: K7, p2, k1, p2, k7.
Row 2: P7, C5F, p7.
Row 4: P6, C3b, k1, C3f, p6.
Row 5 and foll alt rows: K the k sts and p the p sts.
Row 6: P5, C3b, k1, p1, k1, C3f, p5.
Row 8: P4, C3b, (k1, p1) twice, k1, C3f, p4.
Row 10: P3, C3b, (k1, p1) three times, k1, C3f, p1.
Row 12: P2, C3b, (k1, p1) four times, k1, C3f, p2.
Row 14: P2, C3f, (p1, k1) four times, p1, C3b, p2.
Row 16: P3, C3f, (p1, k1) three times, p1, C3b, p3.

Row 18: P4, C3f, (p1, k1) twice, p1, C3b, p4.
Row 20: P5, C3f, p1, k1, p1, C3b, p5.
Row 22: P6, C3f, p1, C3b, p6.

Double Cable 2

worked over 26 sts
Rows 1, 3 and 5: P3, k20, p3.
Rows 2, 4 and 6: K3, p20, k3.
Row 7: P3, C10B, C10F, p3.
Rows 8, 10 and 12: K3, p20, k3.
Rows 9 and 11: P3, k20, p3.

Plaited Cable 2

worked over 24 sts
Row 1: Knit.
Row 2 and foll alt rows: Purl.
Row 3: C6B four times.
Row 5: Knit.
Row 7: K3, C6F three times, k3.

Diamond and Moss Stitch Cable 2

worked over 16 sts
Row 1: P6, k4, p6.
Row 2: K6, p4, k6.
Row 3: P5, C3bk, C3f, p5.
Row 4: K5, p2, (begin Irish moss st for centre with k1, p1), p2, k5.
Row 5: P4, C3bk, p1, k1, C3f, p4.
Row 6: K4, p2, (k1, p1) twice for Irish moss st, p2, k4.
Row 7: P3, C3bk, 4 sts in Irish moss st, C3f, p3.
Row 8 and foll alt rows: K the sts each side of the diamond, p2 for the diamond and work the centre in Irish Moss st.
Row 9: P2, C3bk, 6 sts in Irish moss st, C3f, p2.
Row 11: P1, C3bk, 8 sts in Irish moss st, C3f, p1.
Row 13: C3bk, 10 sts in Irish moss st, C3f.
Row 15: C3f, 10 sts in Irish moss st, C3b.
Row 17: P1, C3f, 8 sts in Irish moss st, C3b, p1.
Row 19: P2, C3f, 6 sts in Irish moss st, C3b, p2.
Row 21: P3, C3f, 4 sts in Irish moss

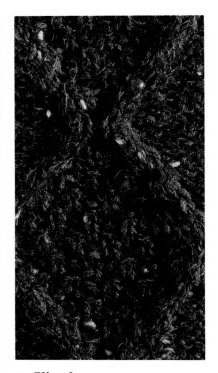

st, C3b, p3.
Row 23: P4, C3f, 2 sts in Irish moss st, C3b, p4.
Row 25: P5, C3f, C3b, p5.
Repeat from row 2.

Large Honeycomb Pattern

multiple of 8
Row 1: Knit.
Row 2: Purl.
Row 3: *C4B, C4F; repeat from *
to end of row.
Rows 4 and 6: Purl.
Row 5: Knit.
Row 7: *C4F, C4B; repeat from *
to end of row.
Row 8: Purl.

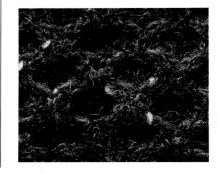

Bell and Diamond Cable

worked over 19 sts
Rows 1 and 3: K7, p2, k1, p2, k7.
Row 2: P7, C5B, p7.
Row 4: P6, C3b, p1, C3f, p6.
Row 5: K6, p2, k3, p2, k6.
Row 6: P5, C3b, p1, (k1, yon, k1, yon, k1) in next st, p1, C3f, p5.
Row 7: K5, p2, k2, p5, k2, p2, k5.
Row 8: P4, C3b, p2, k5, p2, C3f, p4.
Row 9: K4, p2, k3, p5, k3, p2, k4.
Row 10: P3, C3b, p3, sl.1, k1, psso, k1, k2 tog, p3, C3f, p3.
Row 11: K3, p2, k4, p3, k4, p2, k3.
Row 12: P2, C3b, p1, (k1, yon, k1, yon, k1) in next st, p2, sl.1, k2 tog, psso, p2, (k1, yon, k1, yon, k1) in next st, p1, C3f, p2.
Row 13: K2, p2, k2, p5, k2, p1, k2, p5, k2, p2, k2.
Row 14: P1, C3b, p2, k5, p5, k5, p2, C3f, p1.
Row 15: K1, p2, k3, p5, k5, p5, k3, p2, k1.
Row 16: P1, C3f, p2, sl.1, k1, psso, k1, k2 tog, p5, sl.1, k1, psso, k1, k2 tog, p2, C3b, p1.
Row 17: K2, p2, k2, p3, k5, p3, k2, p2, k2.
Row 18: P2, C3f, p1, sl.1, k2 tog, psso, p2, (k1, yon, k1, yon, k1) in next st, p2, sl.1, k2 tog, psso, p1, C3b, p2.
Row 19: K3, p2, k1, p1, k2, p5, k2, p1, k1, p2, k3.
Row 20: P3, C3f, p3, k5, p3, C3b, p3.
Row 21: K4, p2, k3, p5, k3, p2, k4.
Row 22: P4, C3f, p2, sl.1, k1, psso, k1, k2 tog, p2, C3b, p4.
Row 23: K5, p2, k2, p3, k2, p2, k5.
Row 24: P5, C3f, p1, sl.1, k2 tog, psso, p1, C3b, p5.
Row 25: K6, p2, k1, p1, k1, p2, k6.
Row 26: P6, C3f, p1, C3b, p6.

Interlaced Cable

worked over 16 sts
Row 1: K2, p4, k4, p4, k2.
Row 2 and foll alt rows: K the k sts
and p the p sts.
Row 3: K2, p4, C4B, p4, k2.
Row 5: C3f, p2, C3b, C3f, p2, C3b.
Row 7: P1, C3f, C3b, p2, C3f, C3b,
p1.
Row 9: P2, C4B, p4, C4B, p2.
Row 11: P2, k4, p4, k4, p2.
Row 13: as row 9.
Row 15: P1, C3b, C3f, p2, C3b, C3f,
p1.
Row 17: C3b, p2, C3f, C3b, p2, C3f.
Row 19: K2, p4, C4B, p4, k2.

Rope and Diamond Cable

worked over 18 sts
Row 1: K7, p4, k7.
Row 2: P6, C3bk, C3fk, p6.
Row 3 and foll alt rows: K the k sts
and p the p sts.
Row 4: P5, C3bk, k2, C3fk, p5.
Row 6: P4, C3b, C4B, C3f, p4.
Row 8: P3, C3b, p1, k4, p1, C3f,
p3.
Row 10: P2, C3b, p2, C4B, p2, C3f,
p2.
Row 12: P1, C3b, p3, k4, p3, C3f,
p1.
Row 14: P1, k2, p4, C4B, p4, k2,
p1.

Row 16: P1, C3f, p3, k4, p3, C3b,
p1.
Row 18: P2, C3f, p2, C4B, p2, C3b,
p2.
Row 20: P3, C3f, p1, k4, p1, C3b,
p3.
Row 22: P4, C3f, C4B, C3b, p4.
Row 24: P5, C3f, k2, C3b, p5.
Row 26: P6, C3f, C3b, p6.
Row 28: P7, C4F, p7.

Plaited Cable 3

worked over 29 sts
Row 1: K1, p1, k3, (p4, k6) twice,
p3, k1.
Row 2 and foll alt rows: K the k sts
and p the p sts.
Row 3: K1, p1, k3, (p4, C6F) twice,
p3, k1.
Row 5: K1, p1, (C5f, C5b) twice,
C5f, p1, k1.
Row 7: K1, p3, (C6B, p4) twice, k3,
p1, k1.
Row 9: K1, p1, (C5b, C5f) twice,
C5b, p1, k1.
Repeat from row 3.

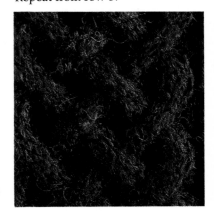

Cable and Ladder Pattern

multiple of 14 sts plus 1
Row 1: (wrong side) K1, *p2 tog, yon, p11, k1; repeat from * to end of row.
Row 2: K1, *sl.1, k1, psso, yon, C6B, k6; repeat from * to end of row.
Row 3: K1, *p2 tog, yon, p11, k1; repeat from * to end of row.
Row 4: K1, *sl.1, k1, psso, yon, k12; repeat from * to end of row.
Row 5: K1, *p2 tog, yon, p11, k1; repeat from * to end of row.
Row 6: K1, *sl.1, k1, psso, yon, k3, C6F, k3; repeat from * to end of row.
Row 7: K1, *p2 tog, yon, p11, k1; repeat from * to end of row.
Row 8: K1, *sl.1, k1, psso, yon, k12; repeat from * to end of row.

Moss Filled Cable with Bobbles

worked over 17 sts
Rows 1, 3, 5 and 7: K6, p5, k6.
Row 2: P6, k2, *(k1, p1, k1, p1, k1, p1, k1) into next, st, lift each st separately in sequence over the 1st st*, k2, p6.
Row 4: P6, work from * to *, k3, work from * to *, p6.
Row 6: P6, k2, work from * to *, k2, p6.
Row 8: P5, C3b, p1, C3f, p5.
Row 9: K5, p2, k1, p1, k1, p2, k5.
Row 10: P4, C3b, k1, p1, k1, C3f, p4.
Row 11: K4, p3, k1, p1, k1, p3, k4.
Row 12: P3, C3b, (p1, k1) twice, p1, C3f, p3.
Row 13: K3, p2, (k1, p1) three

times, k1, p2, k3.
Row 14: P3, k3, (p1, k1) twice, p1, k3, p3.
Row 15: K3, p2, (k1, p1) three times, k1, p2, k3.
Row 16: P3, C3f, (p1, k1) twice, p1, C3b, p3.
Row 17: K4, p3, k1, p1, k1, p3, k4.
Row 18: P4, C3f, k1, p1, k1, C3b, p4.
Row 19: K5, p2, k1, p1, k1, p2, k5.
Row 20: P5, C3f, p1, C3b, p5.

Mixed Colour Knitting

Knitting in two or three colours featuring allover tweeds, classic checks and traditional Fair Isles

Check Pattern 1

multiple of 6 plus 4
Row 1: With A, knit.
Row 2: With A, purl.
Row 3: With B, k4, *sl 2, k4; repeat from * to end of row.
Row 4: With B, p4, *yfwd, sl 2, p4; repeat from * to end of row.
Rows 5 and 6: With A, work as for rows 1 and 2.
Row 7: With B, k1, *sl 2, k4; repeat from * to last 3 sts, sl 2, k1.
Row 8: With B, p1, *yfwd, sl 2, p4; repeat from * to last 3 sts, sl 2, p1.

Check Pattern 2

multiple of 2
Row 1: With A, *sl.1, k1; repeat from * to end of row.
Row 2: With A, purl.
Row 3: With B, *k1, sl.1; repeat from * to end of row.
Row 4: With B, purl.

Slip Stitch Ladder Pattern

multiple of 6 plus 5
Row 1: With A, k2, *sl.1, k5; repeat from * to last 3 sts, sl.1, k2.
Row 2: With A, sl the sl sts, p the other sts.
Row 3: With B, *k5, sl.1; repeat from * to last 5 sts, k5.
Row 4: With B, *k5, yfwd, sl.1, ybk; repeat from * to last 5 sts, k5.

Houndstooth Check

multiple of 4
Row 1: K1A, *k1B, k3A; repeat from * to last 3 sts, k1B, k2A.
Row 2: *P3B, p1A; repeat from * to end of row.
Row 3: *K3B, k1A; repeat from * to end of row.
Row 4: P1A, *p1B, p3A; repeat from * to last 3 sts, p1B, p2A.

Cardigan with contrast bands and short sleeved sweater both patterned with diamonds worked from a chart, knitted in ANI Shetland 2 ply yarn

Triangular Check

multiple of 6 plus 3
Row 1: With B, purl.
Row 2: With A, k1, *sl.1, k5;
repeat from * to last 2 sts, sl.1, k1.
Row 3: With A, k1, *yfwd, sl.1, p5;
repeat from * to last 2 sts, sl.1, k1.
Row 4: With B, k3, *sl 3, k3; repeat
from * to end of row.
Row 5: With B, k1, p2, *yfwd, sl 3,
p3; repeat from * to end of row.
Row 6: With A, k1, sl 2, *k3, sl 3;
repeat from * to last 6 sts, k3, sl 2,
k1.
Row 7: With A, k1, sl 2, *yfwd, p3,
sl 3; repeat from * to last 6 sts, p3,
sl 2, k1.
Row 8: With B, k4, *sl.1, k5; repeat
from * to last 5 sts, sl.1, k4.
Row 9: With B, k1, p3, *yfwd, sl.1,
p5; repeat from * to last 5 sts, sl.1,
p3, k1.
Repeat from row 2.

Diagonal Tweed Pattern

multiple of 6 plus 2
Row 1: With A, purl.
Row 2: With B, k1, *sl 2, k4; repeat
from * to last st, k1.
Row 3: With B, k1, *p4, yfwd, sl 2;
repeat from * to last st, k1.
Row 4: With A, k1, *k4, sl 2; repeat
from * to last st, k1.
Row 5: With A, k1, *yfwd, sl 2, p4;
repeat from * to last st, k1.
Row 6: With B, k3, *sl 2, k4; repeat
from * to last 5 sts, sl 2, k3.
Row 7: With B, k1, p2, *yfwd, sl 2,
p4; repeat from * to last 5 sts, sl 2,
p2, k1.

Rows 8 and 9: With A, work as for
rows 2 and 3.
Rows 10 and 11: With B, work as for
rows 4 and 5.
Rows 12 and 13: With A, work as
for rows 6 and 7.
Repeat from row 2.

Check Pattern 3

multiple of 4 plus 1
Row 1: With A, purl.
Row 2: With B, k1, sl.1, *k1, sl 3;
repeat from * to last 3 sts, k1, sl.1,
k1.
Row 3: With B, k1, *p3, yfwd, sl.1;
repeat from * to last 4 sts, p3, k1.
Row 4: With A, k2, *sl.1, k3;
repeat from * to last 3 sts, sl.1, k2.
Row 5: With A, purl.
Row 6: With B, k1, *sl 3, k1; repeat
from * to end of row.
Row 7: With B, k1, p1, *yfwd, sl.1,
p3; repeat from * to last 3 sts, sl.1,
p1, k1.
Row 8: With A, k4, *sl.1, k3;
repeat from * to last st, k1.

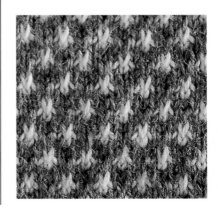

Fleur de Lys Pattern

multiple of 4 plus 2
Row 1: With A, knit.
Row 2: With A, purl.
Row 3: With B, k1, ∗k3, sl.1; repeat from ∗ to last st, k1.
Row 4: With B, p1, ∗yfwd, sl.1, ybk, p3; repeat from ∗ to last st, p1.
Row 5: With C, k2, ∗sl.1, k3; repeat from ∗ to last 4 sts, sl.1, k3;
Row 6: With C, p3, ∗yfwd, sl.1, ybk, p3; repeat from ∗ to last 3 sts, sl.1, p2.
Rows 7 and 8: With A, as rows 3 and 4.
Rows 9 and 10: With B, as rows 5 and 6.
Rows 11 and 12: With C, as rows 3 and 4.
Rows 13 and 14: With A, as rows 5 and 6.
Repeat from row 3.

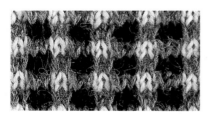

Check Pattern 4

multiple of 4 plus 2.
Row 1: With A, purl.
Row 2: With B, k1, sl.1, ∗k2, sl 2; repeat from ∗ to last 2 sts, sl.1, k1.
Row 3: With B, p1, yfwd, sl.1, ∗p2, yfwd, sl 2; repeat from ∗ to last 2 sts, sl.1, p1.
Row 4: With A, knit.
Row 5: With C, p2, ∗yfwd, sl 2, p2; repeat from ∗ to end of row.
Row 6: With C, k2, ∗sl 2, k2; repeat from ∗ to end of row.

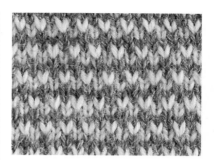

Tweed Pattern 1

uneven number of stitches
Row 1: With A, purl.
Row 2: With B, k1, ∗sl.1, k1; repeat from ∗ to end of row.
Row 3: With B, purl.
Row 4: With A, k1, ∗sl.1, k1; repeat from ∗ to end of row.
Row 5: With A, purl.
Row 6: With B, k2, ∗sl.1, k1; repeat from ∗ to last st, k1.
Row 7: With B, purl.
Row 8: With A, k2, ∗sl.1, k1; repeat from ∗ to last st, k1.
Row 9: With A, purl.
Repeat from row 2.

Three Colour Check Pattern

multiple of 4 plus 3
Row 1: With A, knit.
Row 2: With A, p1, ∗p1, y2on, p3; repeat from ∗ to last st, p1.
Row 3: With B, k1, ∗sl.1 dropping yons, k3; repeat from ∗ to last st, k1.
Row 4: With B, p1, ∗yfwd, sl.1, p3; repeat from ∗ to last 2 sts, sl.1, p1.
Row 5: With C, k1, ∗sl 2, k2; repeat from ∗ to last 2 sts, sl.1, k1.
Row 6: With C, p1, yfwd, sl.1, ∗p2, yfwd, sl 2; repeat from ∗ to last st, p1.

Ridged Brick Pattern

multiple of 4
Rows 1 and 2: With A, knit.
Row 3: With B, *k3, sl.1 purlwise;
repeat from * to end of row.
Row 4: With B, *sl.1 purlwise, p3;
repeat from * to end of row.
Rows 5 and 6: With A, knit.
Row 7: With B, k2, *sl.1 purlwise,
k3; repeat from * to last 2 sts, sl.1,
k1.
Row 8: With B, p1, sl.1, *p3, sl.1;
repeat from * to last 2 sts, p2.
Rows 9 and 10: With A, knit.
Row 11: With B, k1, *sl.1 purlwise,
k3; repeat from * to last 3 sts, sl.1,
k2.
Row 12: With B, p2, sl.1, *p3, sl.1;
repeat from * to last st, p1.
Rows 13 and 14: With A, knit.
Row 15: With B, *sl.1 purlwise, k3;
repeat from * to end of row.
Row 16: With B, *p3, sl.1; repeat
from * to end of row.

Latticed Diamond Pattern

multiple of 12 plus 3
Row 1: With A, purl.
Row 2: With B, k1, *sl.1, k11;
repeat from * to last 2 sts, sl.1, k1.
Row 3 and foll alt rows: Using the
same colour as for previous row,
purl, slipping all sl. sts with yfwd.
Row 4: With A, k4, *(sl.1, k1) three
times, sl.1, k5; repeat from * to
last 4 sts. k4.
Row 6: With B, k3, *sl.1, k7, sl.1,
k3; repeat from * to end of row.
Row 8: With A, k2, *sl.1, k3, sl.1,
k1; repeat from * to last st, k1.
Row 10: With B, k5, *sl.1, k3, sl.1,
k7; repeat from * to last 5 sts, k5.

Row 12: With A, k2, *sl.1, k1, sl.1,
k5; (sl.1, k1) twice; repeat from *
to last st, k1.
Row 14: With B, k7, *sl.1, k11;
repeat from * to last 7 sts, k7.
Row 16: With A, work as for row
12.
Row 18: With B, work as for row
10.
Row 20: With A, work as for row 8.
Row 22: With B, work as for row 6.
Row 24: With A, work as for row 4.
Row 25: With A, work as for row 3.
Repeat from row 2.

Star Tweed Pattern

multiple of 4 plus 1
Row 1: With B, purl.
Row 2: With A, k1, *ybk, sl.1,
insert needle under loop before
next st and k1, ybk, sl.1, k1, pass
1st sl st over 3 sts, k1; repeat from
* to end of row.
Row 3: With A, purl.
Row 4: With B, k3, *sl.1, insert
needle under loop before next st
and k1, ybk, sl.1, k1, pass 1st sl st
over 3 sts, k1; repeat from * to last
2 sts, k2.
Row 5: With B, purl.
Repeat from row 2.

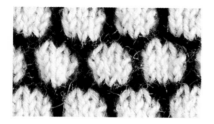

Blister Check Pattern

multiple of 4 plus 1
Row 1: With A, knit.
Row 2: With A, purl.
Rows 3 and 5: With B, knit.
Rows 4 and 6: With B, purl.
Row 7: With A, k2, *unravel next st four rows down, insert needle into this colour A st and under the four loose strands of B and k, k3; repeat from * to last 2 sts, k2.
Row 8: With A, purl.
Rows 9 and 11: With B, knit.
Rows 10 and 12: With B, purl.
Row 13: With A, k4, *unravel next st and k it as for row 7, k3; repeat from * to last st, k1.
Repeat from row 2.

Broken Zig Zag Pattern

multiple of 16 plus 3
Row 1: With A, knit.
Row 2: With B, k1, *(k1, sl.1, k3, sl.1) twice, k3, sl.1; repeat from * to last 2 sts, k2.
Row 3 and foll alt rows: Using the same colour as for previous row, sl all sl sts with yfwd, k all other sts.
Row 4: With A, k1, *sl.1, k3; repeat from * to last 2 sts, sl.1, k1.
Row 6: With B, k4, *sl.1, k1, (sl.1, k3) twice, sl.1, k5; repeat from * to last 4 sts, k4.
Row 8: With A, k2, *sl.2, k3, (sl.1, k3) twice, sl.2, k1; repeat from * to last st, k1.
Row 10: With B, k4, *(sl.1, k3) twice, sl.1, k1, sl.1, k5; repeat from * to last 4 sts, k4.
Row 12: With A, work as for row 4.
Row 14: With B, k2, *(sl.1, k3) twice, sl.1, k1, sl.1, k3, sl.1, k1; repeat from * to last st, k1.
Row 16: With A, k3, *sl.1, k3; repeat from * to end of row.
Row 18: With B, k2, *(sl.1, k1, sl.1, k3) twice, sl.1, k3; repeat from * to

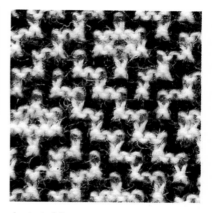

last st, k1.
Row 20: With A, work as for row 4.
Row 22: With B, k4, *sl.1, k1, sl.1, k5, (sl.1, k3) twice; repeat from * to last 2 sts, k2.
Row 24: With A, k3, *sl.1, k3, sl.2, k1, sl.2, k1, sl.2, k3, sl.1, k3; repeat from * to end of row.
Row 26: With B, k2, *sl.1, k3, sl.1, k5, sl.1, k1, sl.1, k3; repeat from * to last st, k1.
Row 28: With A, work as for row 4.
Row 30: With B, k4, *(sl.1, k3, sl.1, k1) twice, sl.1, k3; repeat from * to last 2 sts, k2.
Row 32: With A, work as for row 16.
Repeat from row 2.

Beaded Stripe Pattern

multiple of 6 plus 5
Row 1: With A, knit.
Row 2: With A, purl.
Row 3: With B, k1, *sl.3, k3; repeat from * to last 4 sts, sl.3, k1.
Row 4: With B, p2, *yfwd, sl.1, p5; repeat from * to last 3 sts, sl.1, p2.
Row 5: With B, knit.
Row 6: With B, purl.
Row 7: With A, k4, *sl.3, k3; repeat from * to last st, k1.
Row 8: With A, p5, *yfwd, sl.1, p5; repeat from * to end of row.

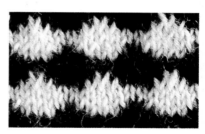

Linked Stripe Pattern

multiple of 4.
Row 1: With A, knit.
Row 2: With A, purl.
Row 3: With B, k1, *sl.2, k2; repeat from * to last 3 sts, sl.2, k1.
Row 4: With B, p1, *yfwd, sl.2, p2; repeat from * to last 3 sts, sl.2, p1.
Row 5: With A, knit.
Row 6: With A, purl.
Row 7: As row 3.
Row 8: As row 4.
Row 9: With B, knit.
Row 10: With B, purl.
Row 11: With A, k1, *sl.2, k2; repeat from * to last 3 sts, sl.2, k1.
Row 12: With A, p1, *yfwd, sl.2, p2; repeat from * to last 3 sts, sl.2, p1.
Row 13: With B, knit.
Row 14: With B, purl.
Row 15: As row 11.
Row 16: As row 12.

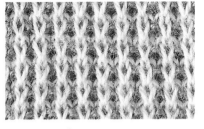

Tweed Pattern 2

multiple of 2 plus 1.
Row 1: With A, knit.
Row 2: With A, purl.
Row 3: With B, k1, *sl.1 purlwise, k1; repeat from * to end of row.
Row 4: With B, *k1, yfwd, sl.1, purlwise, ybk; repeat from * to last st, k1.

Diamond Pattern

multiple of 10 plus 3
Row 1: With A, purl.
Row 2: With B, k1, *sl.1, k9; repeat from * to last 2 sts, sl.1, k1.
Row 3 and foll alt rows: Using the same colour as for previous rows, purl, slipping sl sts with yfwd.
Row 4: With A, k3, *(sl.1, k1) three times, sl.1, k3; repeat from * to end of row.
Row 6: With B, k2, *sl.1, k7, sl.1, k1; repeat from * to last st, k1.
Row 8: With A, k4, *(sl.1, k1) twice, sl.1, k5; repeat from * to last 4 sts, k4.
Row 10: With B, (k1, sl.1) twice, *k5, (sl.1, k1) twice, sl.1; repeat from * to last 4 sts, (sl.1, k1) twice.
Row 12: With A, k5, *sl.1, k1, sl.1, k7; repeat from * to last 5 sts, k5.
Row 14: With B, k1, (k1, sl.1) twice, *k3, (sl.1, k1) three times, sl.1; repeat from * to last 5 sts (sl.1, k1) twice, k1.
Row 16: With A, k6, *sl.1, k9; repeat from * to last 6 sts, k6.
Rows 18 and 19: With B, as rows 14 and 15.
Rows 20 and 21: With A, as rows 12 and 13.
Rows 22 and 23: With B, as rows 10 and 11.
Rows 24 and 25: With A, as rows 8 and 9.
Rows 26 and 27: With B, as rows 6 and 7.
Rows 28 and 29: With A, as rows 4 and 5.
Repeat from row 2.

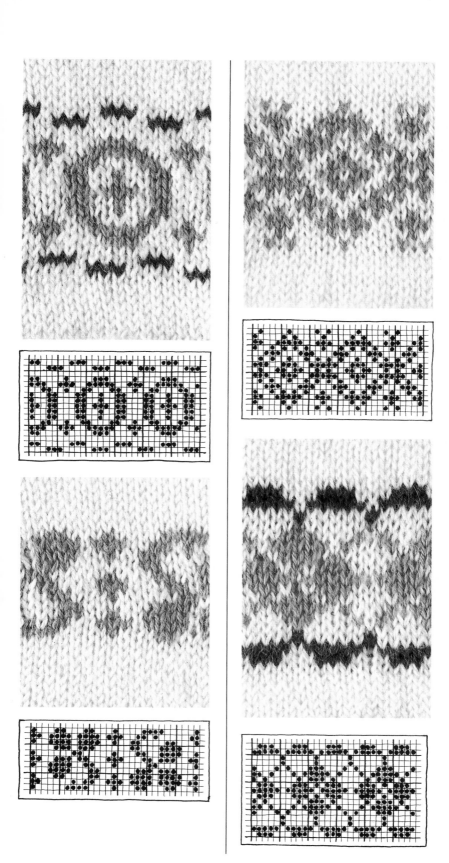

MIXED COLOUR KNITTING

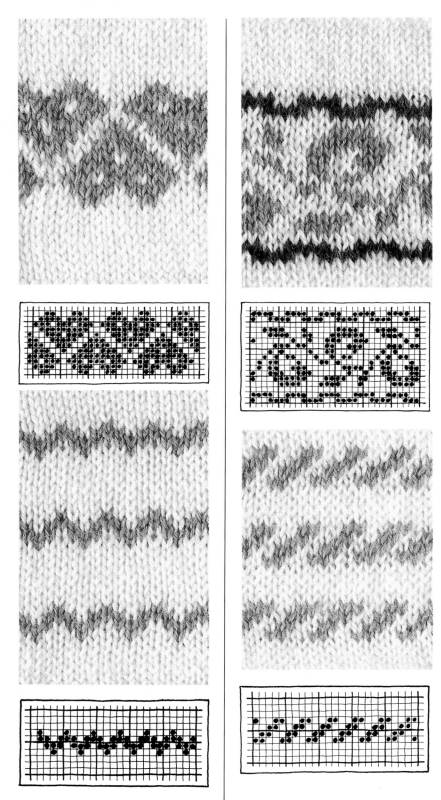

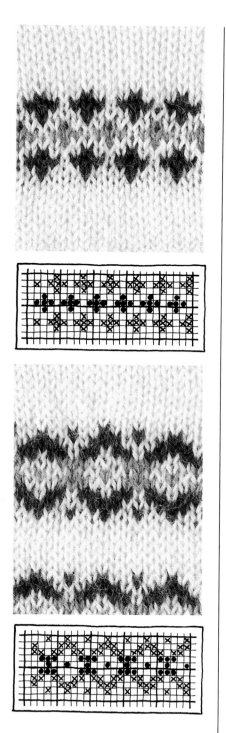

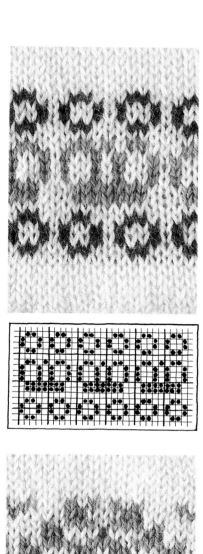

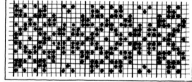

MIXED COLOUR KNITTING

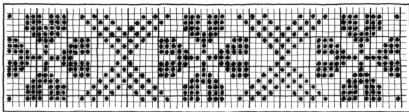

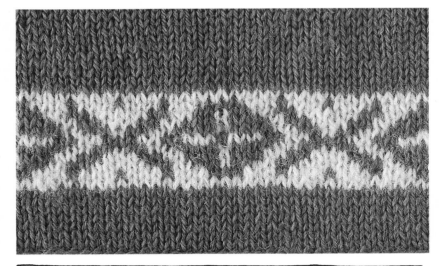

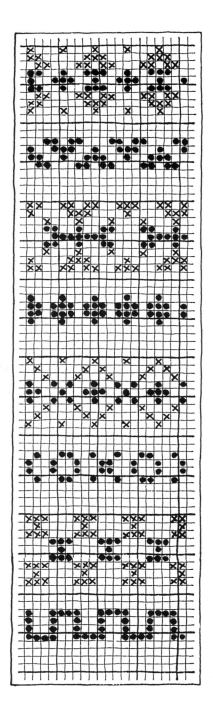

165

MIXED COLOUR KNITTING

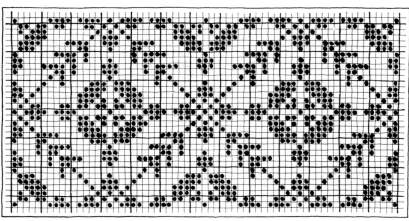

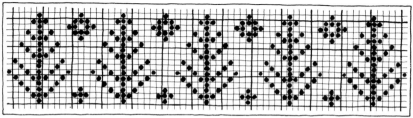

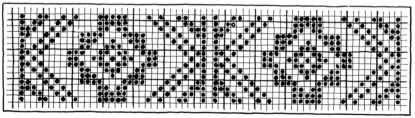

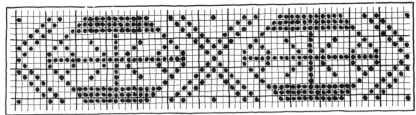

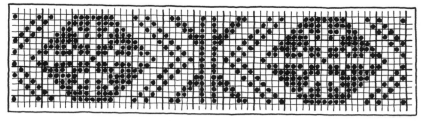

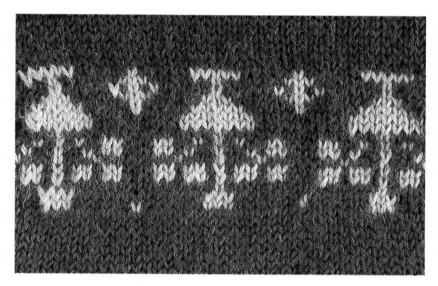

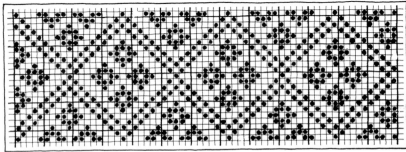

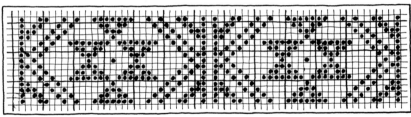

MIXED COLOUR KNITTING

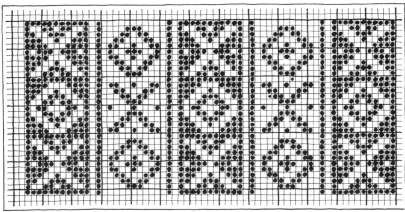

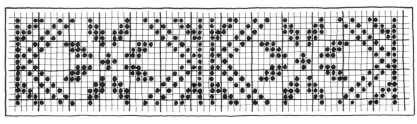

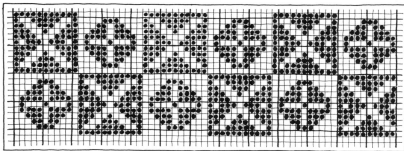

Casting On

Each method of casting on has its own characteristics. The thumb and the 2 needle cable edge are the most often used as each gives an elastic and hardwearing edge. A chain edge or looped method with one needle is used for designs where the hem is to be knitted up or where a less firm edge is needed as in some lace knitting. Neither is suitable for main edges because they are less hard wearing.

On rib edges, invisible casting on gives a neat professional finish. An open cast on is used when the edge will later have stitches knitted up along it.

Thumb method

1. Leave a length of yarn at least 3 times the length of the edge to be cast on (about 1 metre). Make a slip loop and place on needle.

2. Tighten the loop and take the needle in the right hand. Hold the main yarn in the right hand, the free end in the left.

3. Make a loop on the left thumb and put the needle through the loop. Wind the main yarn around the needle and draw this loop through it (fig 1).

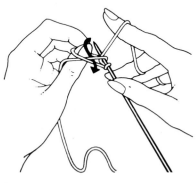

1

4. Slip the loop from the thumb and gently tighten the left hand thread.

Cable method with 2 needles

1. Make a slip loop on the left hand needle.

2. Put the right hand needle into the loop and wind the yarn round.

3. Draw the yarn through the loop on the left hand needle and transfer the loop to the left hand needle.

4. Put the right hand needle between the two stitches on the left hand needle (fig 2) and wind the yarn round. Draw the loop through and transfer the stitch to the left hand needle (fig 3).

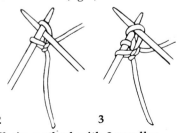

2   **3**

Chain method with 2 needles

1. Make a slip loop on the left hand needle.

2. Put the right hand needle into the loop and wind the yarn round.

3. Draw the yarn through the loop on the left hand needle with the right hand needle and transfer loop to the left hand needle (fig 4).

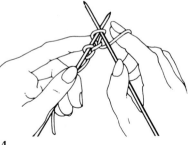

4

Invisible cast on method

(for k1, p1 rib)

1. Using a contrast yarn, cast on half the number of stitches required. If it is an odd number, increase one stitch when the edge is complete. Work 1 row purl, 1 row knit.

2. Row 1: purl using the correct yarn for the garment. Row 2: knit. Repeat rows 1 and 2 once more. Row 5: purl the first stitch, knit up the first loop that shows through the contrast yarn, purl the next stitch, knit up the next loop. Repeat to end of row when the number of stitches will have doubled.

3. Remove the contrast yarn and then follow the pattern instructions.

This same method can be used to give a firm, corded edge on stocking stitch. At row 5, purl the first stitch and purl the first loop that shows through the contrast yarn.

Looped method with one needle
1. Make a slip loop on the needle held in the right hand.
2. Loop the yarn round the left thumb and put the loop on the needle (fig 5).

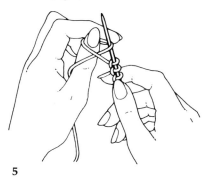

5

Open cast on hem method
1. With a contrast yarn, cast on and work two rows in stocking stitch.
2. With the correct yarn, continue in pattern until the work has been completed.
3. When ready to work from the cast on edge, remove the contrast yarn and place the open stitches on to the needle ready for knitting.

Selvedges

The edges of knitting are as important as the knitting itself. Neat edges give a professional finish.

Slipped stitch edge
Slip the first stitch at the beginning of each row, slipping the stitch purlwise on a knit row and knitwise on a purl row.

Knit stitch edge
Knit the stitch at the beginning and the end of each row. This forms a line of knobby loops on either side which make it easy to match row for row when seaming.

Slip stitch edge for garter stitch
Slip one stitch purlwise at the beginning of each row.

Shaping

In knitting, shaping is put into designs by the use of increases and decreases in the number of stitches worked.

Simple increasing
Increase one stitch by knitting or purling into the front and then into the back of the same stitch.

At edges this makes an untidy finish and looks much better if the increase is worked two or three stitches in from the edge. Knit one or two stitches, increase in the next stitch, knit to the last three or four stitches, increase in the next stitch, knit two or three stitches.

Less visible increases are made by picking up the loop of yarn between two stitches and knitting or purling into the front or the back of the stitch. Working into the back makes the increase even less

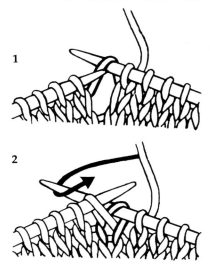

1

2

noticeable (fig 1). Or, on a knit or purl row, increase one stitch by knitting or purling the stitch *below* the next stitch and then knitting or purling the next stitch (fig 2).

When increasing stitches to make openwork and lace patterns, the term yon is often used in instructions. The method used to work it though depends on whether the extra stitch is to be made between 2 knit stitches, 2 purl stitches or a purl and a knit stitch. Between 2 knit stitches, simply bring the yarn

3

forward and knit the next stitch. This automatically makes the new stitch (fig 3). Between two purl stitches, take the yarn over and round the needle and purl the next stitch in the usual way (fig 4). Be-

4

tween a purl and a knit stitch, take the yarn over the needle and knit the next stitch in the usual way. Similarly, between a knit and a purl stitch, bring the yarn from the back and over the needle then purl the next stitch.

Simple decreasing

On a knit row: decrease one stitch by putting the right hand needle knitwise into two stitches and knitting the two stitches together.

On a purl row: decrease one stitch by putting the right hand needle purlwise into two stitches and purling the two stitches together.

On a knit row: decrease one stitch by slipping the next stitch purlwise on to the right hand needle. Knit the next stitch and with the left hand needle pass the slipped stitch over the knitted stitch.

As with increasing, a better effect is obtained by making decreases one or two stitches in from the edge and a more professional look when decreases are chosen to emphasise shaping.

All methods of decreasing slope either to the left or right. Pattern instructions often use k2 tog for the right slope and sl.1, k1, psso or k2 tog tbl for the left slope. A nicer matching decrease though is worked by slipping 2 stitches knitwise and knitting them together through the front loops. Another method matches the left sloping sl.1, k1, psso with the right sloping k1, sl.1, psso where the stitch is slipped knitwise and returned with the knitted stitch to the left hand needle and the slipped stitch passed over.

On purl rows, where p2 tog is worked at the beginning of the row the better matching decrease is made by slipping 2 stitches separately and knitwise, returning them to the left hand needle and purling them together through the back loops. Where knit rows have used sl.1, k1, psso at the beginning and k1, sl.1, psso at the end, the purl row equivalent is to begin by slipping 1 stitch knitwise, purling the next stitch then passing the slipped stitch over. The row ends p1, slip 1 stitch knitwise, return the two stitches to the left hand needle and pass the slipped stitch over.

Knitting up Stitches

With some designs the neckband or front bands are knitted on to an already knitted piece. To ensure an even finish, mark off the edge in 2ins sections and divide the number of stitches to be picked up by the number of sections. Where there are long and short edge stitches, knit up through the short stitches and always knit up stitches along the same row. With a needle one size smaller than that used for the main knitting, put needle through the front of the work, pick up a loop of yarn and bring it through to the front. Alternatively a crochet hook can be used to make the stitches in the same way and the stitches then placed on to the knitting needle. When picking up stitches round a curve, space the stitches remembering that more stitches go round an outward than an inward curve.

Casting Off

The general rule for casting off unless otherwise stated in pattern instructions is to work the stitches as they appear, ie, knit the knit stitches and purl the purl.

Basic casting off

1. On a knit row, knit the first two stitches. Lift the first over the second with the left hand needle. Knit the third stitch and lift the second over the third stitch. Continue in this way until all the stitches have been cast off. Break off the yarn leaving an end of about 15cms (6ins) and draw the end through the remaining stitches, pulling it tight.

2. On a purl row, purl the first two stitches and work as for step 1.

Casting off in pattern

Cast off each stitch by knitting or purling according to the pattern being worked.

This is the basic method of casting off but there are other methods too. Where there is a risk of casting off too tightly, there are several choices.

One is to use a needle several sizes larger for working the cast off row. Another is to use the single decrease method where the first two stitches are knitted together and the stitch thus formed is returned to the left hand needle and then knitted together with the next stitch on the needle. Yet another is the delayed cast off method. Here the first two stitches are knitted then the first stitch is lifted over the second stitch. Keeping this stitch on the left hand needle, pass the right hand needle in front and knit the next stitch. Slip both stitches from the left hand needle to the right hand needle and with the left hand needle, lift the first stitch over the second.

Where shoulder seams are straight, not shaped, and have the same number of stitches, a good looking way to finish them is to knit them together. With the right side of the work on the outside and with both sets of stitches on needles, knit one stitch from the front together with one stitch from the back. Do this once more and then lift the first stitch over the second. Continue until all stitches have been cast off. This method forms a neat ridge on the outside but the ridge can be formed on the inside by working with the wrong side of the work to the outside.

More often though shoulder seams are sloped. The standard cast off often gives an ugly 'staircase' effect. A smoother edge is obtained by not knitting the last stitch, turning the work and passing the first stitch over this stitch then continuing to cast off as usual. Another method is to leave the stitches to be cast off unknitted on each row, bring the yarn forward, slip one stitch, take the yarn back and replace the stitch without knitting it. When all the stitches to be cast off have been left in this way, cast them all off together.

Seams

Use the same yarn where possible and a blunt ended wool or tapestry needle for seaming. If the yarn is very heavy or textured, use a matching 4 ply yarn or tapestry wool.

Back Stitch

Lay the two pieces of work together, right sides facing and match up as nearly as possible, row by row. Pin the edges together or baste about 2 stitches in from the edge. Back stitch the pieces together one stitch in, keeping the stitching straight or where the work is curved, keeping the stitching parallel to the edge of the work. Recommended for most seams, for set in sleeves, heavily patterned edges and shoulder seams.

Invisible Seaming

With the edges of the work side by side, put the needle under the strand of yarn between the first and second stitches and draw the thread through.

Put the needle under the same strand on the other side and draw the yarn through then return to the first side and repeat the process. While working the stitches the edges are drawn together to make a neat seam.

Where pieces have a knobby edge, see page 175, they can be sewn together by threading through the knobs from side to side.

Recommended for garments in stocking and garter stitch, patterns which end with 1 or more stocking stitch stitches and for joining in bands or borders.

Flat or woven seam

With the right sides of the work facing, put the forefinger between the two pieces of work and bring the needle through the first stitch across to the same stitch on the other side. Return the needle through the second stitch back to the second stitch on the first side, drawing the edges close.

Recommended for ribbing, joining on bands, raglan sleeves and fine knits.

Setting in sleeves

Raglan sleeves are simple to flat seam together but more skill is needed to set a sleeve in well.

Mark the centre of the sleeve head and pin it to the shoulder seam. Pin the sleeve shaping to the armhole shaping and then work from the sleeve head down either side, easing the pieces together so that any excess fullness goes into the lower curve of the armhole. Stitch round the sleeve with the body of the garment facing, taking care to keep the stitching within the same two lines of stitches on the straight of the work.

Buttonholes

Where only a small buttonhole is needed as in a child's garment, the simplest way is to knit it as yon, k2 tog. Once the next row has been worked, a small, neat buttonhole is formed.

The standard way to make buttonholes is to cast off a given number of stitches in one row and to cast on the same number in the second row. This can make a rather untidy buttonhole though. A better way is to bring the yarn to the front, slip a stitch from the left hand needle and take the yarn back. Slip the next stitch and with the left hand needle, lift the first slipped stitch over the second. Continue in this way, leaving the yarn at the back until the number of stitches to be cast off has been worked. Slip the last stitch back to the left hand needle. Turn the work and with the yarn at back, cast on with cable method one more stitch than stitches cast off but bring the yarn forward through the needles before placing the last cast on stitch on to the left hand needle. Turn the work and slip the first stitch on to right hand needle passing the extra cast on stitch over it. This method makes a very neat finish on either side.

Buttons

When sewing on buttons use the pins marking the position to raise the button slightly and wind the yarn several times round the stem of yarn before fastening off. For all but the smallest buttons, reinforce by sewing the button through to a small, flat button or disc on the wrong side of the work. Covered buttons add a nice finish. Button moulds, ready to cover button shapes can be used as can any spare buttons with shanks. The number of stitches to be cast on and rows to be worked will depend on the size of button to be covered but as a guide, for a ¾ins button, with double knitting yarn and 3 or 3¼mm needles, cast on 3 sts. Increase 1 stitch each end of every row, working in stocking stitch until there are 11 stitches. Work four rows and then decrease 1 st at each end of every row until 3 stitches remain. Cast off. Cover the button with the knitting by running some matching thread round the edge, drawing the edges together tightly and fastening off securely.

Classic Round Neck Sweater

MATERIALS
Yarn
Pingouin Pingolaine 4 ply
7(7:8:8)×50g balls
Needles
1 pair 3mm (11)
1 pair 3¼mm (10)
MEASUREMENTS
Bust
82(87:92:97) cms
32(34:36:38) ins
Length
54(55:56:57) cms
21¼(21½:22:22¼) ins
Sleeve Seam
45(45:46:46) cms
17¾(17¾:18:18) ins
TENSION
28 sts and 36 rows = 10cms (4ins)
square on 3¼mm (10) needles.
ABBREVIATIONS see page 187

BACK
**Cast on 109(117:125:133) sts using
3mm (11) needles.
Row 1: K2, *p1, k1; repeat from * to
last st, k1.
Row 2: K1, *p1, k1; repeat from * to
end of row.
Rep these 2 rows until work
measures 6cms (2¼ins) ending
with a 2nd row. Change to 3¼mm
(10) needles and st. st. Beg with a k
row, work 2 rows in st.st then inc 1
st each end of the 9th and every foll
10th row until there are
117(125:133:141) sts. Cont without
shaping until work measures
36cms (14ins) ending with a p row.
Armhole Shaping
Cast off 4 sts at beg of next 2 rows,
2 sts at beg of next 2(2:4:4) rows
and 1 st at beg of next 4(8:6:10)
rows. **Cont on rem 101(105:111:
115) sts until armholes measure
18(19:20:22) cms, 7(7½:7¾:8½) ins
ending with a p row.
Shoulder and Neck Shaping
Cast off 8(8:9:9) sts at beg of next
4 rows.
Row 5: Cast off 8(8:9:9) sts, k
17(19:18:20) sts, cast off next
19(19:21:21) sts, k to end. Finish
this left side first. (25:27:27:29) sts.
Cast off 8(8:9:9) sts at beg of next
row. Cast off 10 sts at beg of foll
row, k to end. Cast off rem sts.
Rejoin yarn to neck edge of rem
sts with wrong side facing.
Cast off 10 sts, p to end.
Cast off rem 7(9:8:10) sts.

FRONT
Work as for back from ** to **. Cont
on rem 101(105:111:115) sts until
armholes measure 12(13:14:14)
cms, 4¾(5:5½:5½) ins ending with
a p row.
Neck Shaping
K 42(44:46:48) sts and leave on
holder or spare needle, cast off next
17(17:19:19) sts, k to end. Cont on
rem 42(44:46:48) sts for right front.
Work 1 row straight. * Cast off 3 sts
at beg of next row, 2 sts at beg of
foll 3 alt rows and 1 st on foll 2 alt
rows. (31:33:35: 37) sts.
Cont straight until armhole
matches back armhole in length,
ending at armhole edge.
Shoulder Shaping
Cast off 8(8:9:9) sts at beg of next
and 2 foll alt rows. Work 1 row.
Cast off rem 7(9:8:10) sts*. With
wrong side facing, rejoin yarn to
neck edge of left front sts. Work as
for right front from * to *.

SLEEVES
Cast on 59(61:63:65) sts using 3mm
(11) needles. Work rows 1 and 2 of
back until work measures 6cms
(2¼ins) ending with a 2nd row.
Change to 3¼mm (10) needles and
work in st.st beg with a k row. Inc 1
st at both ends of every 6th row
until there are 93(97:101:105) sts.
Cont straight until work measures
45(45:46:46) cms, 17¾(17¾:18:18)
ins from beg.
Shape Top
Cast off 4 sts at beg of next 2 rows,
2 sts at beg of next 6(8:8:10) rows,
1 st at beg of next 30(30:32:32) rows,
2 sts at beg of next 10 rows and 3 sts
at beg of next 2 rows.
Cast off rem 17(17:19:19) sts.
NECKBAND
Sew right shoulder seam.
With right side of work facing,
using 3mm (11) needles, pick up
and knit 67(73:79:85) sts round
front neck edge and 46(46:48:48) sts
across back neck. Beg with 2nd row
and work in rib as for back for 11
rows. Cast off loosely ribwise.

MAKING UP
Sew left shoulder and neckband
seam. Sew in sleeves.
Sew up side and sleeve seams.
Press very lightly with a warm iron
and damp cloth.

Foreign Language Terms

French

Fournitures	Materials
fils	yarn
aiguilles (aig)	needles
aiguille auxi-liere (aig aux)	cable needle or stitch holder
aiguille cir-culaire	circular needle
bouton(s)	button(s)
crochet	crochet hook
jeu d'aiguilles	double pointed needles
jeu de 4 aiguilles	set of 4 double pointed needles
pelotes (pel)	balls

Taille	Measurements
36, 38, 40, 42, 44	31, 32, 34, 36, 38 ins bust
petit, moyenne, grand, patron	small, medium, large, extra large
tour de poitrine	chest measure-ment
unique	one size
hauteur (ht)	long, length
hauteur totale	complete length

Points employes	Stitches used
côtes 1×1	k1, p1 rib
côtes 2×2	k2, p2 rib
point de boules	bobble pattern
point de dentelle	lace pattern
point de riz	moss stitch
point fantaisie	patterns for which the in-structions are given separ-ately
point jersey endroit (end)	stocking stitch
point jersey envers (env)	reverse stocking stitch
point mousse	garter stitch

Echantillon	Tension
24m×35rgs = 10cms	24 sts and 35 rows = 10cms

Explications	Instructions
assembler	join

attente (att)	leave
augmentation (aug)	add, increase
ayant	having
bandes des devant	front bands
bord en chainette	selvedge
bordures de devant	front borders
bouche	loop
boutonniere	buttonhole
casser le fil	break the yarn
ce point s'execute avec un n. de m. div par (0) plus (0) m.	work on a multiple of (0) plus (0) sts
changement	change
chaque	each, every
col	collar
comme	as
commencant	begin
côté	side
côte	rib
coudre	sew
couleur	colour
couture	seam
de * à *	from * to *
dernier (dern)	last
derriere (der)	behind
dessous	under
dessous de bras	underarm
devant (dev)	front
devant droit	right front
devant gauche	left front
diminuer (dim)	decrease
diminution (dim)	decrease
dos	back
droite (dr)	right
emmanchure (emman)	armhole
empiecement	yoke
en couleur	in colour
encolure	neck
endroit (end)	front of work
envers (env)	back to work
ensemble (ens)	together
epaules	shoulders
explication	instructions
fermer	sew seams
faire	make
faire vis à vis	reverse shapings
fermenture des mailles	cast off stitches, end of work

fil	yarn
fil devant	yarn forward
fil derrière	yarn back
fois (fs)	time, times
former	shape
gauche	left
glisser (glis)	slip (a st)
grille	graph
inversant les explications	reverse the instructions
jété a l'endroit	yon before k st
jété a l'énvers	yon before p st
jété	yon
laisser (lais)	leave
laisser en attente	place on stitch holder
maille(s) (m)	stitch(es)
maille central	central stitch
maille endroit (m. end)	knit stitch
maille envers (m. env)	purl stitch
maille glissée à l'endroit	slip stitch knitwise
maille glissée à l'énvers	slip stitch purlwise
maille impair	odd number of sts
manche	sleeve
même	same
même travail que le dos	work as for the back
milieu	middle
montage	making up
monter	cast on
nombre (nbre)	number
ourlet	hem
overture	opening
partager	divide
partager au milieu	divide at the centre
placer	to place
poche(s)	pocket(s)
poignet	cuff
point (pt)	stitch, pattern
première	first
prendre	change to
puis	then
quelque	each, every
rabattre (rab)	cast off
rab comme les m. se present-ent	cast off in pattern
rab pour l'epaule	cast off for shoulder
rab tout les m.	cast off all sts
rang (rg)	row
rang impair	odd number row
rang pair	even number row

1 rg end	knit row
1 rg env	purl row
rg suivant	following row
rayé	striped
rayures	stripes
relever x m.	pick up x sts
répéter	repeat
répéter tjrs ces x rgs	repeat these x rows
restante(s)	remaining
sans	without
seconde	second
semblable	alike
separement (separem)	separately
simult	at the same time
soin	care
suivre (suiv)	follow
surjet simple	sl.1, k1, psso
surjet double	sl.1, k2 tog, psso
temps	times
total	total
toujours (tjrs)	always
tourner	turn
tous (ts)	all
travail (trav)	work
tricoter (tric)	knit

German

Material	Materials
yarn	yarn
Häkelnadel	crochet hook
Hilfsnadel	stitch holder or spare needle
Rundstrick-nadeln	circular needle
Stricknadeln	needles
Spiel stricknadeln	double pointed needles
Knopf, Knöpfe	button(s)

Masse	Measurements
Grösse	size
36, 38, 40, 42	32, 34, 36, 38 ins bust
Oberweite	actual chest measurement
Ganze Länge	total length

Grundmuster/ Strickmuster	Stitches used
glatt links	reverse stocking stitch
glatt maschen/ glatt rechts	stocking stitch
kraus gestricht	garter stitch
1M re, 1M 1i	k1, p1 rib
2M re, 2M 1i	k2, p2 rib

Meschenprobe 14 M und 20 R = 10cm im Quadrat	**Tension** 14 sts and 20 rows = 10cms
Arbeitsfolge	**Knitting instructions**
ab	from
ab*wiederholen	repeat from *
abnehmen (abn)	decrease(ing)
abketten der Maschen (abk)	cast off sts
abschrägen	shape (of V necks)
alle	all
Anfang	beginning
anfang der R(eihe)	beginning of row
anschlagen (anschl)	cast on
arbeit (arb)	work
armausschnitt	armhole
Armel	sleeve
auf	on
aufnehmen (aufn)	increase
ausarbeiten/ Ausarbeitung	making up
aussen	outside
beenden	finishing
bei	at
beidseitig	both sides/on each end (of row)
Beitragstet	contribution/to contribute
bleiben	remain
bis	until
Borte	border, edging
dabei	yet at the same time/thereby
dann	then
darüberstricken	work (knit) across
dauern	last
davon	away, thereof, thereby
der	the
Doppel	double
1 Doppel Umschlage	y2on
eine	one
einmal	once
einsetzen	insert
ersten	first
Faden nach hinter Legen	ybk
Farbe, Farben	colour, colours
Farbflächen	colour change
Farbfolge	colour sequence
Farbwechsel	area of colour
folgen, folgt (folg)	follow
für	for
gerade	straight
gestreift	striped
gestrickt	knitted
gleich zeitig	at the same time
glatt re	stocking stitch
glatt li	reverse stocking stitch
gleich(e)	alike, same
Hals	neck
Halsausschnit	neck shaping/ neck opening, neckline
hinter	behind
hoch	high
immer	always
jede, jeder	each, every
jedoch	still
Kante	edge
Knopfloch	buttonhole
Kragen	collar
lassen	leave
linke M (li M)	purl stitch
links	left
locker	loosely
Masche(n) (M)	stitch, stitches
2M überzogen zus, stricken	sl. 1, k1, psso
3M überzogen zus stricken	sl 2, k1, p2sso
maschenzahl teilbar durch mit	stitches divisible by with
mittel/mittleren	middle, centre
muster	stitch pattern
muster satz	pattern repeat
nach	after
nach hinten einstechen	in back of stitch, tbl
nadel (N)	needle, row
nahen	sew
Naht, Nähte	seam, seams
noch	still, yet, in addition
oben	at the top
obersten	top
öffnung	opening
offen	open
ohne	without
Rand	side
Randmasche (Rdm)	edge stitch
rechte M (re M)	knit stitch
rechts	right
Reihe (R)	row
Restliche (restl)	remaining
Rollkragen	polo neck
Rückenteil	back
Rückseite	wrong side of work

Rückseite oben	wrong side showing
Runde (Rd)	round, circular
schliessen	close, sew up
Schulter	shoulder
Schulter schrägung	shoulder shaping
Schulterstück	yoke
seitennaht/ Seitenähte	side seam(s)
sind	are, there are
strickschema	diagram of pattern
stricken (str)	knit
Strickschrift	of knitting pattern
Tasche	pocket
Teil, teilen	part, parts
uber	over
Umschlag (U)	yon, yrn, yo, yfwd
umschlag fallen lassen	drop the yo
umlegen	fold over
und	and
unter	under
Unterarm	underarm
Veränderung	change
verbinden	join, unite
Verdrehte	crossed, twisted
verschränkt	back of stitch
verteilt	distribute
von	of
vor	before, in front of
Vorderseite	front of work
wechseln	change, turn
weiterarb	continue to work
weiterhin	from now on, continue to
wenn	when
wie	as
wiederholen (wdh)	repeat
Zahl	number
zusammen (zus)	together
zwei	two
zweite	second
zweimal	twice

Italian

Occorrente	Materials
filati	yarn
ferri (f)	needles
ferro ausiliario (trecce)	cable needle
ferro circolare	circular needle
gioco di ferri	set of double pointed needles
bottone	button

Misure	Measurements
taglia (tg)	size
42, 44, 46, 48	32, 34, 36, 38 ins
altezza, lunghezza	length

Punti impiegati	Stitches used
coste 1×1	k1, p1 rib
coste 2×2	k2, p2 rib
maglia rasata (m. ras)	stocking stitch
maglia rasata rovescia	reserve stocking stitch
punto fantasia	patterns for which the instructions are given separately
punto a grano di riso	moss stitch
punto legaccio	garter stitch

Campione	Tension
23 m. e 27 f. = un quadrato di 10cm di lato	23 sts and 27 rows = 10cms

Esecuzione	Instructions
accavallare (acc)	pass, slip
accavallato (acc)	sl.1, k1, psso
accavallato doppia (acc doppia)	sl.1, k2 tog, psso
alternatamente	alternately
altezza totale (alt tot)	total length
altri	another
ancora	again, more
apertura	opening
attacare	sew, attach
assieme (ass)	together
aumentare, aumenti (aum)	to increase, increases
avviare (avv)	cast on
bordo, bordino	border
cambiare	change
centrale	central, centre
chiudere	cast off
collo, colletto	collar
colore (col)	colour
come	like, as
con il filo dav	with yarn at front
con il filo dietro	with yarn at back

confezione	making up	a metà	in half
contempor-aneamente	at the same time	morbidamente	loosely
		nello stesso modo	in the same way
continuare (cont)	cont	occhielli	buttonholes
cucitura	seam	ogni	each, every
davanti	front	pari	even number (of rows)
a destra	on the right		
dietro	back	passare 1 dir senza lavorarlo	sl.1 knitwise
diminuire, diminuzione (dim)	to decrease, decreases	passare 1 rov senza lavorarlo	sl.1 purlwise
diritto (dir)	knit stitch	per	through, for
dir crociato	k 2nd st, k 1st st and slip both off needle tog	piegare	turn, fold
		piu	more
		proseguire (pros)	continue
disegno	diagram	punti divisi da	stitches divis-ible by
dispari	odd number (of rows)		
		punto scivolato (passato) a dir	sl.1 knitwise
distribuendo nel corso del ferro	spacing evenly across the row	punto scivolato (passato) a rov	sl.1 purlwise
doppio	double, twice	quando	when
due	two	quindi	then
eseguire	make, work	raglan	raglan
ferro, ferri (f)	row, rows	regolarmente	evenly
2° f e f pari	2nd and every alt row	rimanente, rimasto	remaining
filo (fil)	yarn	rip(etere) da * a *	repeat from * to * of pattern
foretti	holes, slots for ribbon		
		rip il disegno	repeat the pattern
gettato (gett)	yon, yrn, yfwd	riprendere (riprend)	pick up
giro	round		
incavo manica	armhole	rovescio (rov)	purl stitch
iniziare (iniz)	bein	scalfo manica	armhole
insieme (ins)	together	sbieco	slope, shaping
in senso inverso	reversing shaping	scollo	neck
		sequito	following
intrecciare	cast off	a sinistra	on the left
intrecciare a costa	cast off in rib	sotto	under
		spalle	shoulders
lato	edge, side	sparse	evenly distributed
lavorare in tondo (lav in tondo)	work in rounds	spiegazione	instructions
		sul diritto del lavore	on right side of work
lavorare su un numero di m multiplo de x plus x	worked on a multiple of x plus x stitches	sul roviescio del lavore	on wrong side of work
		successivo	following
lav le m come si presentano	k the k sts and p the p sts	tenere in attesa (sospeso)	leave unworked
maglia, maglie (m)	stitch, stitches	terminare (term)	end
maglia doppio	k into next stitch 1 row below	traforato	lacy
		treccia	cable
		uguale	alike
2 m. ins a dir	k2 tog	ultimo	last
2 m. ins a rov	p2 tog	vivagno (viv)	selvedge stitch
m. dir ritorto	k through back of loop	volte	times
		una volta	once
m. rov ritorto	p through back of loop		

Spanish

Materiales	**Materials**
hilos	yarn
agujas (ag)	needles
aguja auxiliar (ag.auxil)	cable needle
aguja circular	circular needle
aguja sujeta-puntos	stitch holder
juego de agujas	set of double pointed needles
botón	button

Medidas	**Measurements**
talla	size
40, 42, 44, 46	32, 34, 36, 38
alto, largo	length

Puntos empleados	**Stitches used**
elástico 1×1	k1, p1 rib
elástico 2×2	k2, p2 rib
punto de arroz	moss stitch
punto de jersey	stocking stitch
punto de jersey revés	reverse stocking stitch
punto fantasía	patterns for which instructions are given separately
punto musgo, (punto bobo)	garter stitch

Muestra de orientación	**Tension**
20 p. y 26 v. = un cuadro de 10cm tejido con las ag del no. 5 a p de jersey	20 sts and 26 rows = 10cm in stocking stitch using 5mm needles

Marcha de la labor	**Instructions**
abrochar	fasten
acabar	finish
alto total (alt tot)	total length
anillo	loop
antes	before
armado	making up
arrollado	yfwd, yon, yrn
aumentar, aumentos (aum)	increase, increases
aún	still
a cada extremo	at each end
bolsillo	pocket
borde	edge, border

calado	lacy, slot for ribbon etc
cambiar	change
canesú	yoke
centro, central	centre
cerrar	cast off
clave	key (to chart)
color	colour
con	with
continuar (cont)	continue
coser	sew
cruzar	cross (cable)
cuello	collar
de (en) una sola vez	in one row, in one time
dejar en espera	leave unworked
delantero	front
derecho (de la labor)	right (side of work)
después	after
deslizar	slip
disminuir (dismin)	decrease
dividir (div)	divide
dobladillo	hem
doble (hebra)	double (yarn)
empezar	begin
escote	neck, neckline
espalda	back
fino	fine
fruncir	gather
grueso	thick
hebra (h.)	yarn or yon, yrn, yfwd
hombro(s)	shoulder(s)
igual	equal, the same
impar	odd (rows)
invertir la explicación en sentido inverso	reversing shaping or instructions
izquierdo	left (opposite to right)
labor	work
lado	side, edge
levantar	pick up
manga	sleeve
menguar (meng)	decrease
mitad	half
montar (mont)	cast on
número de puntos múltiplo de x más x	number of stiches divisible by x plus x
ojal	buttonhole
orillo	selvedge
ovillo	ball
ochos	cables
par	even (rows)
planchar	iron, press
proceder igual	work in same way

proseguir	continue	seguir	continue
punto derecho (p. d. or p. der)	knit stitch	siempre	always
		siguiente (sig)	following, next
punto revés (p. r. or p. rev)	purl stitch	simultánea-mente	at the same time
1 p. d. retorcido	k1 through back of loop	sin	without
		sisa	armhole
1 p. r. retorcido	p1 through back of loop	1 surjete (sencillo) (1 surj or 1 ss)	sl.1, k1, psso
1 p. doble	k into st 1 row below	1 surjete doble (1 surj dbl or 1 sd)	sl.1, k2 tog, psso
2 p juntos al der (2 p. j. d.)	k2 tog		
2 p juntos al rev (2 p. j. r.)	p2 tog	tejer (en redondo)	knit (in rounds)
1 p. deslizado (pasado) al der	sl. 1, k1	tejer los puntos tal como se presentan	k the k sts and p the p sts
1 p. deslizado (pasado) al rev	sl. 1, p1	terminar	finish
puño	cuff	tira	strip, border
raglán	raglan	todo	all, every
recto	straight, without shaping	trabajar (trab)	work
		trenza	cable
repetir de * a * (rep)	repeat from * to *	unir	join
		veces	times
restante	remaining	vuelta (v)	row
revés	wrong side of work	2a v. y. todas las pares	2nd and every alt row

Abbreviations

alt	alternate
beg	beginning
C2B	sl 1 st to cable needle and hold at back, k1, k st from cable needle
C2B tbl	sl 1 st to cable needle and hold at back, k1 tbl, k st from cable needle tbl
C2b	sl 1 st to cable needle and hold at back, k1, p st from cable needle
C2bp	sl 1 st to cable needle and hold at back, pl, p st from cable needle
C2b tbl	sl 1 st to cable needle and hold at back, k1 tbl, p st from cable needle
C2F	sl 1 st to cable needle and hold at front, k1, k st from cable needle
C2F tbl	sl 1 st to cable needle and hold at front, k1 tbl, k st from cable needle tbl
C2f	sl 1 st to cable needle and hold at front, pl, k st from cable needle
C2fp	sl 1 st to cable needle and hold at front, p1, p st from cable needle
C2f tbl	sl 1 st to cable needle and hold at front, p1, k st from cable needle tbl
C3B tbl	sl 1 st to cable needle and hold at back, k2, k st from cable needle tbl
C3b	sl 1 st to cable needle and hold at back, k2, p st from cable needle
C3bk	sl 1 st to cable needle and hold at back, k2, k st from cable needle
C3bp	sl 1 st to cable needle and hold at back, p2, p st from cable needle
C3b tbl	sl 1 st to cable needle and hold at back, k2 tbl, p st from cable needle
C3F tbl	sl 2 sts to cable needle and hold at front, k1 tbl, k2 from cable needle
C3f	sl 2 sts to cable needle and hold at front, pl, k2 from cable needle
C3fk	sl 2 sts to cable needle and hold at front, k1, k2 from cable needle
C3f tbl	sl 2 sts to cable needle and hold at front, pl, k2 tbl from cable needle
C4B	sl 2 sts to cable needle and hold at back, k2, k2 from cable needle
C4b	sl 2 sts to cable needle and hold at back, k2, p2 from cable needle
C4F	sl 2 sts to cable needle and hold at front, k2, k2 from cable needle
C4f	sl 2 sts to cable needle and hold at front, p2, k2 from cable needle
C5B	sl 3 sts to cable needle and hold at back, k2, put the p st on left hand needle and p it, k2 from cable needle
C5b	sl 2 sts to cable needle and leave at back, k3, p2 from cable needle
C5F	sl 2 sts to cable needle and hold at front, k2, put the p st on left hand needle and p it, k2 from cable needle
C5f	sl 3 sts to cable needle and hold at front, p2, k3 from cable needle
C6B	sl 3 sts to cable needle and hold at back, k3, k3 from cable needle
C6B tbl	sl 3 sts to cable needle and hold at back, k3 tbl, k3 tbl from cable needle
C6F	sl 3 sts to cable needle and hold at front, k3, k3 from cable needle
C6F tbl	sl 3 sts to cable needle and hold at front, k3 tbl, k3 tbl from cable needle
C8B	sl 4 sts to cable needle and hold at back, k4, k4 from cable needle
C8F	sl 4 sts to cable needle and hold at front, k4, k4 from cable needle
C10B	sl 5 sts to cable needle and hold at back, k5, k5 from cable needle
C10F	sl 5 sts to cable needle and hold at front, k5, k5 from cable needle
dec	decrease
foll	following
inc	increase
k	knit
LT	pass needle behind 1st st,

	k into back of 2nd st leaving it on needle, k 1st and 2nd sts tog tbl and slip from needle	Tw2L	pass needle behind first stitch, knit second stitch, knit first stitch and slip both stitches off needle
m 1	make one stitch	Tw2R	pass needle in front of first stitch, knit second stitch, knit first stitch and slip both stitches off needle
psso	pass slipped stitch over		
p2sso	pass 2 slipped stitches over		
p	purl		
rep	repeat	Tw3R	pass needle in front of first two stitches, knit the third stitch, then the second and first stitches and slip all three stitches off needle
RT	pass needle in front of 1st st, k into 2nd st leaving it on needle, k 1st and 2nd sts tog and slip from needle		
sep	separately	wrh	wool round hook
SKPO	slip one stitch, knit one stitch, pass slipped stitch over	ybk	yarn back
		yfwd	yarn forward
		yo	yarn over
sl	slip	yon	yarn over needle once
SSK	slip next two stitches singly to right hand needle knitwise, insert tip of left needle through front loop of both stitches and knit together	y2on	wind yarn round needle twice
		y3on	wind yarn round needle three times
		y4on	wind yarn round needle four times
st(s)	stitch(es)	Yp2	yarn forward, yarn round needle, p2, pass made stitch over the two purled stitches
st st	stocking stitch		
tbl	through back of loop		
tog	together		

Index